Global Trajectories
of Brazilian Religion

Bloomsbury Studies in Religion, Space and Place

Series editors: Paul-François Tremlett, John Eade, and Katy Soar

Religions, spiritualities, and mysticisms are deeply implicated in processes of place making. These include political and geopolitical spaces, local and national spaces, urban spaces, global and virtual spaces, contested spaces, spaces of performance, spaces of memory, and spaces of confinement. At the leading edge of theoretical, methodological, and interdisciplinary innovation in the study of religion, Bloomsbury Studies in Religion, Space, and Place bring together and give shape to the study of such processes.

These places are not defined simply by the material or the physical but also by the sensual and the psychological, by the ways in which spaces are gendered, classified, stratified, moved through, seen, touched, heard, interpreted, and occupied. Places are constituted through embodied practices that direct critical and analytical attention to the spatial production of insides, outsides, bodies, landscapes, cities, sovereignties, publics, and interiorities.

Religion and the Global City,
edited by David Garbin and Anna Strhan

Religious Pluralism and the City,
edited by Helmuth Berking, Silke Steets, and Jochen Schwenk

Global Trajectories of Brazilian Religion

Lusospheres

Edited by Martijn Oosterbaan,
Linda van de Kamp and Joana Bahia

BLOOMSBURY ACADEMIC
LONDON • NEW YORK • OXFORD • NEW DELHI • SYDNEY

BLOOMSBURY ACADEMIC
Bloomsbury Publishing Plc
50 Bedford Square, London, WC1B 3DP, UK
1385 Broadway, New York, NY 10018, USA
29 Earlsfort Terrace, Dublin 2, Ireland

BLOOMSBURY, BLOOMSBURY ACADEMIC and the Diana logo
are trademarks of Bloomsbury Publishing Plc

First published in Great Britain 2020
This paperback edition published in 2021

A catalogue record for this book is available from the British Library.

Library of Congress Cataloging-in-Publication Data
Names: Oosterbaan, Martijn, 1975- editor.
Title: Global trajectories of Brazilian religion : Lusospheres / edited by
Martijn Oosterbaan, Linda van de Kamp, and Joana Bahia.
Description: 1 [edition]. | New York : Bloomsbury Academic, 2019. | Series:
Bloomsbury studies in religion, space, and place | Includes
bibliographical references and index.
Identifiers: LCCN 2019019100 | ISBN 9781350072060 (hardback) |
ISBN 9781350072084 (epub)
Subjects: LCSH: Brazil–Religion.
Classification: LCC BL2590.B7 G56 2019 | DDC 200.981–dc23
LC record available at https://lccn.loc.gov/2019019100

ISBN: HB: 978-1-3500-7206-0
           PB: 978-1-3502-5250-9
           ePDF: 978-1-3500-7207-7
           eBook: 978-1-3500-7208-4

Typeset by Integra Software Services Pvt. Ltd.

To find out more about our authors and books visit www.bloomsbury.com
and sign up for our newsletters.

Contents

Notes on Contributors   vii

Acknowledgments   x

1   Lusospheres: The Globalization of Brazilian Religion *Martijn Oosterbaan, Linda van de Kamp, and Joana Bahia*   1

Part One   Media, Tourism, and Pilgrimage   21

2   How Religions Travel: Comparing the John of God Movement and a Brazilian Migrant Church *Cristina Rocha*   23

3   Appropriating *Terra Santa*: Holy Land Tours, Awe, and the "Judaization" of Brazilian Neo-Pentecostalism *Matan Shapiro*   37

4   The Ark of the Covenant in Angola: Connecting a Transnational Pentecostal Network *Claudia Wolff Swatowiski*   57

Part Two   Human Rights, Gender, and Sexuality   69

5   Brazilian Gay Pastorate in Mission to Cuba: Shaping a Transnational Community of Speech *Aramis Luis Silva*   71

6   Identity Reconstructions of Brazilian Women in Pentecostal Spaces in Portugal *Kachia Téchio*   85

7   Where Do the Prostitutes Pray? On *Travestis, Mães de Santo, Pombagiras*, and Postcolonial Desires *Joana Bahia*   101

8   Moving Homes: Transnational Meanings and Practices of the Brazilian Catholic Charismatic Renewal Movement in the Netherlands *Andrea Damacena Martins*   117

Part Three   Heritage, Embodiment, and Spirituality   133

9   Between Brazil and Spain: Structure and *Butinage* in the Trajectories of Santo Daime and União do Vegetal *Jessica Greganich*   135

10 "Pray Looking North": Change and Continuity of Transnational
    Umbanda in Uruguay *Andrés Serralta Massonnier*   153
11 The Constitution of a Transnational Sphere of Transcendence:
    The Relationship between the Irmãos Guerreiros Capoeira
    Angola Group and Ilê Obá Silekê in Europe *Celso de Brito*   169

Notes   183
References   201
Index   227

Contributors

Joana Bahia is Professor of Anthropology at the State University of Rio de Janeiro (UERJ), Brazil, and Associate Researcher at the Interdisciplinary Center for Migration Studies (NIEM) at the Rio de Janeiro Institute for Urban Research and Planning (IPPUR/UFRJ). She coordinates the research laboratory Identities, Migrations and Representations of the Brazilian National Council for Scientific and Technological Development (CNPQ). She has researched and published widely in the areas of religious transnationalization, Afro-Brazilian religions, ethnic identities, and migration.

Andrea Damacena Martins is a postdoctoral research fellow at the Federal University of Pernambuco, Recife (Brazil), in the Department of Cultural Anthropology. Since 2003 she has been living and working as an independent researcher in the Netherlands. Her research interests include Catholicism, Brazilian migration, and transnationalism. She has published several articles and book chapters on religious heritage, cultural diversity, identity, and religious and social practices of Portuguese-speaking immigrants in the Netherlands.

Celso de Brito is Adjunct Professor in the Department of Social Sciences and the Postgraduate Program in Anthropology at the Federal University of Piauí (UFPI), Brazil. He earned his doctorate at the Federal University of Rio Grande do Sul (UFRGS), Brazil. He has been a research fellow at the Center for Research in Anthropology, Universidade Nova de Lisboa, Portugal (CRIA/FCSH/UNL), the Tropical Research Institute (IICT), Portugal, and in the Department of Anthropology at Lumière Lyon 2 University, France. His areas of interest include anthropology of Afro-Brazilian populations, anthropology of transnationalism and economic and political anthropologies. He has published numerous journal articles and book chapters in these areas.

Jessica Greganich obtained her PhD in Social Anthropology at the Federal University of Rio Grande do Sul (UFRGS), Brazil, and the Vrije Universiteit Amsterdam, the Netherlands, in collaboration with the Graduate Institute Geneva, Switzerland. Currently she is a postdoctoral researcher at the Federal

University of Pernambuco, Brazil. She has done extensive research on *ayahuasca* religions and religious butinage.

Andrés Serralta Massonnier is Professor at the Holocaust Remembrance Centre of Montevideo, Uruguay. He has researched and published in the areas of Contemporary History, Political Science of Religion, History of Religion, and Genocide Studies. His most recent book is *Enseñar El Genocidio Armenio: Teoría, Metodología y Didáctica* (*Teaching the Armenian Genocide. Theory, Methodology and Didactics*, De La Plaza, 2017, with Marcelo Decena).

Aramis Luis Silva is a visiting professor at the Federal University of São Paulo, Brazil. Focused on political anthropology, social communication, and religion, he has published about museums and ethnographic collections, Catholic missions, and the relationship between religion and sexuality. Concerning religious phenomena, he analyzes the contemporary social forms of subjectivation and the circulation of the categories from which the intersected subjects are constituted of.

Martijn Oosterbaan is Associate Professor of Cultural Anthropology at Utrecht University, the Netherlands. His research is situated at the crossroads of Urban Studies, the Anthropology of Religion, and Media Anthropology, and he has done much research on evangelical and Pentecostal movements in Brazil and beyond. His recent book is *Transmitting the Spirit: Religious Conversion, Media, and Urban Violence in Brazil* (Penn State Press, 2017), and he is currently starting a project on religious vigilantes in megacities in the Global South.

Cristina Rocha is Professor in Anthropology and Director of the Religion and Society Research Cluster, Western Sydney University, Australia. She is President of the Australian Association for the Study of Religion, and coedits the *Journal of Global Buddhism* and the *Religion in the Americas* series, Brill. Her research focuses on the intersections of globalization, migration, and religion. Her most recent book is *John of God: The Globalisation of Brazilian Faith Healing* (OUP, 2017).

Matan Shapiro is a postdoctoral research fellow in the Department of Social Anthropology at the University of Bergen, Norway. Premised empirically on several fieldwork periods in the Brazilian state of Maranhão (2007–8, 2009–10, and 2016), and in Israel–Palestine (2004–5, 2014–15, 2015–17) he has written mainly (but not exclusively) on the links between kinship, ritual, and cosmology in the Brazilian and Israeli societies. His current research focuses on techno-utopianism among bitcoin enthusiasts in Tel Aviv, Israel.

Claudia Wolff Swatowiski is Adjunct Professor of Anthropology at the Federal University of Uberlândia, Brazil. She received her PhD in Social Sciences from the State University of Rio de Janeiro in 2010. Between 2007 and 2008, she was a visiting fellow at the Institute of Social Sciences of the University of Lisbon. Her numerous publications in the fields of Religious and Urban Anthropology include her book *Novos cristãos em Lisboa: reconhecendo stigmas, negociando estereótipos* (New Christians in Lisbon: Recognizing Stigmas, Negotiating Stereotypes) (Garamond, 2013).

Kachia Téchio received her PhD in Anthropology in 2011 from the Universidade Nova de Lisboa, Portugal. She is Assistant Professor at the Federal University of Rondônia, Brazil, where she coordinates the Master's Program Teaching Natural Sciences. Her research interests include identity representations, multiculturalism, traditional knowledge, Pentecostalism, and teacher training for science education. She has published various articles and book chapters on these topics.

Linda van de Kamp is a Cultural Anthropologist and Assistant Professor in the Department of Sociology at the University of Amsterdam, the Netherlands. She carries out interdisciplinary research on urban transformations, religion and ritual, transnational circulation, and industrial and cultural heritage. Her current project, titled "Yoga, Bingo and Prayer in Urban Regeneration Areas," was awarded with a VENI grant from the Netherlands Organization for Scientific Research (NWO). Linda has done in-depth research on the emergence of Brazilian Pentecostalism in Mozambique. She is the author of *Violent Conversion: Brazilian Pentecostalism and Urban Women in Mozambique* (James Currey, 2016).

Acknowledgments

The birth of this volume is the result of an international collaboration of scholars of Brazilian religion who we first encountered during a conference of the International Society for the Sociology of Religion in Louvain la Neuve, Belgium, in 2015. Since then, the editors of this volume have organized meetings in different configurations in Europe and Brazil with the aim of extending our understanding of the global trajectories of Brazilian religious movements, ideas, and practices. We are grateful to all contributors of this volume who have shared their insights and enthusiasm that made this volume possible. We specifically want to thank several members of the collective who could not be part of this volume but whose input over the years has been invaluable: Ronaldo de Almeida, Elisabeth Mareels, Carlos Gutierrez, and Marcelo Natividade. Beyond these scholars we would like to thank all the participants of the panel "*Tradução, conexões e re(criações) culturais das religiões brasileiras na Europa e em outros contextos nacionais*" at the 30th conference of the Brazilian Anthropological Association (*Associação Brasileira de Antropologia*, ABA) in João Pessoa, Brazil, in 2016, and all the participants of the panel "Lusospheres: Global Trajectories of Brazilian Religion" at the 2017 conference of the Dutch Association for the Study of Religion (*Nederlands Genootschap voor Godsdienstwetenschap*, NGG) in Utrecht, the Netherlands. In particular, we want to thank Katja Rakow for her excellent discussion during the NGG panel. Lastly, we would like to thank the series editors: John Eade, Katy Soar, and Paul-François Tremlett for their commitment to this volume and Camilla Erskine and Lucy Carroll of Bloomsbury Publishing for their support and pleasant cooperation.

Lusospheres

The Globalization of Brazilian Religion

Martijn Oosterbaan, Linda van de Kamp, and Joana Bahia

Introduction

Over the last several decades, Brazil-born religious forms and practices have expanded globally. Religious movements as diverse as Santo Daime, Candomblé, Capoeira, John of God, and Brazilian-style Pentecostalism and Catholicism have become immensely popular in many places outside Brazil. One may encounter people of German descent in the Candomblé temples in Berlin, people of Dutch descent participating in Santo Daime rituals in Amsterdam, or Brazil-born people congregating in a neo-Pentecostal church in Barcelona. Brazilian religions are among the world's most appealing and widespread religiocultural forms and, as one of "the major actors in the new global geography of the sacred" (Rocha and Vásquez 2013), Brazilians have become crucial players in the creation of global religious networks.

The driving forces of this development can be identified in processes we commonly call "globalization" (see also Beyer 2006). Over the last two decades, Brazil has emerged as a country which exports its culture and religions on a large scale as a consequence of the growing mobility of persons and the increasing possibilities of fast and long-distance communication (Rocha and Vásquez 2013; see also Roett 2010). While Brazil has had a long history of receiving immigrants from Europe, Japan, and other Latin American countries, since the 1980s, it has become an important "emigration country" (Sales 1999: 20–21). In response to multifaceted social, economic, and political circumstances, Brazilian citizens—and middle-class professionals in particular—began to emigrate to destinations across the world (Beserra 2003; see also Rocha, this volume).

In the early 2000s, Brazil's economy started to grow and the country became recognized as one of the emerging economies in the world, which is exemplified by its admission to the international coalition of BRICS countries (Brazil, Russia, India, China, South Africa).[1] Moreover, Brazil entered the global stage of international affairs when the former president Luis Inácio Lula da Silva replaced the G8 with the G20, which attests to the shifting dynamics in the global power constellations. Nevertheless, substantial social and economic inequalities continued to exist in Brazilian society, and large-scale corruption, scandals, and decreasing commodity prices culminated with a failing economy. Currently, Brazilians face an unstable socioeconomic, political, and cultural situation, and citizens have continued to leave the country.[2]

Studies by the United Nations and the International Organization for Migration indicate that most Brazilians emigrate to the United States, followed by Europe (see also Oliveira Assis 2013; Povoa Neto 2007; Siqueira 2014).[3] In general, studies show that the emigration of Brazilians is related to the existence of migration networks in the destination countries that encourage and facilitate the journey (Padilla 2006). Within Europe, most Brazilians go to Portugal, followed by Spain, the UK, Germany, Italy, France, Switzerland, and Belgium. The majority of the migrants come from lower-middle-class and working-class backgrounds. Strikingly, these individuals are increasingly being criminalized, particularly women (Padilla 2006; Pontes 2004), a phenomenon that intensified after the 2001 attacks on the New York City World Trade Center (see Oliveira Assis and Martins 2010a, b).

While economic factors play an important role in emigration, migration also involves multiple economic, social, and cultural factors (Patarra 2005), including religious ones (Levitt 2007; Martes 1999). Brazilian religious entrepreneurs emigrate for missionary purposes, and Brazilian religious spaces become crucial for the creation and continuity of transnational social networks (Beserra 2006; Dias 2006; Sherringham 2013).

Although migration is important for the spread of religious ideas and practices, as we will see, this volume seeks to go beyond an explanatory framework of religious globalization merely in terms of migration patterns. For example, though travel plays a key role, non-Brazilians often seek and find Brazilian religions in their home country without the mediation of a Brazilian emigrant. The spread of Brazilian religions also occurs through spiritual seekers and tourists traveling to and from Brazil, and through the circulation of religiocultural performances, objects, and media. This book contributes to a growing body of work that demonstrates that we need to adjust our imagination and analysis of global religious spread (Rocha and Vásquez 2013; van de Kamp 2016a, 2017).

We focus on Brazilian religions because the presence of Brazilian forms of spirituality and worship outside Brazil complicates many scholarly representations of religious globalization. In addition, globalized Brazilian religion elucidates, *par excellence*, the contemporary mechanisms that allow religious life to blossom in distinct locales throughout the world. We aim to show the particular ways in which religious images and practices were "culturalized" and "patrimonialized" during Brazil's anthropophagic history.[4] Consider the Afro-Brazilian martial art Capoeira, for example, which allows these practices to travel across the globe in different guises, sometimes posing as "more-than-religion" or "not-really-religion" and at other times as deeply spiritual phenomena, that is highly attractive to non-Brazilians living outside Brazil.

This book examines the multidirectional character of Brazilian religious flows in a variety of case studies that demonstrate new religiocultural cross-fertilizations. We argue that Brazilian religious practices, objects, and media play a central role in the making of transnational *lusospheres*. The concept lusosphere refers to the historical Portuguese colonial reach[5] that is often identified by way of its linguistic footprint—the so-called "Lusophone world"—or by way of places where Portuguese expansion has wielded an influence—so-called *Lusotopoi*. Nevertheless, the concept lusosphere signals cultural interactions in a different geopolitical age, one in which imagination plays a crucial role (Appadurai 1996). In a dynamic space of historical and cultural production, Brazil is often imagined and re-created as "a cool territory," an authentic, tropical, spiritual, and sensual place, capable of bringing forth extraordinary avenues that connect humans to the transcendental and providing the material and aesthetic forms that allow for heightened collective experiences and a sense of community (see Meyer 2009).

Rather than describing the flows in terms of places of origin or the language that is spoken, we have searched for a concept that allows us to capture both the multipolarity of contemporary religious globalization and the experience of community, supported by material environments. What characterizes a lusosphere, then, is a "peculiarity of intersection" (Cahen 2013: 10) with various features and flows that, on the one hand, include practices that open up entities and create assemblages (Deleuze and Guattari 1987) and, on the other hand, consist of delimitations that create shared spherical spaces of experience (Sloterdijk 2003, 2009). We will explain this dynamic of "flow and closure" (Geschiere and Meyer 1998) in more detail below.

Brazilian religious forms play a crucial role in the creation of lusospheres, which is partly related, we believe, to the fact that transnational Brazilian religious forms are exemplars of blended ideologies and practices. Capoeira and Santo Daime, for example, are the products of intersecting religious *and* cultural traditions from Europe, Africa, and Latin America, and can be perceived and experienced as both leisure and religion. Strikingly, these traditions and their practices cross both territorial and conceptual domains (see also de Vries 2008; Meyer and Houtman 2012). Moreover, the religious practices and financial investments that aim to make Brazil the new Holy Land and the center of spiritual healing demonstrate how political, economic, cultural, and religious domains intersect and thus signal the need to investigate how religious traditions connect to other social phenomena and how traditions change as a result of new cultural interactions. It is our aim to discuss these issues in this book, taking the globalization of Brazilian religion as a starting point.

The globalization of Brazilian religion: Multipolar connections

Many publications convey a unipolar view on religious globalization, in which religious spread was imagined as a unidirectional diffusion of European religions into the Americas, Africa, and Asia as a consequence of the travels of European explorers, missionaries, and merchants. While this historical presentation needs to be scrutinized critically (Velho 2009), it also inadequately represents the current growth of transnational religious flows. We are witnessing the growth of many religious styles in Europe, ranging from various forms of Buddhism that can be traced to origins in Asia to the presence of Pentecostal churches that have been founded in Africa.

Although these examples frequently appear as indications of contemporary directions of religious spread, we are not entirely satisfied with the historical description or with the prevalent assumptions about the production of religious life in distinct places. Looking at Brazilian religious movements from past to present complicates the perception that distinct religions can travel from one place to the other, after which they continue to live their atomistic lives in a different environment. This is, we hold, the unfortunate effect of thinking in terms of exportation or migration models. Similarly, the notion of diaspora does not fully capture the dynamics of religious globalization, which is understood to spring from religious, doctrinal sources. The concept thus contains the notion of an original center (and home) from which "a tradition" or "a people" sprung (see e.g., Cohen 2008).

Yet, the Brazilian religions that are featured in this volume were, in many ways, the product of earlier forms of religious globalization that emerged under colonialism and were important components of it (Naro, Sansi-Roca, and Treece 2007). For instance, when Candomblé appeared in contemporary Berlin, we encountered a complex and wondrous amalgam of Yoruba related deities, fused with Brazilian Baroque Catholicism that is packaged in a "spiritual" workshop for urbanites who seek to discover the energetic force of their bodies (Bahia 2016; see also Brito, this volume).

This brief example not only points to earlier fusions of African religious practices that arrived in Brazil with the enslaved, and a particular form of Catholicism that arrived with the Portuguese colonizers, but also to the fact that what is produced in Berlin is something new and different. The presence of African or Latin American migrant churches in Europe today; the growth of transnational Islam; and the worldwide travels of Brazilian, Asian, and African spiritual healers (e.g., Becci et al. 2013; Garbin and Strhan 2017; Hüwelmeier and Krause 2009; Oro and Rodrigues 2015) force us to shift our focus from places of religious origin to movements between places as processes of religious creativity and innovation (van de Kamp 2016b; see also Keim et al. 2014).

Having said this, we also need to engage with another dominant representation of religious globalization that is frequently used to counter a picture of atomistic religions that are transported from one place to the other. This concerns recounting the globalization of religion as a process of homogenization. Several scholars have described booming global religious movements—such as Pentecostalism and Buddhism—as principal exemplars of this kind of cultural globalization (e.g., Csordas 2009). The doctrines, organizational formats, media, and bodily practices found in these types of religion are adopted all over the world, seemingly irrespective of local cultural variation. The religious activities in Rio de Janeiro, Singapore, Lagos, Amsterdam, or Chicago are often described as strikingly similar to each other, both in the scholarly literature as by the religious organizations themselves. From the perspective of the pursuit of a universal cultural–religious identity, it hardly seems to make any difference where one attends a Pentecostal church service or a Buddhist ritual (Miller and Yamamori 2007; Pinxten and Dikomitis 2009; Rocha 2005).

While by no means we want to deny the many resemblances between different temples and churches throughout the world, descriptions of global religions regularly pose a number of questions. Broadly speaking, they concern two interrelated problems: First, globalization is often treated as a global cultural flow that originates in one place, country, or continent and from there expands all over the globe, encroaching on various local settings. Religion then becomes part of a local reaction and response to globalization, colonization, and missionization (Comaroff and Comaroff 1991; see also Meyer 2004; Robbins 2004). This view presents us with a distorted image of cultural and religious exchange and transformation we feel, because it is deeply problematic to describe and understand the spread of certain forms, doctrines, and practices as a relation between *the global* and *the local* (Robertson 2012).

Based on the research presented in this book, we argue that religious globalization is not about local adoptions of a global phenomenon. We concur with the important critique of Ana Tsing (2000), which posits that it is a misconception to think of cultural change in terms of local reactions to global forces (see also Mazzarella 2004). There are no global forces outside of the forceful connections produced between specific places and people in specific settings. Analytically speaking, religions seem to travel well because of (some of) their non-territorial characteristics and practices; however, we argue that we cannot take certain doctrinal qualities for analytical facts. Surely, it does matter that religious leaders generally perpetuate the idea that one need not be in a particular place to be in touch with the spiritual; however, in practice, routes, trajectories, languages, and environments are essential in co-producing divine presence (Abreu 2005; de Witte 2009; Oosterbaan 2017).

As the contents of this book will demonstrate, we found that Portuguese-speaking religious adherents in different places in the world display particular similarities that go beyond the sharing of language and involve shared conceptualizations of spiritual presence, sacred music, and visual cultures and styles, yet we could not grasp them in terms of *one* of the common descriptions that are often used to analyze particular religious groups in terms of territorial origins and spatial spread. Rather, in any given religious setting, we found *different* combinations between presented imaginaries of global presence, connection, and movement, and actual connections as displayed by the travels and routes of people and things.

To be a bit more precise, one very large church with Brazilian roots—the Universal Church of the Kingdom of God (UCKG)—generally presents itself as universal and nondiasporic, yet, in several of its European locations it attracts predominantly Brazilians (e.g., Oosterbaan 2011; Moreira forthcoming), never shedding entirely a diasporic Brazilian identity or able to really accomplish the "reverse missionization" (Freston 2010; Jenkins 2011) that is sometimes suggested. At the same time, in the European cities of Brussels, Paris, and London, for example, the church's audience consists of a considerable number of Caribbeans and West- and Luso-Africans who find the church's approach toward African and Afro-Brazilian spirits appealing (Almeida and Gutierrez 2015; Mareels 2016: 304–07; Miller and Anderson 2003). In addition, in Luanda, Angola, and in Maputo, Mozambique, the Brazilian connections of the Universal Church are crucial to enact a sacred connection to a Biblical-Jewish past through the replica of the Temple of Solomon that the Universal Church constructed in Brazil, bringing a part of Jerusalem and its past to Brazil, and from Brazil to Angola and Mozambique (Openshaw 2018: 137–53; Reis Santos 2018: 183–216; Swatowsiki, this volume; see also Shapiro, this volume). Looking at these and other religious connections and practices in different parts of the world, we see that cultural–religious forms are not best described in terms of universal modern forms but rather as assemblages of different connections, traditions of thought, and practices that are shaped by different historical and contemporary political and economic conditions.

In addition, authors such as Andreas Wimmer and Nina Glick Schiller (2003), and Peggy Levitt and Nina Glick Schiller (2004) have stressed that religious scholars should analyze the global flow of religious movements by looking at the networks that stretch across the borders of nation-states, through which ideas, practices, and resources circulate. Inspired by these ideas, we suggest to approach religious spaces as sites of performances that create belonging to connections and trajectories (see also Coleman and Maier 2013; Heck 2013; Krause and van Dijk 2016). More than a "translocal" phenomenon (Smith 2005), religious agents extend the borders of their localities by making themselves part of developments and practices elsewhere, which is facilitated by the borderless power of spirits and gods. In other words, based on the material presented in this book, we propose to approach religion as spheres shaped by local, global, and transnational forces in which religion is not a mere idiom, but an important force in re/creating worlds or a "worlding process" (Roy and Ong 2011; see also Lanz and Oosterbaan 2016; Meyer 2014). Globalizing Brazilian religion illuminates this process in numerous and impressive ways, erasing unipolar understandings of global religion.

The different social–cultural, spatial, and temporal bearings of Brazilian religious connections that involve different power mechanisms demonstrate the multipolarity of religious globalization. Brazilian religion is not only varied geographically, but also in its practices and discourses that are dependent on different connections and social relations, as we aim to demonstrate in this volume. Brazilian religious multipolarity highlights the multidirectional and multiscalar character of its flows that expose the continuities and changes in the creation of ethnic, Brazilian, transnational, and historical representations and identifications in religious circuits.

Religion and *butinage* in Brazil

The rise of Brazil as a religiocultural center in today's polycentric global geography of the sacred (Rocha and Vásquez 2013) is related to its history of cultural hybridism and religious creativity (Andrade 1990; Bastide 1978; Siqueira 2003), as well as to an imagination of Brazil as exotic, spiritual, original, and full of energy; the country of soccer, capoeira, and carnival (Da Matta 1991).

For a long time, Brazil was officially considered a Catholic country as a result of the Portuguese colonization of Brazil and the relation between the Portuguese crown and the Holy See at the time. But, from the beginning, Luso-Catholicism in Brazil was a complex amalgam of Portuguese Catholicism, African religions that had arrived with the enslaved, and indigenous religions. A popular form of Catholicism emerged that incorporated the veneration of saints, indigenous traditions and African spirits with their accompanying rituals, miracles, festivals, and pilgrimages that gave way to the creation of "hybrid" and "syncretic" religions (Greenfield and Droogers 2003) such as Candomblé. Spiritist movements that fused the belief in reincarnation with scientific practice, such as proposed by Allan Kardec, became widely influential in the nineteenth and twentieth century and heavily influenced the creation of the Afro-Brazilian religion Umbanda— perhaps the best example of Brazilian religious fusion of the past century (Hess 1991). These religious innovations have continued through the blending of spiritual traditions such as the Ayahuasca religions Santo Daime and União do Vegetal (Greganich, this volume; Groisman 2009), and a variety of esoteric mystical movements (Siqueira 2002).

The growth of Evangelical Protestantism and Pentecostalism in Brazil's major cities as part of a process of industrialization since the 1950s has become the marker of the continuing and growing religious pluralism in Brazil, accompanied by the emergence of mass media and the cultural industries of music, lifestyle, and sports. While Protestantism arrived in the country with European and North American missionaries (Mafra 2001), home-grown Pentecostal churches such as the UCKG have been expanding all over the world since about the 1980s. Churches as the UCKG strongly show the unified fusion between religion, business, global sports (Rial 2012), mass media (Birman and Lehmann 1999), and popular culture (Oosterbaan 2017). Born-again Brazilian soccer players, for instance, are the new face of contemporary Christian mission, acting as superior religious entrepreneurs at a mediatized and spectacular global stage (Rial 2012).

These types of fusions are also visible in the global spread of the Afro-Brazilian dance, fight, and sport game Capoeira. Stephen and Delamont (2013: 272) show that Brazilian teachers of capoeira in the UK may not openly connect it to Umbanda and Candomblé; nevertheless, the notion of *axé*, the central force that—according to Afro-Brazilian religions—animates all beings, continues to be vital to the culture of capoeira in London. Here, it is framed as "good energy, which produces good capoeira play." Similarly, the Afro-Brazilian priest who teaches Afro-Brazilian dance in a cultural center in Berlin also provides insights into the modus operandi of Candomblé (Brito, this volume). Afro-Germans, for example, participate in these courses because they are seeking their African roots, and in the process, they might learn about their spiritual connections (Bahia 2016). These examples demonstrate the intersections of political, economic, cultural, and religious domains, and particularly the specific religiocultural assemblages of different connections, traditions of thought and practices that are shaped by distinctive historical trajectories, and contemporary conditions of tourism, migration, mass media, and entrepreneurship.

Against the background of Brazil's religiocultural multiplicity, it is revealing that recently, a group of scholars (Gez et al. 2017) proposed the concept of *butinage* on the basis of research in Brazil (Soares 2009). Butinage, a French term taken from the world of *apiculture*, refers to the social practice of foraging for flower pollen and nectar. "This metaphor captures religion as actor-centered and inherently polymorphous and changeable. The practitioner of religious butinage—the *butineur*—is situated between multiple religious institutions, whose formal prescriptions he or she overflows through the dynamism of de facto practice" (Gez et al. 2017: 141–42).[6] Religious butinage refers to people's engagements in multiple religious traditions without necessarily conforming to one overarching and dominant religious order. In analogy with the behavior of bees that move from flower to flower, foraging for nectar and gathering and distributing pollen as they go, the notion of butinage points to the networks of relations that are built over time. This metaphor of butinage could also help to describe the cross-fertilization of religious and nonreligious activities and traditions. As Lee (2017: 153) writes in response to Gez et al.:

> A person might for example, participate in activities of religious traditions that they perceive as "exotic" and be influenced both by the contours of those traditions and by their sense of otherness from them (Lee 2015). Or, on the

other side of the coin, we can describe the way in which nonreligious identities are shaped by the individual's knowledge and experience of particular religious cultures (Davie 2013).

In addition, the practice of butinage can lead to the creation of new religious assemblages that restructure existing religious institutions and practices (Greganich, this volume).

Lusospheres

The conceptual power of butinage stems not only from its reference to reproduction and change across religious and cultural domains but also from its spatiotemporal dimension. From the outset, Gez et al. (2017) make clear that they are arguing against those scholars who erroneously take religious identities as solid and stable, and who lose sight of the flexibility of individuals and their capacity *to move*. While we certainly agree, the efforts to criticize those who assume stable religious identities produce the risk of negating stasis as the spatiotemporal counterpart of mobility (see also Oosterbaan 2014). As Devaka Premawardhana (2017: 154) states in response to Gez et al., butinage also "accounts for the way that birds—or, for that matter, bees—that go on the move do not always stay on the move: they stop and perch, and they nest and rest." The metaphor of nesting and resting not only points to the spatial embeddedness of new assemblages, according to Premawardhana, it also refers to "strategic antisyncretism" and to the pragmatic and situational nature of identity claims (2017).

This point strikes a chord with earlier critical remarks on global mobility. At the high point of the anthropological focus on globalization, which emphasized "cultural flows," Peter Geschiere and Birgit Meyer already (1998) pointed out that, in fact, people engage in processes of "fixing" the flows in efforts to affirm and reestablish boundaries and difference. Fifteen years later, Nina Glick Schiller and Noel Salazar (2013: 2) urged scholars to reconsider the "analytical category of mobility and its relationship to social theory and global transformation" to take notice of the fact that neither mobility nor stasis should be taken as *a priori* social facts.

In the field of religious studies, Thomas Tweed (2006) has incorporated the dialectics of flow and closure, mobility and stasis, syncretism and antisyncretism most explicitly by making it the core of his definition of religion. For Tweed (2006: 54), religions are "confluences of organic-cultural flows that intensify joy and confront suffering by drawing on human and suprahuman forces to make homes and cross boundaries." Whereas we do not necessarily think that "home" is the only or best category to describe place making, we are inspired by Tweed's emphasis on religion as a catalyst of "crossing and dwelling" and also somewhat surprised that neither Gez et al. (2017) nor their commentators (2017) refer to his work. Though Tweed's notion of home arguably encompasses more than a narrowly defined "domicile," we think the concept of *sphere* as presented by the philosopher Peter Sloterdijk (2003, 2009), in combination with the notion of assemblages as presented by the philosophical tandem Gilles Deleuze and Félix Guattari (1987), ultimately helps us better to understand how religious–cultural fusions produce spatial–material environments across the world.

Before setting out to elucidate why the term lusosphere helps us to recognize and describe the global travels of Brazilian religion, it is important to take up the question of how we understand the relation between spheres and assemblages, concepts derived from different philosophical projects. Following Judith Wambacq and Sjoerd van Tuinen (2017), the projects of Sloterdijk and Deleuze and Guattari have often been described as opposing, given the fact that the two projects present diverging understandings of the relation between interiority and exteriority—between an entity and its *umwelt*. As suggested, Sloterdijk emphasizes immunity and closure whereas Deleuze and Guattari focus on openness. Nevertheless, as Wambacq and van Tuinen show, the apparent opposition is largely resolved when the two projects are examined in detail. According to Wambacq and van Tuinen, Sloterdijk—not much unlike Deleuze and Guattari—recognizes the ontological necessity of movements that open up interiorities, but such openings face existential obstacles which result in the continuing efforts to close the spheres that make life possible: "An organism comes to be in and through these delimiting, identifying movements" (2017: 3). Nevertheless, spheres are "not self-concealed and isolated but reach out for accompaniment" (2017: 5). According to Sloterdijk, contemporary life consists of spheres that are connected to one another the way bubbles form agglomerates of "foam." The bubbles that constitute foam both form and influence each other as two bubbles share what separates them and, in the words of Schinkel and Noordegraaf-Eelens (2011: 13), thus form a "pluralist universe of rhizomatic co-isolation."

Despite the fact that spheres are ontologically related to other spheres, Sloterdijk maintains that social life is produced by (or in) bubbles and that humans reproduce bounded spheres in which social life is made possible. "A sphere is thus a shared psychospatial immunological edifice. It might be positively compared with Latourian actor-network chains or with Deleuzian assemblages. It has elements of a Foucaultian dispositif in its mesh of discourse, practice and objects and in its potential of shaping man" (Schinkel and Noordegraaf-Eelens 2011: 13).

We argue that Brazilian religiocultural multiplicity produces lusospheres. Both the imagination and materiality of the global connections that shape particular Brazilian religious spaces turn out to display very specific forms, which, in our cases, are heavily influenced by colonial lusophone relations (see Sarró and Blanes 2009) in which Brazil has played a particular role. Notably, the environments in which the various religious actors operate often encompass not only a specific place or city, but larger sacroscapes (Tweed 2006) that connect different countries with each other—for instance Angola, Brazil and Israel or Brazil, the USA and Cuba.

Our interlocutors, in different places and with varying religious perspectives, locate themselves according to particular understandings of space and movement and how they experience their presence in a particular location. For instance, a Brazilian pastor of the Metropolitan Community Churches (MCCs) in Cuba was able to articulate a sense of transnational community building on religious discourse and practice *and* on collective experiences of "homosexuality," "liberation," and "exclusion" in Brazil and Cuba. The pastor preached: "Wherever we [the LGBT community] are, we can find a piece of ourselves. And I can see myself here. To embrace myself and to meet myself in you—that communion has a transforming power" (in Silva, this volume). He and the larger MCC articulate a sense of space as being open *and* closed through their interconnections. Through their public actions the MCC creates a sphere that encompasses safe places in Cuba and Brazil, but that operates across scales and capacities to incorporate an international network in order to realize their full capacity as believers, citizens, and LGBT-ers committed to achieving human rights. In other words, we need to examine how differing spatialities allow actors to create ways of operating and moving in a religious–cultural place, and to understand a religious place as being located not only materially, but also socially and spiritually. In this way, we can understand the space as being open and closed at the same time.

Adding the concept of assemblages to our reflections on lusospheres is thus not meant to indicate that the ontological perspective of openness and exchange is missing in Sloterdijk's spherical approach, but rather to stress that these spheres are the product of intersecting material and symbolic artifacts. As Delanda (2016: 20) explains, "assemblages are always composed of heterogeneous components." It is important to highlight the nonhierarchical heterogeneity of assemblages because this gives us the possibility to go beyond static notions of religion and religious life. When we take the example of the Brazilian pastor working in an MCC in Cuba, we see that the lusosphere he helps to create is as much the result of an international LGBT movement and ideology as it is part of a global Christian ideology, intermeshed with human rights discourse (Silva, this volume).

Beyond this example, one might also think of other emerging intersections between Christianity and global neoliberal values and mechanisms that produce the so-called "prosperity gospel" that so many people find hard to explain in terms of Christian traditions that preach humility and simplicity. Nevertheless, when one understands churches such as the UCKG as an example of entrepreneurial religion (Lanz and Oosterbaan 2016), one might see that its spectacular services (Kramer 2005) and its emphasis on exorcism and self-actualization through entrepreneurialism and material gain demonstrates a new form of religion that is not reducible to either "Christian" values or "neoliberal ideology." Likewise, it does not help to pose the question if the UCKG is really a church *or* a business (or a political force). The interesting thing is that it is all of these at the same time (see also Campos 1997).

These two examples demonstrate that the assemblages at the core of contemporary lusospheres are not confined to one specific domain of interaction between religious and sociocultural phenomena, but that new and unexpected fusions are becoming visible. In this volume, we have subdivided these interactions in three book parts that each highlight different domains: (1) Media, tourism, and pilgrimage; (2) Human rights, gender, and sexuality; and (3) Heritage, embodiment, and spirituality. Our emphasis on specific domains in each part does not mean we hold that lusospheres are only formed in relation to these domains or only in that particular configuration. Notions of authenticity, for example, play an important part in tourists' discourses and practices and in "heritage regimes" (Bendix 2009) and embodiment is as much a feature of sexuality as it is of spirituality. Nevertheless, we do see that certain domains of social life particularly show "thick" relations with each other and with religious practices.

Media, tourism, and pilgrimage

Media and tourism are among the keywords of contemporary cultural globalization, highlighting the dissemination of images of selves and others, the desire to travel, and the effects of mass mobility. Much has been written about spiritual tourism and pilgrimage as two contemporary intersections of religion and tourism (Badone and Roseman 2004; Coleman and Eade 2004; Eade and

Sallnow 1991). This part of the book builds on that work yet focuses specifically on contemporary "religious transportability" (Csordas 2009) as a continuous process. The part particularly focuses on consecutive religious travels that produce layered religious phenomena that we here conceive of as lusospheres. Our notion of pilgrimage, emphasized in this part, extends beyond the common use of the concept to include both traditional understandings of religious travels to a religious shrine or center and to what Nick Couldry (2003) has termed "media pilgrimages": "journeys to points with significance in media narratives" (2003: 76). Couldry emphasizes that these media pilgrimages are not necessarily religious; however, we are interested in the crossroads between mediated symbolic centers (in the world) and religious practices and imaginations; for these two often enforce each other, as we will see.

This volume opens with a chapter by Cristina Rocha, who analyzes a Brazilian Pentecostal church in Australia and a faith healer in Brazil to understand how imagination (Appadurai 1996) and a historically constructed global power geometry (Massey 1993) interact with religious ideas and practices, which together produce different envisioned routes for people who seek spiritual and earthly support. By contrasting multiple destinations, each with its own sense of community, Rocha shows us that Brazil can be imagined as center on a global spiritual map, though primarily for non-Brazilians who entertain a "nostalgia for a preindustrial world" and see Brazil as an ecological–spiritual hub. The Pentecostal Brazilian migrants who travel to Australia envision their new country as temporally advanced, reproducing a similar spatiotemporal axis as the non-Brazilian travelers, yet with a different destination in mind. Rocha's focus on two Pentecostal churches—Hillsong and Assemblies of God—shows that Brazilian migrants regard the Assemblies of God as a protective and homely community, yet one that does not entirely match their aspirations of upward mobility and their desire to become part of a fashionable global community of Pentecostal believers. The neo-Pentecostal church Hillsong matches such an imagination and experience much better, therefore many Brazilians "migrate" from the Assemblies of God to Hillsong.

The second chapter, written by Matan Shapiro, insightfully shows how Brazilian Pentecostal churches are currently utilizing Old Testament symbols and materials to mediate spiritual power. Brazilian neo-Pentecostal churches, which are themselves the product of New-World Protestant Christian movements and African spiritual traditions that emphasize spirit possession, are looking at Holy sites in Israel as spatiomaterial gateways to a Biblical past and at Jewish rituals and symbols as concrete examples of Old Testament practices that allow congregants to ground their faith. The Holy land tours and the importation of material from Israel to Brazil demonstrate that even though Pentecostalism is often conceived of as a highly mobile religion "with no historical links to tradition and no territorial roots or identity" (Casanova 2001: 434), neo-Pentecostal churches are emphasizing spiritual rootedness and thus producing specific spiritual centers connected to each other by means of a global web with a spatial hierarchy. In the next chapter of this volume, written by Claudia Swatowiski, we will see that this web is built upon historical colonial pathways and held together by linguistic and cultural practices.

The chapter by Claudia Swatowiski forms a striking counterpart to that of Shapiro because it focuses on the presence of the neo-Pentecostal UCKG in Angola. It specifically looks at the material religious elements that mediate the relations between Angolan adherents and a divine sphere while connecting them to Brazil, Israel, and a global community of born-again Christians. As both Swatowiski and Shapiro describe, the UCKG has built a new global headquarters, the "Temple of Solomon" (*Templo de Salamão*) in São Paulo, Brazil, using stones that were brought from Hebron, Israel, to authenticate the church's connection to the Biblical Holy Land. The Temple, a replica of the Biblical Temple of Solomon in Jerusalem, was inaugurated in 2013 and nowadays serves as new divine center for adherents of the UCKG and those attracted to its religiomaterial universe. In her chapter, Swatowiski shows how this centrality is reproduced by the so-called *caravanas* (expeditions) from Angola to Brazil that guide Angolans to the Temple in São Paulo, as well as the transnational circulation of a replica of the Biblical Ark of the Covenant beyond Brazil. While the first movement follows the logic of pilgrimage, the second movement follows a logic of procession (Kong 2005), in which a sacred object moves out of the center to the periphery and back. In 2017, a replica of the Ark of the Covenant, a gold-covered wooden chest, was taken from São Paulo to Angola and taken on a procession through the streets of Luanda, witnessed by thousands of people. Beyond the detailed description of the power emanating from a replica of the Biblical Ark, Swatowiski demonstrates how the global spiritual circuit produced by the UCKG builds on earlier colonial connections and on spatiomaterial network that resembles a Roman Catholic model (see also Rickli 2016).

Human rights, gender, and sexuality

The chapters in this second part demonstrate the nuanced intersections of gender, migration, sexuality, and religion. In general, the part shows how global religious movements allow for the expression of alternative identifications vis-à-vis hegemonic representations of gender and sexuality and, *vice versa*, how global rights discourses infuse religious practices and networks. The chapters make evident how homosexuals, transsexuals, travesties, and women contribute to the expansion of religious practices, often creating different views about sexuality and ways of thinking about bodies and gender. This part elucidates how bodies can function as vehicles for political action and the mediation of spirits, while challenging (post-)colonial geopolitical and religious hierarchies. Without denying the structuring force of the global labor market or the bureaucratic and juridical powers of modern states, this part emphasizes the agency and power of spirits, saints, and *orixás* (Lambek 2014; Latour 2005) to intervene and co-produce religious subjectivities that challenge the hegemonic norms and state regulation and control. One could thus say that this part also shows how religious transnationalization "from below" (Freston 2010) works.

In the first chapter of this part, Aramis Silva looks at the roles that Latin American religious leaders (and Brazilians in particular) play in creating new spheres of communication, which has been very important for the expansion of the MCCs in the Cuban context. The MCC addresses a host of global challenges such as the inequalities produced by hierarchical notions of race, gender, and sexual orientation. In his chapter, Silva analyzes the speech regimes of MCC's leaders and he shows how these regimes allow new forms of political activism. MCC was founded in Cuba at a time in which Pentecostal fundamentalist groups were expanding on the island. Armed with the so-called prosperity gospel, these Pentecostal groups criticized the Cuban regime while pushing traditional gender and sexuality norms and inciting homo- and transphobia. Around the same time, homosexual rights were included in Cuba's revolutionary agenda and LGBT groups were becoming more visible in Cuban society. Throughout his chapter, Silva describes the fusion of religious and political speech and the emergence of new forms of religiopolitical subjectivity, and he shows how these speech regimes are embedded in sociotechnological networks, supported by Whatsapp and similar electronic platforms. In doing so, Silva sheds light on the material and linguistic aspects of lusospheres.

In the following chapter, Kachia Téchio discusses how the performances of Brazilian women who attend the Deus é Amor Pentecostal church in Portugal (IPDA) produce new representations of Brazilian femininity that help them (and possibly others) to obtain jobs in the Portuguese labor market. To increase their chances of gaining acceptance in the cleaning and service trade, the Brazilian women try to immerse themselves in the local landscape and speak Portuguese without their regional Brazilian accent. Moreover, their performances seek to represent respectable Brazilian "non-women," mothers who have transformed their bodies, devoid of desire and sensuality, and sanctified by body hair. Such representations mark an opposition to the prevailing ideas about Brazilian woman in the European context, where they are frequently stereotypically portrayed as carefree and sensual. Pentecostal religious discourses of the IPDA in Portugal support the portrayal of women who are different from the Brazilian women who perform sex work in Portugal and allow the church attendants to communicate to Portuguese women that "here are women who will not steal your husbands," who have no sexual capital and no sensual dispositions. In addition, the Pentecostal women experience the setting where the IPDA is headquartered in Lisbon as a womb or a "bubble" (Sloterdijk 2003) within which they can generate a new "Portuguese" and Pentecostal identity among the continuous flow of new immigrants who come and go.

In the third chapter of the part, Joana Bahia begins her analysis with a note that the Afro-Brazilian "sexual" spirit *pombagira* has an Iberian origin which, by way of the Afro-Brazilian religious practices, was carried by Brazilian migrants. It thus returns to the peninsula, full circle. Her chapter explores the relationship between a travesti and her *pombagira* and analyzes how this spirit allows her priestess to move between the worlds of prostitution and religion, transmitting knowledge from one universe to the other. Besides supporting movements between street and temple, the *pombagira* also supports the travesti's capacity to reverse sexual hierarchies, which is closely linked to the colonial past, and penetrate "European bodies" instead of being penetrated by them. Sexual, spiritual, and corporeal metaphors sustained by the spirits' actions reverse hegemonic readings of postcolonial hierarchies, attributing religious and sexual powers to socially stigmatized transsexuals and allowing Brazilian bodies and spirits to invade Europe and Europeans.

Bahia's chapter speaks to Téchio's chapter, as the two authors present opposing configurations of sexuality, religion, and Brazilian identity in the Portuguese context. The colonial trope of Brazilian sensuality that made structural exploitation and the reproduction of desires and sexual hierarchies possible still operates as a powerful regime that harnesses imaginations and performances in the postcolonial context. Nevertheless, this regime operates and is dealt with in different ways in relation to different spiritual traditions and sociocultural positions. The attendants of the IPDA attempt to produce a different "Brazilian woman" among others by means of Pentecostal techniques aimed at expelling *pombagira* spirits. The travesti, who is a *mãe de santo* (a high position in the

Afro-religious hierarchy) in a Candomblé temple, embraces the stereotype to employ its sexual power.

In the last chapter of the part, Andrea Martins shows the daily practices and discourses of Brazilian women involved with the Charismatic Catholic Church and demonstrates how their worldview as migrants and religious activists makes a sense of belonging in Dutch society possible at a time when local nationalist groups are attempting to affirm a homogenous social reality. In her analysis, Martins opposes the ideas of house and home, showing that although migrants favor the welfare and social security offered by the Dutch state, this does not mean that they feel that they have a home in their host country. "Home," to them, reflects a sense of belonging identified in such things such as acts of spontaneity in personal relationships and in diverse social groups that they feel characterizes the Brazilian urban environment, which they feel is largely absent in the Dutch context. In this sense, the church is a place of reconstruction of this sense of belonging. In order to understand the transformation of the church into a home, Martins shows that the use of traveling saints and devotional objects in rituals is a way for Brazilians to strengthen their cultural and religious identity in the face of the Portuguese migrant community and to expand a Brazilian nationality in the context of religious transnationalization in the Netherlands. Our Lady of Aparecida and the Archangel Michael are particularly important in this respect. Both religious symbols are considered signs of affirmation of Brazilian identity and as spiritual powers that mediate the internal conflicts between Brazilians and Portuguese, through which the migrant women create a "Brazilian" Catholic lusosphere of multicultural belonging.

Heritage, embodiment, and spirituality

The last part of the volume focuses on heritage, embodiment, and spirituality. Although various studies have already indicated the importance of heritage and authenticity as constitutive concepts for global religious practices (see also Meyer and Van de Port 2018; Meyer and de Witte 2013), this part specifically looks at cultural–religious groups that portray their roots as lying elsewhere, in an original spiritual center, while simultaneously claiming privileged transnational connections to such centers by means of performances and embodiment. These performances are perhaps best characterized by what Birgit Meyer and Mattijs van de Port (2018) have called the "aesthetics of persuasion." At the core of such acts of persuasion stand "attempts to orchestrate shared sensations and experiences in authenticating a heritage form as an essence rather than a mere construction. The point is that a sense of authenticity as an essence is effected through a particular *aesthetics* to which it owes its reality effects" (2018: 20, emphasis original).

Similar to previous chapters, Jessica Greganich's work highlights the attraction of Brazil as an ecological–spiritual center and, in her case, as a point of origin of *ayahuasca* religions, in particular Santo Daime and União do Vegetal. *Ayahuasca* is a tea brewed with the plants *Banisteriopsis caapi* and *Psychotria viridis,* of which the latter contains a psychoactive substance. With the help of the concept of *butinage* (see above), Greganich argues that the appearance of these two religious movements in Spain is not only the result of the movements of Brazilian migrants who exported their practices, but also the effect of the travels of spiritual seekers from Europe to Brazil and back. The chapter not only provides an important alternative way of writing about the transnationalization of religion in terms of deterritorialization and reterritorialization (Deleuze and Guattari 1987), but is also a good example of an effort to maintain a dynamic perspective on religious reproduction by showing that it stems from desire.

The following chapter by Andrés Serralta Massonnier takes us across the Brazilian border into Uruguay. In this chapter, Massonnier questions why Umbanda spread relatively quick in Uruguay in comparison to other Latin American countries that border Brazil. He argues that the reason is largely due to the particular qualities of the border region where many Uruguayans speak a regional dialect *Portunhol,* which greatly facilitated the adoption of Portuguese Umbandist language, among other things. One of the strong points that Massonnier makes in the chapter is that contrary to what is sometimes suggested: it was not immigration of Brazilians into Uruguay that prompted and sustained the growth of Umbanda temples in Uruguay. The diffusion of Umbanda (a relatively young Afro-Brazilian religious movement) took place almost simultaneously on both sides of the border. Strikingly, Umbanda practices and symbols are widely adopted by Afro-Uruguayans and by people who identify with Charrúa culture and identity. Charrúa were Amerindian people that lived in the region but were largely extinct. The adoption of Umbanda as a privileged collection of ethnic and religious signifiers to express and experience heritage in Uruguay in our opinion marks some of the core elements of our notion of lusospheres. The spread of Umbanda took place along colonial and linguistic pathways, and yet Umbanda—itself a fusion of Afro-spiritualism and European scientism—also allows for new imaginations of local heritage.

In the last chapter of this volume, Celso de Brito analyses the transcendental strategies and senses produced by the members of the Capoeira group *Irmãos Guerreiros* (based in Bremen, Germany) together with the *Babalorixá* of a Candomblé temple in Berlin to expand Capoeira to other European countries. Brito eloquently shows how in the German context Candomblé adherents and European Capoeira practitioners foreground their shared spiritual characteristics, bypassing the fact that the development of Capoeira in Brazil during the twentieth century was characterized by the rigorous patrimonialization and secularization of the martial art form. During the German Capoeira lessons that Brito describes, practitioners are taught that music, dance, and ritual are fundamental to the production of *mandinga* (seductive spiritual power), and the *mestres* (capoeira teachers) invite their pupils to understand their transcendental experiences as part of Afro-Brazilian traditions and heritage. Brito's chapter is not only important because it shows how certain Afro-Brazilian religious and cultural practices are (re)connected to each other *outside* Brazil, but the chapter also hints at the influence of the German art scene, demonstrating that shared notions of black heritage are not necessarily related to a black diaspora or to a historical colonial past (see also Bahia 2014, 2016). Brazilians and Germans share neither a close linguistic affinity nor a strong colonial relationship. Nevertheless, in Germany, at the crossroads of Capoeira, Afro-Brazilian religious, cultural, and artistic practices emerge in new spaces of spiritual experience that allow for the imagination of a "transnational pan-Africanism" beyond diasporic communities.

In Brito's chapter, several of the threads of this volume come together. Not unlike Yoga, capoeira is a bodily tradition and a set of corporeal techniques that, for some, are nearly devoid of religion and are full of spiritual power for others. Moreover, both have the capacity to travel easily and emerge in various places in the world that do not have a historical colonial relation with the place of origin. Capoeira reproduces notions of Afro-Brazilian spirituality throughout the world; yet to understand its spread we cannot rely on an analysis of Brazilian migration patterns. We must also see that the attraction of Capoeira stems from a genuine desire of people who were born *outside* Brazil, who are not Brazilians, to participate in an art form that unites notions of heritage, bodily exercise, and spirituality, and invites outsiders to enter the *roda* (circle), which is characteristic of Capoeira and similar to other cultural–religious bubbles we encounter in the world.

Part One

Media, Tourism, and Pilgrimage

How Religions Travel

Comparing the John of God Movement and a Brazilian Migrant Church

Cristina Rocha

Introduction

In this chapter I address the different ways in which religious movements travel and are able to establish transnational connections. Drawing on two different research projects on the global expansion of Brazilian religions that I have conducted over a decade (2006b, 2013, 2017a, b), I show that religious mobility takes place through diverse but overlapping vectors: the work of the imagination, the mobility of people (migrants, spiritual tourists, religious leaders, international students), religious artifacts, and old and new digital/ media. The Brazilian faith healer John of God has established a global movement by alluring Western spiritual tourists to Brazil through the sales of religious artifacts (crystals, rosaries, herbs, crystal beds),[1] his own travels overseas, and old and new/digital media (newspaper stories, TV documentaries, followers' books, tour guides' websites, and blogs and social media). The smaller Brazilian Pentecostal church in Sydney, Australia, grows its congregation among young Brazilian students who learn about and are attracted to Australia through annual Australian education fairs in Brazil; Brazilian agencies that sell study-abroad packages; media stories on the country; fellow Brazilians who report their stories on social media; and the marketing and tours of Hillsong United, the world-famous band of the Australian Pentecostal mega-church Hillsong.[2]

I argue that in both cases it is the work of the imagination and a historically constructed global power geometry (Massey 1993) which prompts mobility. On the one hand, John of God's followers go to Brazil attracted by the global imaginary of the developing world as deeply spiritual, where people lead authentic and pristine lives. As such, they are moved by a sense of nostalgia for a preindustrial world. This imaginary is reinforced by tour guides' construction of John of God's healing center as a magical place akin to Shangri-La.[3] On the other hand, Brazilians are enticed to Australia by a diametrically opposite but correlated imaginary. For Brazilians, Australia, as a "First World" country, is imagined as a perfect place: its streets are clean and safe; its locals are completely honest; its public transport works well; it lacks class divisions; and it is technologically sophisticated. In a sense, like John of God's healing center, Australia is constructed as a mythical Shangri-La, but this time because of its "perfection."

Remarkably, Australia is also perceived as perfect because of its supposed similarities with Brazil—its beach culture, laid-back lifestyle, and multiculturalism—which makes it more desirable a place to live than the "cold" countries of the North (in a literal and figurative sense). In a way, both countries' history of colonialism and their location in the southern hemisphere give Brazilians a sense of familiarity that, in their imagination, tones down Australia's patent otherness. This sense of familiarity facilitates Brazilians' desire to travel. The oft-quoted phrase *A Austrália é o Brasil que deu certo* (Australia is like Brazil but it succeeded) that circulates in conversations among Brazilians on social media and in face-to-face interactions points to an acknowledgment of similar histories of colonization but also to the fact that Australia became a developed country while Brazil never reached that stage. In other words, for them Australia is like Brazil minus crime, violence, bureaucracy, poverty, and corruption.

As a consequence of these imaginaries and the asymmetry of power between the Global North and South, while the John of God movement is able to expand among Western followers, migrant Pentecostal churches from the Global South such as the one studied here face unsurmountable obstacles in their reverse missionizing project (cf. Oro 2014). Similar to my findings, Freston (2010) points to, on the one hand, migrants' marginal position in and lack of understanding of the host society, and their prioritizing "ministering to the diaspora community" over the native population; and, on the other hand, Westerners' (particularly European) prejudices against Charismatic Christianity coming from the Global South. Charismatics are perceived as "primitive" to a largely secular population. Unlike for the John of God followers, here primitive has a negative connotation. As Bruner (2005) has argued in his anthropological study of tourism, while Westerners are happy to travel to the developing world to gaze at and mingle with local populations,[4] the latter are not necessarily welcome in the West as migrants. In a similar way, Brazilian Pentecostalism is regarded as matter out of place in Australia. To be sure, as I show elsewhere (Rocha 2017a), at the John of God's healing center there have been hostilities between locals and pilgrims from the Global North. However, my point here is that Westerners are able to spread their newly found beliefs and practices in the Global North more easily than Brazilian migrants are able to spread Pentecostalism in these countries.

In what follows I first discuss the ways in which religions move and the work of the imagination regarding Brazil and Australia. I then explore how this work of the imagination is deeply entangled in the almost effortless globalization of the John of God movement, and in the difficulty the Brazilian church faces to grow in Sydney. In doing so I attend to the roles that exoticism, (post)colonial desire, nostalgia, aspiration for modernity, and cosmopolitanism play in the establishment of a lusosphere.

Globalization and imagination: The persistence of a power geometry

In an increasingly globalized world, the flows and patterns of cultural influence and absorption are inevitably enmeshed in what Massey (1993: 61) calls a "power-geometry of space-time compression." That is, the issue of who holds power in relation to flows and movement cannot be overlooked. Globalization is a process by which dispersed places become increasingly interconnected; however, inequalities persist. The historical predominance of North–South flows demonstrates the structures of power in place, and the ways in which globalization is in fact gated, that is, while capital may cross borders easily, that is not the same for labor (Turner 2007). Indeed, Cunningham (2004: 335) has shown that "border crossings reinforce differences and, in some cases, prevent crossings." This is because global flows do not travel in empty space, but have established historical trajectories (Ang and Stratton 1996: 28). Their histories of colonization mean that there has been little cultural interaction between peripheral nations (Mosquera 2003: 21). Although there are obviously barriers to flows of people, more recently we have seen more interaction and new routes of migration among countries of the South which are reinforced by digital media— particularly through the use of smart phones and social media. Consequently, many scholars have been focusing on these growing South–South connections (Hearn 2016; Rocha 2009; van de Kamp 2016).

In our previous work, Vásquez and I (2013) argued that the global dissemination of religions originating in Brazil into the Global North and across Africa, Asia, and Oceania has contributed to the complication in the direction, entanglement, and content of global flows. We identified diverse but overlapping vectors that have contributed to the worldwide construction, diffusion, and consumption of Brazilian religious identities, worldviews, and lifestyles: migration, spiritual tourism, the work of imagining and consuming Brazil and Brazilian culture and religions, mass media, and the internet. These vectors can be isolated for analytical purposes, but on the ground, they often interact with each other, alternatively reinforcing each other or generating "zones of friction" (Tsing 2005). For instance, the work of the imagination is facilitated by mediatization and the internet, particularly social media. The ways in which mass media construct a locale influences the mobility of others, who may travel as migrants, international students, tourists, or spiritual tourists. This is also true of people posting pictures and comments about a particular locale on social media to acquaintances and friends. Thus, mobility and media create "transnational imaginaries."

As Appadurai (1996: 3) has posited long ago, the intensification of the global flows of media and migration has had a deep influence on the "work of the imagination as a constitutive feature of modern subjectivity." For him (1996: 31):

> The image, the imagined, the imaginary—these are all terms that direct us to something critical and new in global cultural processes: the imagination as a social practice. No longer mere fantasy (opium for the masses whose real work is somewhere else), no longer simple escape (from a world defined principally by more concrete purposes and structures), no longer elite pastime (thus not relevant to the lives of ordinary people), and no longer mere contemplation (irrelevant for new forms of desire and subjectivity), the imagination has become an organized field of social practices, a form of work (in the sense of both labor and culturally organized practice), and a form of negotiation between sites of agency (individuals) and globally defined fields of possibility. ... The imagination is now central to all forms of agency, is itself a social fact, and is the key component of the new global order.

As we will see in my discussion of the two case studies, because the work of the imagination is central to agency, it also prompts mobility. However, since globalization does not erase a global power geometry (Massey 1993) in which "different social groups, and different individuals, are placed in very distinct ways in relation to these flows and interconnections," historical imaginaries that exoticize and essentialize both the Global North and South persist. The former is perceived as wholly industrialized, rich, rational, while the latter is constructed as homogeneously poor, primitive, religious, chaotic, and hypersexualized.

Hall (1992) has argued that "the West" is neither a geographical territory nor a natural entity, but is rather a historically produced category. For Hall, the binary opposition between "The West" and "The Rest" is a discursive formation that emerges as a result of a set of historical forces that were central to the formation of Europe's identity. These include the processes of Reformation and Enlightenment as well as Europe's encounter with the "New World." Both processes gave Europe a sense of itself, an identity against which other non-Western societies and cultures were measured. The idea of progress that emerged during the Enlightenment was defined in terms of a single linear model of development according to which societies and cultures were hierarchically ranked as more or less "civilized" or "developed" depending on either their temporal distance or proximity to modernity (Hall 1992: 313). Such a view rests on a set of historicist assumptions according to which modernity is understood as "something that became global *over time*" and that certain cultures and societies can only ever experience a *belated* modernity, having been consigned to "an imaginary waiting room of history" (Chakrabarty 2000: 7–8).

Latin American countries have forever struggled with the belief that theirs was a "second-rate version of North Atlantic modernities which they 'failed' to follow" (Schelling 2000: 2). Throughout much of Latin American, and particularly Brazilian history, the theme of modernity has been the central pole around which the idea of national identity was woven (García Canclini 1995; Oliven 2000; Ortiz 2000; Schelling 2000; Souza Martins 2000). Although there was never any doubt about Brazil being part of the West, its colonial history along with its sense of its geographical distance from Europe and North America have given rise to a pervasive uncertainty regarding its status as a thoroughly modern nation. Modernity has always been viewed as something foreign, which Brazil is perceived to have lacked, and thus had to import from "metropolitan" centers of power. Brazil and its upper and middle classes have historically sought to become modern and cosmopolitan in several ways, among them by establishing policies to attract white European migrants in the nineteenth century (Rocha 2006a; Seyferth 1990) and traveling to these metropolitan centers. These strategies endure, as we will see in regard to Brazilians traveling to Australia.

In a complementary fashion, in the European and North American imagination, Brazil is associated with, on the one hand, tropes of sensuality, passion, beauty, vivacity, sexual freedom, and on the other hand, with a pristine past which industrialized countries have lost, one in which spirituality is present in everyday life. Therefore, in the collective imagination of the West, Brazil becomes the primitive, traditional, exotic Other. Aparicio and Chávez-Silverman (1997: 8) explain a similar process in their analysis of the ways in which Anglo culture in the United States represents Latin American literature. They coined the term "tropicalization" and argued that to tropicalize "means to imbue a particular space, geography, group, or nation with a set of traits, images, and values that are circulated and perpetuated through official texts, history, literature, and the media." As we will see in the following sections, the ways in which the global expansion of the lusosphere is enabled or hindered is through such "tropicalization," that is, the circulation and consumption of these imaginaries associated with Brazil.

John of God: A global Brazilian healer

The question of how a faith healer from the Global South becomes a global phenomenon, feted by celebrities such as Oprah Winfrey and the performance artist Marina Abramovic, guided my recent book (Rocha 2017a). A subsequent question was how his cosmology, and spiritual practices and religious artifacts traveled and were translated or caused friction in other societies. The more apparent reason for the healer's success is that if people are terminally ill and have been told by their doctors that biomedicine cannot do anything else for them, they may consider alternative forms of healing. Moreover, there is the fact that John of God performs extraordinary surgeries. He cuts people's skin with a scalpel, scrapes their eyes with a kitchen knife, or inserts surgical scissors deep into their noses, all without asepsis or anesthetics. People do not seem to feel pain or develop infections. Thus, the promise of healing and having a radical experience of transcendence through these surgeries are big drawcards.

Nevertheless, I would argue that John of God's cosmology, practices, and sacred objects are able to become global and be accepted by Westerner followers for additional reasons that have to do with the location of the healer in the Global South, particularly in Brazil due to its associated imaginaries presented above. A good example of this is artist Marina Abramovic's travel to Brazil in order to make a documentary of her own experiences with several different local religions of possession. In her 2012 film, "The Space in Between: Marina Abramovic and Brazil," she dabbles with Afro-Brazilian religions, drinks the Amazonian hallucinogenic brew ayahuasca, visits the new religious movement Valley of the Dawn, and spends time with John of God. As a result, the film is a hotchpotch of decontextualized, weird, and definitely primitive religious practices. This is how the film is advertised:

> Marina Abramovic travels through Brazil in search of the *spiritual forces of nature* that are embedded in *the culture of native* Brazilians. Through communing with locals, partaking in *local traditions*, and venturing out into *caves and forests*, she embarks on a *voyage* to elevate her *emotions and consciousness* and create a new piece of art that will lift up the people she meets along the way. (http://www. thespaceinbetweenfilm.com, my italics)

As we can see, the tropes used in this advertisement fit well with an imaginary of Brazil as a primitive, highly spiritual, and enchanted place. These are old tropes associated with the Global South. The European explorer enters "caves and forests" to find exotic and mystical "local traditions." This description above brings to mind something akin to the "Heart of Darkness" (Conrad 1995 [1899]), although it is now given a positive spin. I suggest that this is so because of a prevailing nostalgia for a preindustrialized world. Boym (2007: 7) posited that "the twentieth century began with utopia and ended with nostalgia." By that she meant that the optimism about the future and the faith in progress of the early twentieth century have been supplanted by nostalgia for a past untouched by progress. Industrialization, modernization, and secularization have created a longing for an (idealized) past when time was slower and nature was not degraded, when there was a connection with the "spiritual," and a strong sense of community and belonging. This longing is intensified by the crossroads the twenty-first century has found itself—in peril from climate change, the ravage of wars, and the resulting increasing numbers of refugees. This is compounded by the intense fragmentation and dislocation of globalization.

Western tour guides to John of God also make use of these same tropes to construct Brazil as a place immersed in spirituality. For instance, in the first book published in English by a guide (Pellegrino-Estrich 2001 [1997]: 83) and still one of the main sources of information for foreigners, "primitive" traits are also viewed positively:

> Western society has lost connection with its spirit origins. In countries like Brazil, India and China the existence of a spirit world, living and working around us in our daily lives, is totally acceptable. Most people in these countries live their lives within … the universal laws of love, honesty, morality, humility, charity and consideration.

This description is highly idealized given that Brazil has one of the highest rates of crime and homicide in the world, and violence has assumed pandemic proportions (Zaluar 2014). There have also been instances of crime in the town of Abadiânia, where John of God's healing center is located (Rocha 2017a: 121). However, in order to ensure the globalization of the healer's cosmology, practices, and sacred objects not only do tour guides construct an exoticized Brazil that corresponds to Westerners' imagination of the country, but they also must circumvent friction when the practices at the healing center do not fit this imaginary. One constant issue is the need to explain John of God's Catholicism to foreigners who may have rejected it, may subscribe to another religion, or hold no belief. For instance, daily activities at the healing center start and end with two Catholic prayers: The Lord's Prayer and Hail Mary. An American tour guide who was the Master of Ceremonies for the John of God's healing event in New Zealand in 2007 had a good solution to this conundrum. He told the audience in the first morning of the international event:

> Brazil is the largest Catholic country in the world. We work within a Christian framework but even in Brazil we don't ask people to be Christian. We'll be praying. You'll hear the Hail Mary and the Lord's Prayer. Please use this as something sacred, as an expression of energy, holy energy, as a way of contacting that energy in your heart. If you have an intellectual objection to that, then try to breathe.

By explaining away Catholic prayers as part of the Brazilian culture, and by offering more palatable practices such as just breathing and viewing prayers as "something sacred, expressions of holy energy," this tour guide works as a cultural translator pegging the local, traditional Brazilian symbolic world onto a global, open-ended spirituality to which many foreigners adhere. On other occasions I heard that the prayers were "expressions of the masculine and feminine principles," that they "open a vortex of healing energy," that they "were actually ancient and track back two thousand years ago," and that "they help raise the energy for John of God to enter into trance." In all these examples, foreign cultural translators deploy a global New Age/self-spirituality framework to defuse tensions between what may be seen as an unpalatable Brazilian local practice to foreign followers' own beliefs and practices.[5]

Overall, here I pointed to ways in which an imaginary of Brazil that circulates globally facilitates the globalization of John of God's cosmology, spiritual practices, and sacred artifacts. In the following section, I discuss how an imaginary of Australia constructed in Brazil attracts young Brazilians to the country and has a bearing on the difficulties the Brazilian church faces to establish roots in the country.

The Brazilian diasporic church

The Community of Jesus Church (thereafter CJC, a pseudonym) is an Assembly of God Church created in 2007 by a young Brazilian couple to cater for the increasing number of middle-class Brazilian students in Sydney, Australia. Since the beginning of the twenty-first century, Australia has become a favored destination for this sector of Brazilian society. Australia's beach/surf culture, safe streets, English language, strong economy, and developed-world status are significant attractions (Rocha 2006b, 2013, 2014, 2017b; Wulfhorst 2011). Traditionally the United States, which also has many of these features, has attracted most Brazilian student-migrants. However, Australia's visa system, that allows twenty hours of work per week and the potential for future migration through a point system or an employer-sponsorship scheme, makes the country more attractive. Brazilian students are middle class and, therefore, they either already have tertiary education, or have deferred their university studies halfway through their degree to study English in Australia. They see fluency in English as a way to become cosmopolitan, be able to apply for Permanent Residence in Australia, or if returning to the homeland, convert the cultural capital acquired in Australia into economic capital (Bourdieu 1984, 1986), as they find better jobs in Brazil.[6]

As part of the Global North, Australia is constructed as a perfect country in the Brazilian media, on conversations among Brazilians on social media, and by the Australian government eager to attract foreign students to the country. For instance, when the prominent Brazilian newspaper Folha de São Paulo ran a story on Australia, it titled it: "Everything Works in Sydney, Even Street Traffic" (Barros 2002). The report affirmed that there were no traffic jams in the largest city of Australia. Certainly, this was a construction derived from a desire for what Brazil lacks: organization. Traffic jams are common occurrences in Sydney, as successive governments have prioritized cars and have not built a comprehensive metro system. A more recent report (Prado 2017) once again focused on characteristics which Brazilian cities lacked:

[Australian] cities are extremely safe; you can go out at night and walk back [home], without the danger of being robbed. ... no matter what city you're in, Australians are always willing to help a lost tourist. They are all cordial, polite and very, very helpful.

Safety was a significant reason for leaving the country and the main worry when they thought of returning home for all Brazilians I interviewed in over a decade

(Rocha 2006b, 2009, 2013, 2014, 2017b, 2019). Hence this journalist's emphasis on the issue. However, because of the persistently constructed imaginary of Australia as completely safe as illustrated in this quote, Brazilians are usually shocked when they have their property stolen or have their homes broken into. This is, of course, not as common an occurrence as in Brazil, but it happens. Then Brazilians use Facebook sites created by/for the Brazilian community to voice their dismay and alert others to these dangers. However, more often than not they blame migrants and not Anglo-Australians for these crimes, reinforcing the imaginary of developed countries as perfect.

For their part, the Australian government has been heavily marketing Australian education globally. This is the country's third largest industry after iron ore and tourism, worth $2.4 billion dollars in the 2016/2017 financial year. As in other parts of the world, in Brazil it has been running education fairs for the past decade. In their campaigns, they use the slogan "study and have fun" accompanied by images of beautiful beaches and slick universities. This reinforces an imaginary of Australia as a country similar to Brazil but better. This imaginary is reinforced by young Brazilians who share their experiences in the country on social media. For instance, a young man shared the following on the Brazilians in Sydney Facebook group and received 2.6k "likes":

> I've travelled a lot, [and Australia] is [among] the top-three best countries in the world. Here they teach you how to live. They teach you to be always on time, not just hang out doing nothing. Here you learn things that no teacher, television, or institution teaches you. Australia is a school of life. (August 31, 2016, https://www. facebook.com/groups/brasileirosemsydney/permalink/1404280772919448/)

Here we can see that modernity, with its precise marking of time and industriousness, is what this young man was learning to embody in Australia. Young middle-class Brazilians often see their time in the country as an "adventure," a rite of passage that helps them become adults: learning to live alone and to support themselves without family and friends by their side. Similar to many other middle-class youths elsewhere, what drives their travel is a desire to see the world, and become independent adults and cosmopolitan. However, unlike youth from the Global North, for most of them, this is not only the first time they leave their homeland but also their family home and have to work, budget, buy groceries, cook, and clean.[7] As a consequence, they feel vulnerable, lonely, and anxious about their new adult lives in a foreign country.

Diasporic churches like the Community of Jesus Church (CJC) help them cope with this situation. Scholars have pointed out that by allowing a transnational membership, religion presents itself as a map through which individuals, particularly transnational migrants and organizations, attempt to locate themselves amid fragmentation and dislocation generated by mobility (Vásquez and Marquardt 2003: 53). Indeed, religion is an important aspect in the insertion of migrants in the country of settlement as well in transnational processes (Levitt 2007; Tweed 1997). Diasporic churches assist migrants in the process of overcoming nostalgia, homesickness, and the challenge of adapting to the new country.

Indeed, at the CJC young Brazilians can feel at home by speaking their own language, eating food from homeland, and making friends with other young Brazilians in the same situation. They can also network to find accommodation and jobs. However, this is not enough for many of these Brazilians. Their middle-class sensibility places value on education, consumption of foreign cultures and goods, cosmopolitanism, and professional jobs (O'Dougherty 2002; Ricke 2017; Rocha 2006a, 2019; Torresan 2012). It prompts them to strive to learn English and make friends with Australians in order to find professional jobs and recover their social class position. The CJC cannot offer them a path to belonging in the country since services and church activities are in Portuguese, and the congregation is made up of Brazilians.

For this reason, many Brazilians usually start going to Australian megachurches, where they can meet Australians and practice English. As I showed elsewhere (Rocha 2017b), in particular they choose the megachurch Hillsong because it gives them a chance to participate in global Pentecostal youth culture. Hillsong targets youth, has branches in global cities worldwide, a band which tours the world (including Brazil), and counts foreign and Brazilian celebrities (e.g., Justin Bieber, the footballer David Luis, and soap-opera star Bruna Marquezine) among its congregation. Some students who are fans of the Hillsong band in Brazil travel to Australia to be part of the church congregation; others constantly move between the Brazilian and Australian churches: the former gives them a home away from home, and the latter affords them the opportunity to become Australian and cosmopolitan. In this context, CJC and other churches catering to young Brazilian students find it difficult to build a stable congregation and establish solid roots in the country. They cannot expand among the local population because they cater to a migrant group, and they also cannot have a guaranteed congregation within the Brazilian community. As a Brazilian pastor complained to me:

> It is more "fashionable" to have a picture on Facebook by the Hillsong church than by my church to show that they are in Sydney. Brazilian churches do not give them the glamour that Hillsong does.

A CJC pastor explained how they try to counter this situation:

> We have this difficulty: they want to speak English. We have two ways [to attract students]: we strive to serve the [Brazilian] community in the best possible way regardless whether people are religious or go to another church. First, we make them feel cared for and protected. Second, we show them that the church does not want to make a profit from them, that the church is here to take care of them.

Undeniably, the CJC supports the community in many ways: they offer professional cleaning and barista courses so that they can find jobs; they help them write their CVs; and they give them support when they fall sick, do not have money to pay the rent, or have no place to live. In addition, by showing young Brazilians they are not after their money, the pastor tries to counter the negative image Pentecostal churches have in the Brazilian media and society because of their association with money laundry and predatory behavior toward the poor (Antunes 2013; Loes and Cardoso 2016). Another CJC pastor mentioned an additional way they address the high turnover in their church: they looked up to Australian churches, particularly Hillsong, as sources of ideas for their own church. She said:

> We're such a young church, so we inspire ourselves in churches that are successful. We go to Hillsong and other churches. We see what is cool. Everything the Australian churches do, they do really well. They invest money, they invest in marketing.

This admiration of Australian churches, particularly Hillsong, and the idea that they are "cool" because of their association with fashion, celebrity, and youth cultures and their slick marketing techniques fit within the Brazilian imaginary of Australia, and the Global North in general, discussed above. However, CJC's strategies to attract Brazilians have limited success. That is so because CJC follows a Brazilian style of church service without the glitz of the megachurch, its services are in Portuguese and devoid of Australians, and many in the congregation actually belong to the lower sectors of the Brazilian middle classes. This reflects the significance of class boundaries in Brazil, where cultural capital is constantly used to state class boundaries (Rocha 2006a). Indeed, when I asked a Brazilian student at CJC why he did not go to Hillsong, he remarked:

> Brazilians [who go to Hillsong] have another culture. They are well-off in Brazil. I am poor in Brazil. For example, I don't care about clothes. Most Brazilians I know who go [to Hillsong] are trendy, they all wear their hair and outfits in the same style. They like to go out to eat at shopping malls and I think it is stupid to spend money like that.

Given that most Brazilian students in Australia are well off, and the alluring power of Hillsong and other Australian megachurches because they are deeply connected to an imaginary of developed world in the minds of Brazilians, CJC and other Brazilian churches face a big challenge to their growth in Australia.

Conclusion

In this chapter, I showed that migration, spiritual tourism, exoticism, aspiration for modernity and cosmopolitanism, and the work of the imagination are all entangled in the globalization of Brazilian religions and the establishment of a lusosphere. Religion is not a bounded set of beliefs and practices separate from other spheres of life, thus its capacity to move suffers from a global power geometry. Indeed, religious mobility depends on the imaginary associated to the religion's original location, the direction of travel, as well as their beliefs and practices.

The two religious movements I analyzed here are part of a lusosphere, in which Brazil, its culture, and the Portuguese language receive different meanings according to the diverse networks in which they take part, and their locations within different imaginaries. In other words, the position of Brazil "on the borderlands of the Western world" (Hess and daMatta 1995) has different effects on these religions' mobility. For foreigners, a Brazilian faith healer whose cosmology and practices have strong New Age/self-spirituality undertones, such as John of God, fits in the Global North imaginary of the Global South. His movement expands and can flourish through the postcolonial consumption of the commodified exotic other (Young 1995), although it needs to be culturally translated to Western tastes and expectations.

By contrast, the Brazilian church encounters a much more difficult terrain to expand. Brazilians travel because they aspire to become cosmopolitan and fully modern, something they feel Brazil lacks. As such, they may seek the Brazilian church to feel at home, but they are also attracted to Australian megachurches because they can learn English and meet locals there. Moreover, the church is not able to attract local Australians because of its focus on supporting young Brazilians, and the fact that Australia is a largely secular country and Pentecostalism is negatively portrayed in the media and in society at large.

In both these examples, we can see the ways in which global circulation of imaginaries and the historical differences of power have a bearing on who and what gets to move and where. Indeed, Bruner (1989: 440) has alerted us to the fact that in tourism (and in spiritual tourism, I would add) the "Third World becomes a playground of the Western imaginary, in which the affluent are given the discursive space to enact their fantasies." By contrast, "workers, refugees, and displaced peoples from the periphery move to the capitalist centers, undoubtedly with their own projected images of wealth, security, and power" (Bruner 1989: 444).

Appropriating *Terra Santa*

Holy Land Tours, Awe, and the "Judaization" of Brazilian Neo-Pentecostalism

Matan Shapiro

Introduction

In July 2014 the Brazilian neo-Pentecostal church Igreja Universal do Reino de Deus (hereafter IURD) inaugurated in São Paulo its new world prayer center, a huge structure stretching several blocks across in the central Brás neighborhood.[1] Partially constructed with stones imported to Brazil from the Palestinian city of Hebron in the West Bank, the monumental building has deliberately been designed to resemble the First Temple of the ancient Hebrews, which the Old Testament attributes to King Solomon. The church thus straightforwardly dubbed it "The Temple of Solomon" (*Templo de Salomão*).

The opening ceremony suggested that this explicit linkage with the people of Israel is anything but accidental. It included the Israeli national anthem and other songs in Hebrew; a prayer interval (*oração*) for the people of Israel recited in Hebrew by a pastor wearing a tallit (Jewish prayer shawl) and a yarmulke; and a clip that semantically presented IURD as the direct descendant of the Israelites. A key moment featured a group of "Pentecostal Levites" dressed in white robes and golden waistbands carrying on their shoulders a life-size model of the Ark of the Covenant into the temple. IURD's charismatic leader, Bispo Edir Macedo, preached enrobed in a *tallit*, wearing a skullcap and championing a long white beard that lent him a prophetic demeanor. All in all, as it blended common evangelical ritual practices with a Biblical time frame and Jewish material culture locally perceived as sacred, the spectacle created a powerful simulacrum of the Holy Land on Brazilian soil.

Evangelical churches of diverse denominations in Brazil increasingly enhance such spectacular use of items of "Jewish" content as a means to justify Christian theological and moral traditions (Giumbelli 2013: 34–35). In a pioneering article, Brazilian anthropologist Marta Topel (2011) argues that this phenomenon should be seen as a form of millenarian dispensationalism. From this perspective the status of Jesus as the *Jewish Messiah*—not a Christian one—is the important factor. The intention of living under the Word of God is here related to a root of "Jewish" core sacredness that is taken to precede later Christian cosmological elaborations. If Christianity has not replaced Judaism in God's overall plan for salvation, the people of Israel and those who follow Christ come to constitute an unbreakable unity (cf. Dulin 2015). By emphasizing the Jewishness of Christ, those who live under the Pentecostal Word of God are thus immanently sawn into the very essence of divinity. Topel refers to this contemporary social process as the "Judaization of Brazilian neo-Pentecostalism" (2011: 39–43).

Based on nearly two years of ethnographic research on Brazilian-Evangelical Holy Land trips, in this chapter I seek to elaborate Topel's analysis.[2] I posit that Brazilian evangelical devotional travelers do not passively revel in the elevated cosmic position of the Jewish People. Rather, they also actively reframe the ontological status of Jewish objects while incorporating them in accordance with their own cultural, spiritual, and cosmological frameworks. Going beyond Judeofilia and Christian Zionism (cf. Shapiro 2011), the active appropriation of both the Holy Land and Jewish material culture thus inspires an ontological (rather than merely representational) change in the Brazilian spiritual space. I argue that this apparent historical revisionism of Christian theological routes emanates a particular spiritual "awe" (Meyer 2015), which enables the immediate transformation of Brazilians themselves into a "chosen people" here on earth.

As I elaborate this argument, I will use the term "evangelicals" (*evangelicos/ cas*) in accordance with its common use in Brazil, which popularly includes the ensemble of Historical-Protestant, Pentecostal, neo-Pentecostal, and nondenominational churches. In referring to the devotional travelers with whom I worked in the Holy Land however, I will mainly use the term "neo-Pentecostals." This is because most of the trips I accompanied were organized by churches that scholars identify as part of Third Wave neo-Pentecostalism, a theological and sacramental trend in the global evangelical movement which focuses on Prosperity Theology (Giumbelli 2013: 16–17).

In what follows I will first contextualize the rise of Holy Land tours amongst Brazilian neo-Pentecostals. I will then demonstrate ethnographically that these travelers tend to conceive of the Holy Land as God's physical dwelling place, which is literally infused with a divine substance. Arriving in the Holy Land, purchasing certain objects in it and enacting various rituals to anoint them is thus seen to enhance this divine substance, which metonymically already contains God's eternal bliss. After they have been "charged" with that divine bliss, objects or bodies returning to the home communities in Brazil may thus trigger superhuman miracles in the lives of the faithful. Finally, I will consider how the emergent construction of this cosmology takes part in the contemporary transformations of traditional markers of alterity in the Brazilian spiritual space at large, highlighting a particular lusosphere that in line with the IURD example presented above creates a provisional Holy Land on Brazilian soil.

Evangelical pilgrimage from Brazil to the Holy Land

Protestant revival movements have arrived in Brazil as early as 1910 (Freston 1999), but the number of adherents remained negligible until the 1970s, amounting to no more than 5–6 percent of the Brazilian population (Mariano 2004). In that decade, however, a rapid acceleration in the diffusion of evangelical doctrines among the popular classes began to take place, and today roughly 25 percent of the Brazilian population—approximately 50 million people—define themselves as "evangelicals" (IBGE 2017). In recent years, Brazil has consequently become the largest evangelical national community in the world (Sinner 2012).

While evangelical movements in Brazil since the 1970s have been flourishing mainly in impoverished socioeconomic environments (Fry and Howe 1975; Mafra 2001), in recent year millions of church members have joined the Brazilian lower middle class (Giumbelli 2013). With improved purchasing power many evangelicals have thus begun consuming various new "religious products," including organized tours to the Holy Land. Evidently, in 2008 only 7.3 percent of Brazilian tourists entering Israel declared they were "Protestants travelling for religious motives," whereas in 2013 this figure grew to 22 percent (IMTSS 2013). During this same period the overall number of Brazilians traveling to Israel has doubled while the relative number of travelers who self-identified as "Protestant" within them has tripled (IMTSS 2013).[3] In 2017, an experienced Israeli tour guide working closely with the Brazilian market for decades has affirmed that even after the economic crisis of 2015 Brazilian evangelicals continue to participate in Holy Land excursions in impressive numbers.

This phenomenon can be distinguished internally—as it relates to the "Brazilian spiritual market" (Chesnut 2007)—and externally, as it relates to the wider Holy Land tourism market. Firstly, Brazilian-Evangelicals at large commonly refer to Holy Land trips as *caravanas* (expeditions) rather than as *peregrinação* (pilgrimage), the later being a term mostly used by Catholics. This semantic demarcation, which designates a unique "Brazilian-Evangelical" pilgrimage space, also manifests ethnographically in particular events that differentiate participants from other religious communities in Brazil. For example, healing and exorcism rites that occasionally take place during these tours are heuristically juxtaposed against Afro-Brazilian "demonic" possession (cf. Gonçalves 2007; Selka 2010). Or, such rituals as the Holy Fire Ceremony (*Fogueira Santa*) that some churches enact on Mount Carmel directly contrast with typical events during Catholic pilgrimages in the Holy Land, which tend to focus on symbolic movement *toward* the holy site rather than on cathartic ritual enactments within it (Maues 2013; cf. Bowman 1991: 114–15).[4] Religious mobility abroad here reproduces cultural differences "within" the Brazilian context (Pype et al. 2012).

And, second, spiritual–economic transactions during Brazilian *caravanas* likewise often differ from typical Euro-American Holy Land tour performances. For instance, several Jewish-Israeli tour guides told me that Brazilian neo-Pentecostals emphasize sacrificial money "offering" (*ofertas*) much more than Euro-American groups. Or, while American travelers to the Holy Land generally tend to purchase such "Christian craft" mementos as communion cups, Jerusalem Crosses, and olive-wood Crèches (Feldman 2014), Brazilians tend to engage in conspicuous consumption of such "Jewish" objects as Star of David necklaces, prayer shawls, yarmulkes, and even mundane products like cooking oil or bags of flour.[5] Finally, and more prosaically, while traveling in the Holy Land, Brazilian neo-Pentecostals often use speakers, microphones, and loud music, which in some cases interrupt other evangelical groups in devotional sites and cause arguments and friction. I have personally witnessed several such occasions. Activities taken during the journey consequently accentuate perceived cultural differences between a salient Brazilian-style neo-Pentecostal materiality and worship practice vis-à-vis Euro-American religious conventions and norms (cf. Rocha and Vásquez 2014).

The structure and duration of these trips, as well as most of the sites visited, do not however significantly differ from North American or European evangelical devotional journeys in the Holy Land. Groups most commonly number 30–40 people who are members of one or several affiliated churches and a tour lasts in average 10 days. Aside from the pilgrims, each group usually includes several male and female pastors, of whom one would usually be responsible for the religious dimension of the voyage as a main spiritual leader. This includes the orchestrating of prayer sessions (*oração*) and sermons in religious sites, leading discussions or worship on the bus, and setting the overall schedule (as well as changing it ad hoc, at times). A licensed Israeli tour guide always accompanies the journey (Feldman 2007).[6] These guides oversee the organizational and bureaucratic dimensions of the trip while providing historical, informative, and sometimes even theological explanations in each of the sites visited (Bajc 2007). The bus drivers, who like the guides usually remain with the group throughout the duration of the whole trip, are most frequently Palestinian.[7]

While Holy Land tours take place throughout the whole year, a particularly busy period corresponds annually with the Jewish New Year Holidays across September and October.[8] These are Rosh Hashanah (New Year), Yom Kippur (Day of Atonement), and especially Sukkot (Tabernacles), which, according to the Book of Zechariah, is a cosmic time frame during which God is committed to shed His bliss over those who visit His Holy City Jerusalem.[9] During the Sukkot period some of the largest and most visible Brazilian neo-Pentecostal churches thus organize large convoys and rallies in Israel, which may include hundreds or even thousands of pilgrims at a time. Important contemporary rallies (2017) include Rene Terranova's (Movimento Internacional de Restauraão) CITY in Jerusalem; and Estevam Hernandes' (Renascer) The Jesus March (*Marcha de Jesus*) near the Sea of Galilee. These rallies are intimately linked with the renewal of broken ties as well as prayers for material prosperity, the acquisition of wealth, and healing of chronic health problems.

A characteristic tour begins in the north of Israel. It includes a stop at The Mukhraka on Mount Carmel, where according to accepted evangelical teachings both in the United States and in Brazil Elijah the Prophet had overpowered and destroyed the Baal Prophets. The group then continues north to the Sea of Galilee and nearby Christian sites, which include Caphernaum, Tabgha, Mount of Beatitudes, the lakeside itself, and Yardenit—the Jordan River baptismal site— where travelers often perform a "born again" immersion ceremony. From there, the groups travel south through the Jordan Valley to the Dead Sea and Jericho, sometimes also visiting Herod's palace in Masada and the Qumran Caves.[10] Driving west from the desert up the Judean mountains, the main portion of the tour takes place in Jerusalem, where the group spends three days or more (cf. Bajc 2006).

On arrival to Jerusalem, groups often stop at an outlook point located on top of Mount of Olives, which reveals a magnificent view of the Temple Mount and the surrounding area. Other important sites in Jerusalem include the Garden Tomb (rather than the Holy Sepulcher, which is identified as a "Catholic" site),[11] the Western Wall, the Jewish Quarter, the City of David, and the Siloam Tunnel, as well as sites of cosmic significance in Christian historiography such as the Garden of Gethsemane at the foot of the Mount of Olives. Recently, some groups have begun visiting museums associated with Zionism or the history of the Jewish people, such as the Holocaust Memorial of Yad Vashem, The Israel Museum, and the South Wall Excavations Museum.

In all these sites interaction with locals, whether Arab-Palestinian or Jewish-Israelis, is usually limited to commercial exchanges or short casual conversations with different intermediaries in the tourism industry (Feldman 2011). The bus, the hotel, the sites of worship, and the various rallies thus create a bubble environment almost completely detached from daily life in Israel (cf. Feldman 2007: 354–57). This exacerbates the imaginary of a utopian space abundant with divine meaning, which recursively intensifies the predesignated moral and theological values that are embedded in the rituals pilgrims perform throughout the trip (Kaell 2014). While this simulacra of home-away-from-home in a perfect Bible Land characterizes all pilgrimage journeys in the Holy Land (Ron 2009), in its Brazilian neo-Pentecostal particularity it relies heavily on an ontology of sacredness that is seen to be physically soaked in the land. I now turn to elucidate this claim.

The land of miracles

While Apóstolo Terranova's disciples were baptized *en masse* at the Yardenit site on the Jordan River, seven participants in the *caravana*—four men and three women, all in their late 20s or early 30s—arranged their own private ceremony in an isolated riverside pool a short distance away.[12] Dressed in white robes, they formed a circle in the water and held hands. One of them then recited an *oração*, his voice trembling with emotion[13]:

> Dear Father, our God, we will descend into this supernatural water so that miracles will take place; [and so that] extraordinary things will surprise us when we shall return to Brazil. Surprise us with your power, my father, [because] we claim [your bliss] this morning and declare our Faith [in you] ... Father, eradicate our infirmities, both spiritual and physical. Father, make a miracle in the cartilages of my knee! I want a miracle, my Lord, My God! I did not undergo a surgery in Brazil so that I could come here to Israel. Everything I have

done was to serve you in the best possible way so I will be able to walk ... [And therefore] I ask for a miracle in this morning ... Amen.

The participants washed their faces and then completely immersed themselves in the Jordan River water seven consecutive times. While the ceremony clearly resonates with the general evangelical conviction that "the body is God's Temple," its discursive Brazilian-Evangelical particularity here lies in the phenomenological purification that results from the circumstance of being in a holy space–time while physically absorbing an eternal divine grace through immersion. The entire Holy Land is here taken quite literally to be soaked with a sacred essence, which can be enhanced through *oração* to provoke miracles. The speaker of the small group of pilgrims that enacted this private ceremony has thus given up surgery in Brazil precisely because only in the Holy Land it would have become possible for him to feel God in the flesh and experience a miracle. Doron, an Israeli tour guide who works mainly with Brazilian churches, reiterates this view:

> With the Brazilians every personal story is related to some miracle. In every group I hear stories about at least one person who had no money but all of a sudden received a message from their travel agent that someone they don't even know just paid for their tour. There is also emphasis on healing. In a group I guided some time ago I saw a Pastor doing miracles and causing a woman on crutches to begin walking. The tiniest event that could happen is related to divine presence in the Holy Land, or to God's supervision. They don't just experience these miracles alone but also share stories about that between them on the microphone of the bus, so this encourages others to actively look for these miracles. They almost always find them.

One reason devotional travelers are inclined to find miracles in the Holy Land is that these are already inscribed and predicated in the Holy Scriptures. For example, Bispo Robson Rodovalho, the charismatic leader of Sara Nossa Terra church, produced a clip evocatively called "Walking in the Land of Miracles: A Convoy into the Super-Natural."[14] In the clip Bispo Rodovalho reads some verses from 1 Kings 18, which describe how Prophet Elijah defeated the 450 Baal Prophets on Mount Carmel, thus proving to the Israelites that the Lord is the real God. He then brings rain upon the land after three years of draught.[15] Bispo Rodovalho compares between God's bliss to the elements used by Elijah in that biblical event—water and fire—in order to encourage the faithful to sacrifice money through offerings to the church. The clip then cuts and a telecaster declares: "When Bispo Rodovalho conducted his prophecy a miracle occurred. In the nearby Israeli city—which has not seen rain for many months—raindrops began to fall…. This natural phenomenon is a sign to the presence of God." Bispo Rodovalho then reappears on the screen, claiming that Mount Carmel is a "pure desert" so that the fog on the mountain, as well as the rainfall, is "a supernatural event that confirms the presence of God here."[16]

Divine presence is indeed taken literally. For example, I once challenged a *caravana* participant called Rubens using the familiar Christian argument that God is everywhere, and hence He could not be confined to a particular space. Rubens replied that while this may be true, the Holy Land is nonetheless absorbed with a higher concentration of "divine essence" precisely because God chose it as the site for the fulfillment of His prophecies. Rubens then went on to claim that in one of his annual trips to the Holy Land he actually met Jesus Christ, sat with him for a long conversation, and accepted tips about the exact location of two oil wells and a diamond mine in the Brazilian Amazon. A day or two after this conversation Rubens published a post on a church WhatsApp group in which he claimed he had encountered an Angel of God during a visit to Gethsemane Garden, an experience so strong that it caused the Jewish guide of the group to convert into Pentecostalism.

"This is the land of miracles," said Paulo, a Pastor working for the Igreja Batista Reformada from Bahia, who has been returning to the Holy Land for ten consecutive years. For him, traveling through the Holy Land in itself "liberates" the miracles. "It is action that opens the gate through which the bliss (*benção*) flows," he said. By "action" Paulo meant any sequence of rituals pilgrims uphold during the journey, which thereby switches on a divine current that radiates into the bodies of the faithful. However, for Paulo and almost every other pilgrim with whom I spoke, God's bliss is not preserved exclusively for the pilgrimage time space (see also Kaell 2016). Rather, as I will now show, it can be captured, accumulated, carried away, and manipulated in Brazil by way of directing that divine bliss toward the mundane reality of the faithful.

Techniques of transfer

After a prayer on Mount Carmel during a *caravana* organized by Apostolo Valdemiro Santiago of the Igreja Mundial do Poder de Deus, I observed about twenty pastors sanctifying Jewish religious objects, bottles of olive oil and even huge books containing the names of the members of each of their respective congregations. Holding one of these books, a pastor spoke to the camera: "May

God bless you directly from Mount Carmel … the coming Sunday we will lay our hands upon you in Campinas [state of São Paulo, Brazil], and as we do that God will cause incredible things in your life … prepare yourselves for the great anointment." Another pastor, who stood literally five meters away on a slope overlooking the Megido Valley (Armageddon, in Christian tradition), spoke ecstatically to a different camera, his voice trembling with excitement (emphasis mine):

> As much as the Lord has won here in Armageddon, and as much as the Lord has won all [other] battles, HALLELUIAH! You are an invincible God when it comes to wars; that person who is fighting cancer, my Lord, this person who is fighting extreme poverty (*miséria*), against closed doors, against the crisis in this country [meaning Brazil], she will prevail, she will win. The elderly lady who is there with diabetes or high blood pressure, the elderly man who is there suffering, crying, unemployed, in the name of Lord Jesus—Oh God of Armageddon—halleluiah, He will now join your battle! Oh, he who has cancer be cured! Oh, he who has a high blood pressure be cured!

He then extended his hands toward the camera and said:

> If you believe, touch your television now, halleluiah, because the anointment of this God, the anointment of the All Mighty, *is now entering your life. Halleluiah* … You can now be awaiting this victory [which comes] from this place which is sacred, a place of responses. I will be bringing this soil [to you], the Holy Land, and bless you so there will be much victory of God in your life.

This powerful rhetoric act is representative of similar such blessings and consecrations I saw virtually in every Brazilian neo-Pentecostal *caravana* I accompanied. It includes three stages: first, substantiating the linkage between God as a supernatural entity and the particular Holy Land site in which the recording takes place; then listing the kinds of miracles God will bring about; and finally promising to actively create the physical bridge or contact between God and the faithful. In this case, this is done with a request to touch the television, which is seen to project the sublime power of God from the Holy Land into Brazil.

More frequently, however, a direct connection between God and church integrant is preferred. As they return home, pastors bring with them fragments of the Holy Land itself—including soil and rocks—and, especially, consecrated objects. While every object can be charged with God's essence, Jewish religious objects are considered particularly suitable for that task due to the biblical indication that the Jewish People is God's "Chosen People." Jewish prayer shawls,

mezuzahs, and menorahs—as well as bottles of olive oil or even bags of flour
and salt bought in Israeli supermarkets—are all perceived as "closer" to the
authentic, primordial, Bible Land. This is also the case with such Hebrew terms
as "shekhina" (the presence of God), "rabbi," "moreh" (teacher), Shalom, and
"haiym" (life), which pastors at times utter during prayer sessions.[17] Pastors thus
often use an elaborate arsenal of "Jewish" symbols to enhance and activate God's
power in the lives of the faithful.

Take the following example. In an IURD clip online, Pastor Pedro Alvarenga
is seen standing in front of the Tower of David, which makes part of the walls
of the Old City in Jerusalem, holding a bottle of Israeli olive oil in his hands. He
closes his eyes and then consecrates the bottle:

> God, in the name of Lord Jesus I consecrate this oil and I determine that just
> as the Lord has strengthened David, the Lord will strengthen all those who will
> receive this olive oil; those who are depressed, who lack faith, those who are
> subjected to problems, to debts, to economic vulnerability, bankruptcy of their
> company. My God, those who are downtrodden and fallen, they will stand up,
> because I hereby consecrate [this bottle] with the force of your power. And just
> as much as your force had sprout in the interiority of David, your force will also
> sprout in the interiority of that person [anointed with this oil].

He then invites the faithful to the anointment ritual in church that coming
Monday.[18]

Here, the pastor utilizes the mythical space–time of the Holy Land as an
amplifier that enables a double process of sanctification: first, an immediate
spiritual elevation associated with the actual presence in a holy space, and
second, by actively enhancing the supernatural power of God through prayer
or other ritual action. This technique literally transfers cosmic vitality from
a Biblical-Jewish past to the contemporary Brazilian evangelical reality. The
principles of this practice—presence in the holy site, consecration through
prayer, and transfer through touch—consist in a systematic structure by which
pastors and other brokers mobilize a sublime essence from the Holy Land to
church congregants in Brazil and beyond.

As with Catholic relics—that are heuristically taken to be filled with life—
the act of consecration turns both consecrated objects and the bodies of those
who will touch them into vivid subjects of holiness (Feldman 2016).[19] This is so
because transferring a divine sparkle from the holy place into a still object gives it
life, and thus ignites it with movement and vitality (Sansi-Roca 2007). Charging
human bodies with this totalizing holiness consequently changes the meaning of

any further interaction with that person, whether she is a pastor or a "common" pilgrim (Coleman et al. 2004; Robbins 2004). The blessing hands a Pastor lays upon the body of the faithful in this context then become metonymical to the sacred place and even to God Himself, more abstractly. One fascinating result of this process is that it gradually inspires the conceptual reconstruction of Brazilian neo-Pentecostalism at large as intrinsic to the "Chosen People."

A chosen people in the tropics

On their return to Brazil travelers emphasize the spiritual significance of the trips in different ways. While congregation members usually suffice in framing the "Terra Santa Pilgrimage Certificate" they received on the completion of the journey from their tour operator or church official, pastors and community leaders often adopt a new honorary title to their name, such as "*Bispo/a*" (Bishop), "*Apóstolo/a*" (Apostle), or even "*profeta*" (Prophet). Beyond these nominal or symbolic new markers of identity, however, many of the returning pilgrims also enhance the pilgrimage journey in concretely material ways (cf. Kaell 2016). This includes listening to songs in Hebrew that are circulated online, often with explicit religious meanings, and wearing Star of David necklaces or other Jewish symbols. Likewise, during worship some persons begin using Jewish objects they bought in Jerusalem, such as Jewish prayer shawls or headcaps. These methods consolidate a sociological change in status that also entails a deep cosmological significance (cf. Turner and Turner 1978).

Yet, from a devout Christian perspective the problem with Jewish object is that they are, after all, Jewish. When I once consulted an evangelical friend during my fieldwork in Maranhão in 2016 how to communicate the subject of my research to potential research interlocutors, he insisted I used the term "biblical symbolism" rather than "Jewish materiality." "It sounds better," he told me. As "biblical symbols" rapidly become fashionable among evangelicals all around the world—from Brazil to Ghana to the United States (Dulin 2015)—users must reframe, incorporate, and domesticate them so they can be smoothly integrated into mundane worship practice. It is my contention that in the course of this process, faith culture followers of various neo-Pentecostal denominations across Brazil begin to imagine themselves as somewhat *ontologically* "Jewish" in and of themselves, and thus, as intrinsic to the eternal bliss associated with the Jewish People. I would like to bring several examples for this fascinating contemporary process.

First, take the case of Josias, who in 2010 married his girlfriend Luciana in Maranhão in a ceremony that mimetically followed an orthodox Jewish wedding he downloaded from YouTube. They chose a Jewish setting because both have been procedurally reverting from neo-Pentecostalism to Judaism for several years beforehand, a process they had taken upon themselves following Josias' conviction that Judaism is "contained" in his blood. Evidently, Josias told me, his grandmother used to light candles every Friday night—not knowing this is a traditional Jewish custom—and "as a family we have always been good in business."[20] The wedding included the national flag of Israel, a Jewish wedding canopy *(hupa)* and a Jewish wedding contract in Hebrew *(ketuba)* Josias ordered from São Paulo. The ceremony was administered entirely in broken Hebrew by our mutual friend Wilson, who is a Presbyterian Pastor. Both Wilson and Josias wore yarmulkes and Jewish prayer shawls. Wilson nonetheless opened the ceremony in a typical Pentecostal preacher style:

> *Shalom* everybody, *amén?* … Genesis narrates the story of beginnings and shows us … a divine standard for humanity, which is the family … And this [standard] is so indicative *(marcante)*, that even our Messiah *Yeshua*—Jesus—was invited to a wedding and realized a great miracle there—they lacked wine and wine is the symbol of joy so that Jesus could not let that wedding [remain] in frustration. He entered with providence. This is what *Yeshua* will do in every incidence of your lives. *Amén?*

Wilson and Josias deliberately designed this seamless fusion between Christian and Jewish ritual elements. The Star of David and the *ketuba*, as well as the arabesques Wilson had improvised on the microphone to sound "Jewish," were perfectly integrated in the gospel of Jesus Christ that was pronounced before and during the *hupa*. *Shema Yisrael* and other traditional Jewish tunes (such as *Hava Nagila*) were played during the wedding, but no alcohol was supplied to the predominantly practicing evangelical guests. Whereas Luciana covered her face with a white veil, no separation between men and women was imposed. And while the couple approached the *hupa* to the sounds of *Hatikva*—the Israeli national anthem—at the end of the ceremony Luciana threw her bundle of flowers to the group of unmarried girls that gathered behind her "as if" it was a Christian ceremony. In order to mix these distinctive Jewish and Christian models effectively, Josias's best man Fabio read on the microphone a simultaneous translation in Portuguese from a sheet of paper. For all it mattered, the operational fusion of Judaism and evangelical Christianity constituted here an ontological unity.

If in 2010 this seemed to some of the guests somewhat strange, by 2017 the idea of a complete overlap between Jews, "Zion," and (Brazilian) neo-Pentecostalism has already become normalized. During fieldwork with pilgrims in 2016–2017, research interlocutors told me of persons using blue contact lenses and wearing earlocks in a Hassidic fashion to appear "more Jewish." I even heard of one case of self-mutilation, concerning a person who had tried to circumcise himself and ended up peeling off the skin of his penis. When I visited the Temple of Solomon in July 2016, I spotted in the crowd some people wearing yarmulkes and one couple dressed completely like orthodox Jews. The woman had a long-sleeve blouse and a long skirt that covered her legs down to her ankles. She wrapped her hair with a handkerchief. The man wore a black-and-white suit and a black yarmulke. I could not speak with them, but it seems to me they adopted these costumes because they represented an aesthetic of piety, a kind of origin or authenticity that could be used to "feel" God closer to one's body during the prayer session.

Among many Brazilian neo-Pentecostals ontological intersections with Judaism thus become unlimited in scope. For example, in 2010 I attended a Biblical Geography lesson in a private evangelical college in São Luís. The teacher, Professor Saul, sought to prove in the scriptures that 3,000 years ago the South American continent was only several dozen kilometers away from Africa. He thus pitched that the legendary biblical site Ophir—to which King Solomon had sent ships that returned abundant with gold—was actually the land we now call Brazil. This not only suggests that Brazil is mentioned in the bible as integral part of the prophetic divine plan for the History of Mankind, he exclaimed, but also that from antiquity different peoples migrated into Brazil. Saul concluded: "so this explains why there is no single Brazilian race and why we are all genetically mixed." Here, an unbreakable tie with the eternal biblical God of the Jews is seen to be carried in the blood. Genetics thus stand for a concrete biological connectivity with a divine origin, which is predicated on the conflation of "races" and the transaction of wealth, making ethnic miscegenation in Brazil an indwelling quality of God's predesigned plan for humanity that also attests to the truthfulness of the scriptures.

This incorporation of Judaism "in the flesh" ultimately allows Brazilian neo-Pentecostals to think of themselves as a Chosen People, intimately linked to an extranatural, infinite source of cosmic power. Here, God's earliest choices are eternal and they manifest ontologically in things and people. This may explicate why, according to the IURD internet site, parts of the walls of the Temple of Solomon in São Paulo were built with stones imported to Brazil from Hebron in the occupied West Bank. IURD has in fact fully transferred its Holy Fire (*Fogueira*

Santa) rituals from Mount Carmel in Israel to the Temple in São Paulo. Before 2014 congregants could send written requests and prayers to pastors, who would travel in organized delegations to the Holy Land and burn these requests on Mount Carmel, thus delivering them straight to God. From the inauguration of the temple, however, these rites are done in São Paulo. The altar and the Golden Ark of the Covenant are seen in this context as a sacred ground absorbed with a divine, supernatural essence (see Swatowiski, this volume).

In all these examples Judaism and the Holy Land jointly represent an original bliss because they are imagined to reflect an ancient time frame, whence divine power actively manifested in everyday affairs (Dulin 2015). I now move to consider analytically how the growing "Brazilination" of the cosmic power associated with the Abrahamic God and the Holy Land affects traditional markers of religious alterity in the Brazilian society.

Discussion: The power of biblical awe

When I asked research interlocutors in *caravanas* why they purchased Jewish prayer shawls and bottles of Israeli olive oil seldom did they mention the theological or philosophical appeal of Jewish scholarly tradition. The most common response was that these objects simply helped them feel closer to God. It is therefore not surprising that of the many neo-Pentecostal church integrant I have met during long periods of fieldwork both in Brazil and in Israel only two persons reported they actively sought and downloaded information on Jewish Law, biblical history, or the Hebrew language from the quite substantial body of scholarly works on the Old Testament available online in Portuguese. Or that for IURD church integrant it is completely unimportant that the Golden Ark of the Covenant positioned in the Temple of Solomon is human-made. The power of these "biblical" symbols is intrinsically embedded in their experiential capacity to concretize and condense admiration, reverence, respect, wonder, fear, or, ultimately, a sense of awe.

Birgit Meyer (2015) has recently claimed that the aesthetics of "awe" and the "wow" do not at all mean a conceptual vacuum, empty mimesis, or lack of theological sophistication. Elaborating early twentieth-century writings of Robert Ranulph Marett on spiritual wonder, Meyer agrees that religious materiality should be understood at once as an instrument to intermediate the sublime "beyond" *and* as a vehicle to induce social cohesion. Spiritual objects, sounds, and visions create a sense of awe not merely because worshipers "believe" in the cosmological concepts they are supposed to represent but also—and simultaneously—because they play a key role in an orchestrated, holistic, effervescent social experience (viz. Durkheim 2001 [1912]). In that sense, Meyer insists that the power of awe is self-generated; there is no conspiracy or a cynical deception aimed at deluding the crowd of worshipers by engulfing them in some kind of institutional coercion to comply with the established moral order manifested in certain aesthetical choices. The power of awe is so totalizing and morally abiding precisely because it fuses natural and supernatural elements, immanence and transcendence, the political and the economic, the abstract and the concrete, as well as past and present, which all manifest contextually in an immaculate material artifact, song, rhythm, dance, or otherwise. Summarizing Marett's position on the matter, Meyer writes (2015: 17–18):

> Awe here is understood as a powerful emotion produced and reproduced through specific and authorized methods. In the service of political power, awe is invoked to impress and amaze, sustaining that power with an aura that elevates it beyond the ordinary and makes it be perceived as sublime. Resonating with Durkheim's notion of effervescence—the sublime feeling that erupts when taking part in a ritual performance, yielding in participants a sense of society as a pre-existing transcendent power—Marett's notion of awe allows for a much more fine-tuned operationalization that helps us grasp the process of its actual production.

The institutionalized production of awe in contemporary Brazilian neo-Pentecostalism often links into the aggressive distribution of Prosperity Theology (Kramer 2002; Oosterbaan 2011). This global doctrine holds that those who truly live by the power of the divine Word of God (*a palavra de Deus*) will gain a pure life devoid of any demonic manifestation (Sinner 2012: 104–05). This is accomplished via "sacrifice," most commonly through cash donations toward church institutions. Repeated sacrificial offering will bring about material and spiritual abundance as well as the complete dissolution of illness, emotional difficulties, or other misfortunes, all of which perceived as originating from the evil influence of demons (cf. Shapiro 2015). These convictions are grounded in extravagant collective ritual action—often in the vein of exorcism or healing rites (Kramer 2005)—which deliberately encourage communal emotional effervescence as they transform churchgoers into active performers (cf. Coleman 2004). Focusing on the IURD, Kramer (2005: 101) calls this a "spectacle of power":

> A process of dramatic visualization [that] grounds the authority of universal church leaders, and the efficacy of its rituals. Drawing on a globalized Prosperity

Theology, the spectacular represents power and wealth in the enactment of ritual and authority ... Power and wealth figure, on the one hand, as hidden potential for action in the future and, on the other hand, as the visible realization of past actions. The spectacular mobilizes and translates an invisible dimension of power into visible form.

An invitation to touch consecrated artifacts or to take part in anointment ceremonies, both during Holy Land trips and afterward back in the home communities in Brazil, adheres precisely to this logic. Magic, miracle, and the operation of divine grace are presented in these ritual contexts as sublime responses to acts of sacrifice—most commonly of money—which in their own right are explicitly linked with the allure of defeating demons and the totalizing personal triumph such victory is supposed to bring about (Oro 2005; Reinhardt 2007). They thus embed within them a predictable, although powerful, sense of awe in front of the almighty power of God and His ability to transform lives. Evidently, IURD church integrants frequently testify that a miraculous divine intervention has occurred in their lives following sacrifices conceded on *Fogueira Santa* rituals, whether this has been fulfilled physically on Mount Carmel or in the Temple of Solomon in São Paulo. Here, the power of awe validates, reaffirms, and necessarily also reproduces a cosmology based on miracle that strengthens both a linkage with the beyond and fidelity to particular church institutions that enable the faithful to experience that awe in their personal lives through anointment rituals and other techniques.

As this relates to religious diversity in contemporary Brazil, the awe-inspiring power of Things-Jewish becomes an important boundary maker across the wide ensemble of spiritual doctrines and religious communities that spot Brazil's vast urban landscape (Almeida 2004; cf. Casanova 2013; Birman 2012). Jewish religious objects are seen in this context as symbols of piety that fend off secular temptations as well as the emotional thrill and cosmological appeal of Catholic, Afro-Brazilian, or competing evangelical doctrines. Biblical awe appears here both as an intermediary between people and the sublime, and a very efficient vehicle for the enactment of earthly political action (viz. Meyer 2015; Kramer 2002 and 2005; Shapiro forthcoming). The bliss achieved through the use of Jewish objects is then directed toward a spiritual war against agents of evil (cf. Gonçalves 2007; Almeida 2017; Birman 2012), who may sometimes be profoundly familiar, such as your neighbor or ex-husband (Selka 2010; Birman 2009).

Ultimately, then, when pastors encourage the faithful to donate large amounts of money during and after Holy Land *caravanas*, they do not merely demand a proof for the participants' trust in the sublime power of God. They also conduct essential procedures required for the empirical release of awe, wonder, "wow," magic, or even a supernatural miracle from the still objects in which it is seen to be absorbed. Since the offering that responds to this act of liberation (or opening) of divine power is heuristically compared with the planting of a seed that will yield fruits in due course—and since offering is always contingent on the intermediary role of pastors in consecrating objects and substances—this sense of awe recursively generates institutional authority. And, in a circular fashion, this authority leads to further normalization of the efficacy of Jewish symbolism, which further exacerbates the awe-inspiring allure of the pilgrimage experience in the Holy Land, and so forth. Objects, words, and charged body parts at once represent and reinstate the ancient biblical authenticity required for the validation of certain contemporary faith-based assumptions about the nature of the universe, the sublime power of God, and the role of Jesus Christ in human history (Dulin 2013).

Conclusion: Biblical lusospheres

Ritual engagement with a mythical Bible Land in contemporary Brazilian neo-Pentecostal sacramental practice is efficacious inasmuch as it is done in its own right. To put this more explicitly, pilgrims do not travel to Israel and conduct numerous prayer rituals as well as multiple cash offering to the church in order to achieve something external to these very rituals. Sublime grace— the aspired divine *benção* of the Almighty God—is imbued in the act, which causes the spontaneous emanation of a supernatural power already incarnate in sacred materiality. Following Topel (2011), Kramer (2005), and Meyer (2015), I argued that precisely this type of ritual action produces (or indeed releases) awe, which—apart from constructing a bridge to a proclaimed "beyond" that is verified in the cosmology of the church—also has profound earthly consequences in ascertaining new markers of alterity between spiritual communities. In this context the generation of a Chosen People on Brazilian soil entails a compelling struggle over the definition of social difference on symbolic, moral, and spatial registers both within religious communities in Brazil and across the Lusophone Atlantic (Sarró and Blanes 2009).

The social process I have been outlining here can ultimately be treated as an emerging biblical lusosphere taking shape also on a wider geopolitical scope. As flows of ideas, persons, and things circulate the "Lusophone Atlantic" in various directions, they trigger a "transnationalization of the religious imagination"

(Mapril and Blanes 2013) across spiritual doctrines and nation-states (Pype et al. 2012; Sansi-Roca 2007). Whenever Brazilian neo-Pentecostal organizations gain visibility in Portuguese-speaking mass- and social-media networks (Swatowiski 2010), they accentuate and localize wider theological claims concerning the spiritual authenticity, ritual efficacy, and ethical credibility of the "Judaization doctrine" (Topel 2011). A cosmology that reconstitutes Brazilian faith culture followers themselves as a Chosen People thus becomes intrinsic to the rapid "religious southernization" of Christianity (Jenkins 2002).[21] In fact, the different pilgrimage journeys I accompanied in Israel included delegations from such diverse countries as Mexico, Guatemala, Ghana, Angola, Peru, and China. The emergence of a biblical lusosphere here is two-fold: while it exports prominent Brazilian worship practices and bodily techniques to Europe, for instance, it also reaffirms the truth value of church theologies in the Brazilian social context itself. Theological doctrines and magical practices that we could identify as particularly Brazilian-Evangelical (rather than, for example, North American) are thereby being localized and transnationalized simultaneously.

As this relates to Brazilian sociality, the biblical lusosphere of awe goes beyond the struggle that is taking place between evangelicals, widely defined, to adherents of Afro-Brazilian religious doctrines (viz. Gonçalves 2007) and Charismatic Catholics (de Abreu 2015). Rather it also involves secular segments of the Brazilian society and even competing evangelical doctrines (Almeida 2017; Giumbelli 2013). In fact, Messianic Jews in Brazil condemn this use of Jewish sacred objects as idolatry and a fetishization of Jewish culture.[22] While certain neo-Pentecostal organizations emphasize the adoption of Jewish symbols as a way of linking up with what they see to be a primitive, authentic, original Christianity on the ontological level; those Protestant churches that are generally referred to as "historical" use objects identified with Judaism or Zionism only as a symbolic representation to remind congregants of the place of the Jewish people in the divine plan of history. The tendency toward "Judaization" (Topel 2011) has thus engendered significant dissent in recent years within the Brazilian evangelical world. Some churches reject this tendency completely and continue to embrace Replacement (or Supercessionist) Theology (*substituicão*), the idea that the task of the Jewish people in history ended with the birth, crucifixion, and resurrection of Jesus Christ.

But this is of little concern to my neo-Pentecostal research interlocutors. For them, immersion with the Holy Spirit within the course of a Holy Land pilgrimage journey extends its influence in a linear fashion throughout the years through anointment rituals and other forms of adoration of Things-Jewish back in their home communities. In that sense, and in parallel to questions of social alterity, participants in *caravanas* continue to feel they have acquired access to a marvelous, higher level of holiness. As I claimed above, the transposition of a divine essence into Brazil and the consequent construction of a provisional Holy Land on Brazilian soil are taken very literally as a vector of sublime bliss that is set upon persons, congregations, and even the nation as a whole. Here the awe-abiding dispersal of the supernatural power of a Jewish God and a Jewish Jesus across Brazil becomes a precondition for the reworking of social boundaries, which ultimately accentuate, enhance, and sometimes even invent profoundly new ways to be Brazilian.

The Ark of the Covenant in Angola

Connecting a Transnational Pentecostal Network

Claudia Wolff Swatowiski

Introduction

Created in 1977, the Igreja Universal do Reino de Deus (hereafter "The Universal Church of the Kingdom of God" or the "Universal Church") has rapidly expanded from Rio de Janeiro to the rest of Brazil and the world. This neo-Pentecostal denomination—one of the most successful Brazilian churches in terms of international proselytism[1]—has been present in Angola since the early 1990s. With high visibility in public spaces and growing expansion throughout the country, the Universal Church has a significant number of temples and followers in many Angolan cities. In this chapter, I examine how Angola takes part in a transnational Pentecostal network anchored in Brazil and referencing Israel. My focus here is to analyze how the Universal Church, through temples and objects, re-establishes religious centralities, promotes dynamics of fixation and circulation, and claims legitimacy and visibility—shaping a particular Pentecostal *lusosphere*.

In earlier work (Mafra, Swatowiski, and Sampaio 2013), I have claimed that Edir Macedo, the founder of the Universal Church, has transformed a popular pastoral project into a "globally integrated Pentecostal network." We (Mafra, Swatowiski, and Sampaio 2013) have argued that this neo-Pentecostal denomination can be considered as a vast network of tightly connected transnational temples, offering a theological project undertaken from the global periphery, that responds to the consequences and contradictions of late modernity. In this chapter, I return to this argument and expand it. Looking at recent events related to the inauguration of the Universal Church's Temple of

Solomon in Brazil and to the circulation of a replica of the Ark of the Covenant, I analyze how the Universal Church re-establishes religious centralities and, at the same time, creates flows through rituals, objects, and buildings in a South–South context.

In 2012, I did fieldwork in Luanda.[2] Employing qualitative methodology, I participated in the routines of Universal temples in two Luanda neighborhoods and spoke with worshippers, religious agents, political leaders, and residents of the neighborhoods. After that, I continued to follow the news of the actions of the Universal Church, as well as specific events in Angola and in Brazil that called my attention. The inauguration of the Temple of Solomon in São Paulo and the arrival of the replica of Ark of the Covenant in Luanda stand out. Analyzing these two events will help us to understand some dynamics of the denomination that shape a particular Pentecostal *lusosphere*.

The Universal Church in Angola

A former Portuguese colony, Angola became independent in 1975, immediately entering a period of civil war.[3] The end of the civil war in 2002 generated a wave of international investments, which attracted Angolans from the diaspora, as well as countless foreigners (Brazilians, Chinese, Portuguese, and others). The oil and civil construction industries have become the prime forces in the national economy. Large companies located in the country have created a competitive labor market. In this context, access to the formal economy is very restricted, with a large part of the population surviving through the informal sector of the economy. Many specialized jobs are occupied by foreigners and the demand for professional skills is forcing the local population to obtain formal education.

The high cost of living in the capital Luanda—one of the world's most expensive cities—and the seduction of consumer goods, has generated tension and fueled the desires of those who see scenes of opulence in the media and the streets. But infrastructural expansion has not accompanied the increase of the population in the Angolan capital, which now contains almost seven million residents (INE 2016). Modern buildings have been constructed where old houses once stood and where many residents have sought infrastructure improvements. Socioeconomic abysses have created strong contrasts in the landscape. International reports point to a sharp inequality in the distribution of wealth and to one of the world's largest discrepancies between wealth in resources and promotion of social well-being (Africa Progress Report 2013).

On the religious scene, the Catholic and historical Protestant churches operating in the country since the colonial period have been joined by Pentecostal and neo-Pentecostal churches that have arrived more recently (Viegas 1998; Viegas, Bernardo, and Marques 2008). From 1975 to 1990, religions were repressed by the government of the Movement for the Liberation of Angola (MPLA), which had a communist orientation. Since the 1990s, concomitant with a gradual political opening, various religions began to operate in Angola in a more significant manner. Nowadays, according to the 2014 Census, out of a total population of over 25 million residents, 41.1 percent declare themselves to be Catholics and 38.1 percent Protestants, which includes Pentecostals.[4]

The Universal Church of the Kingdom of God officially established itself in Angola in 1992. Since then, it has invested in buying large halls and building large temples in the capital and the provinces. It also purchased and began to operate radio and television stations, thus gaining visibility in the public sphere. Since 1998, it has counted on the retransmission of broadcasts from its Rede Record television network in Brazil (Fonseca 2003) and on the strong presence of AM and FM radio stations.

In 2004, church leaders announced that the Universal Church had reached all of Angola's 18 provinces through a national network of 124 temples (Freston 2005). The denomination now has some 200 temples throughout the country. Its growth is particularly visible when it holds large public events that mobilize crowds, as it did on December 31, 2012. An event on that day was so popular that there was extreme overcrowding, leading to the deaths by trampling of sixteen people in a stampede. The Cidadela Stadium, where the "Dia do Fim" (The Last Day) was held, is located in front of the Universal Church in Marçal—a lower middle-class area of Luanda, close to the city center—and has a capacity of ninety thousand people. In total 250,000 responded to invitations by the Universal Church. Representatives of the Church said that they had not expected so many people. For this reason, the denomination was barred from conducting services throughout Angola for sixty days. After this, six leaders of the Universal Church were charged and tried for the deaths, but all were absolved in 2015.

The Universal Church came to Angola with a consolidated and centralized transnational structure, organized in an ecclesial hierarchy formed by workers, pastors, and bishops, in a setting of urban expansion and socioeconomic transformation. The denomination brought with it its ritualized routine—consisting of a fixed weekly agenda of thematic services[5]—as well as cosmological perspectives and theological readings offering specific interpretations of and solutions for many of the difficulties experienced by Angolans. The Universal

Church presents itself as an institution dedicated to cooperating with the population and addressing their problems in a "national reconstruction," and as a body with the power to confront demons and the know-how to solve the different problems of the "modern world." Agents of the Universal Church emphasize prosperity, encourage entrepreneurship, and suggest forms of self-presentation for the job market (Swatowiski 2015).

With modern, comfortable, well-equipped temples and a veritable arsenal of cutting-edge media, the Universal Church offers its worshipers the possibility to participate in an expanded universe (Birman 2006; Swatowiski 2006). While the temples become spaces where those in attendance can have a foretaste of the lifestyle of urban middle classes, Universal's media shorten the distance between local religious agents and their audience, allow participation in rituals transmitted from Brazil, or the possibility of hearing Edir Macedo's message from wherever he is preaching. Universal's network of temples and media connect people from around the world to a highly centralized organizational structure. In this sense, the Universal Church is as much a sign of the arrival of modernity as a gateway to a new social world whose boundaries are not limited by the local congregation but extend to a global "imagined community" (Anderson 1983; Oosterbaan 2011).

During the period that I was in Angola, I regularly attended the Universal Church in Marçal and Alvalade, two of the thirty-two Church worship spaces in Luanda. Both churches are located along the main avenue of each neighborhood, supporting the hypothesis that the Universal Church strives to find locations that are highly visible and have high movement of people.[6] The Marçal church has a large warehouse-like structure with capacity for approximately 250 people. The Alvalade church—known as *Catedral da Fé* (Cathedral of Faith) or *Cenáculo do Espírito Santo* (Cenacle of the Holy Spirit)—is the Universal Church's headquarter in Angola and has capacity for more than 3,000 people. It is located next to a five-star hotel in a wealthy and traditional portion of Luanda and has a luxurious and comfortable interior. The pulpit is opulently decorated. The "cathedral" materializes a project of prosperity and wealth that the Universal Church wants to make visible and accessible to worshipers.

Solomon's temple: A central node of a transnational network

The Universal Church has a habit of building large temples to receive many worshippers.[7] The enormity of the temples shapes the landscape of many a city, demonstrating the church's power and ubiquity. They are built in a style described by Bishop Marcelo Crivella, an engineer and the nephew of Edir Macedo, as "eclectic with reference to the neoclassical" (Gomes 2011). The Cathedrals of Faith, like the one in Alvalade, Luanda, usually have a facade with a portico and triangular pediments, supported by cylindrical columns, erected on a landing accessible by stairs. Inside, there are large, airy spaces with comfortable armchairs. These monumental constructions can be seen as a gateway to a new social world. They can also be understood as a public demonstration of power and wealth, which is interpreted from a religious perspective as the proof of God's action and the "activation" of faith; the success of a theology that understands that greatness is the fruit of revolt, sacrifice, and faith.

The central temple and offices of the Universal Church of the Kingdom of God are currently at the "Temple of Solomon," located in a working-class neighborhood of the city of São Paulo, Brazil. The whole complex has about 100 thousand square meters of built area. It was inaugurated on July 31, 2013, in the presence of many great businessmen and authorities, including the president of Brazil at the time, Dilma Rousseff, and the vice president, Michel Temer.

With capacity for more than ten thousand people, the space is intended to be a replica of the original Temple of Solomon in Jerusalem. Regarding the temple, Edir Macedo has declared that "The architectural design followed the Biblical references of the first temple erected by King Solomon, accompanied by studies conducted in Israel and developed by the world's most advanced engineering and technical knowledge" (Macedo 2014: 218).

The effort to execute a perfect reproduction of Solomon's first temple is part of a logic of reconstruction and re-creation—marked by a strong emphasis on technical aspects of the process of re-creation of the past (Gonçalves 1988). It also includes the dramatic aspect of reenactment, with some pastors dressed as old priests, representing biblical characters. In this context, "the past is a time that repeats indefinitely" (Gonçalves 1988: 271), intended to connect directly with the present. As in the example of the tourist village known as Colonial Williamsburg, in the United States, studied by Gonçalves, the architecture and performance of the church workers at the Temple of Solomon in São Paulo do not suggest antiquity, but rather something new and clean, almost ascetic: the shine of recreated things. "Its authenticity is based not on an organic relationship with the past but on the very possibility of technical reproduction of that past," as Gonçalves (1988) said about Williamsburg.

Edir Macedo has said that he thought of the idea to build the Temple of Solomon during a pilgrimage to Israel, when he "expressed the desire that all people could step on the ground and touch the stones that witnessed the events described in the Bible."[8] The Temple aims to be "a piece of Israel in Brazil," and for this, stones were brought from Hebron, Israel and used in the construction of the Temple.

It is important to notice that the idea of bringing Israel to Brazil is not new in the Universal Church. The "World Cathedral of Faith," also called the "Major Temple" in Rio de Janeiro, was built with the same purpose. Stones from Israel were also used to build the wall that surrounds the 10,000 square meter site representing the "Wailing Wall" (or "Western Wall"). The main nave of the temple was inspired by "Herod's Theater," also from ancient Jerusalem. A large model of ancient Jerusalem occupies 200 square meters next to the temple. It intends to accurately reproduce Jerusalem and bring to Rio "the spirit of the sacred city" (Gomes 2011; Kramer 2001).

The establishment of a direct relationship of Brazilian neo-Pentecostalism with Israel and the Jewish universe was extensively studied by Matan Shapiro. In the chapter published in this volume, Shapiro points out this "distinct style of Brazilian-Evangelical piety" in which the Holy Land is "literally infused with a divine substance." This essence "can be captured, accumulated, carried away and manipulated in Brazil," transferring "cosmic vitality from a Biblical-Jewish past to the contemporary Brazilian-Evangelical reality" (Shapiro, this volume).

The idea of building a replica and bringing a part of Jerusalem to Brazil reached its highest expression in the Temple of Solomon. The temple can be considered "the material demonstration of the Universal Church's consolidation as a church and of its bond with the Holy Land," an accreditation of the "confirmation of its religious authenticity" (Contins and Gomes 2007: 10). Moreover, the temple suggests "a direct connection with a remote Jewish history, while simultaneously repudiating a conventional construction of Christian history, which necessarily passes through Europe" (Mafra 2011: 619). If Catholicism made Rome its center, and Protestantism has its roots in Europe, the Universal Church tries to replicate the Christian centrality of the Holy Land—an important place in the constitution of the Christian collective memory[9]—in South America. That means that in its attempt to reorder the religious geography, the Universal Church establishes a globally integrated Pentecostal network that reinforces the importance of Israel and replicates its centrality in Brazil, shaping a particular Lusosphere. The Temple, with the many meanings it carries, works as an anchorage for the denomination, bringing together religious and administrative dimensions in one place.

In this context, the Universal Church emphasizes that the Temple of Solomon is intended to be a site for religious experience, similar to a visitation to the Holy Land. The invocation of Christian memories present in the Holy Land, and its revival in the materiality of the temple erected in São Paulo, with its monumentality and authenticity, is intended to augment the importance of that space and generate a religious experience. The religious agents of the Church highlight that it is also important for the visitors to know the biblical history related to the Temple to understand the various elements reproduced at the Universal Church's Temple of Solomon (which includes a Tabernacle of Moses, a Jerusalem Temple Memorial, and a Garden of Centennial Olive Trees).

Thus, the Temple of Solomon becomes a locus for religious tourism. The Universal Church organizes so-called *caravanas* (expeditions) to the temple from different locations in Brazil and abroad. Instead of going to Jerusalem, the faithful can now go to São Paulo. Meanwhile, there are other unique aspects to the Solomon's Temple in Brazil: (1) the "original" temple in Israel has been destroyed, making the Brazilian building exclusive[10]; (2) the temple offers the comfort and luxury of a modern building to a people deprived of the benefits of capitalism, giving its visitors an experience of social distinction; (3) the monumental building, located in the periphery of capitalism, is the headquarter of a church that uses magical means to produce wealth, accompanying the contemporary dynamics of what were called occult economies (Comaroff and Comaroff 2001: 310); (4) Brazil, as part of the Lusophone circuit, is more familiar to many of the Church's followers, such as Angolans, than Israel; (5) it is cheaper and faster to go from Luanda to São Paulo than to Israel.

When I was in Luanda doing fieldwork, the Temple of Solomon was under construction in Brazil. After a service at the Universal Church in Marçal, I registered the following in my diary on May 16, 2012: "at the end of the meeting, the pastor asked for contributions for the construction of the Temple of Solomon in Brazil—a large project of the Universal Church, which will become a place of pilgrimage for people of all religions who cannot go to Israel."

Since then, at least three *caravanas* have been organized from Angola to visit the Temple of Solomon. But even if only a few Angolans have the means to visit the temple, the "feeling of belonging" to a transnational denomination that has such a monumental headquarters—built with the donations from the faithful— is more important. News of the progress of the construction of the temple also circulated in the churches in Angola, allowing the faithful to accompany the process and participate with donations. In a world that values monuments and patrimony, in which there exists a "process of subjectivation in which a monument is perceived to integrate the biography of an individual" (Contins and Gomes 2008: 174), the Temple can be a source of pride for those who take part in this globally integrated Pentecostal network.

More than this, besides functioning as a new center in a global religious circuit, the Temple of Solomon in Brazil can authenticate elements that circulate in this transnational network. For example, the "oil of the Temple of Solomon," consecrated by Bishop Edir Macedo at the temple in São Paulo, has been distributed at special Church events around the world. It replaces the "oil of Israel," previously consecrated in the Holy Land and also distributed in the Church's temples.

As we can see, the Universal Church generates many connections to the Temple of Solomon. Moreover, a specific point of connection that is being circulated around the world and connects Israel, Brazil, Angola, and other places where there are Universal temples, is the Ark of the Covenant. The Universal Church invests greatly in the circulation of the ark and shaping big events around it.

The Ark of the Covenant in Angola

On June 7, 2017, the Universal Church promoted a special event to celebrate the twenty-five years of its activities in Angola. The entire event focused on the replica of the Ark of the Covenant: a gold-covered wooden chest with a lid designed according to a description in the Book of Exodus, containing two stone tablets with the Ten Commandments, from the Temple of Solomon in Brazil. The denomination publicized that Angola was the first African country to receive the Ark. The Ark was taken on a procession through the streets of Luanda; from the airport, to Talatona (a modern and rich area in Luanda Sul), on a fire truck, covered in a navy blue velvet cloak and accompanied by four men dressed in special suits that replicated the robes of ancient priests. As at the inauguration of the Temple of Solomon in Brazil, the "triumphal entrance of the Ark of the Covenant" was an ostentatious ritual and a big political and media event (see Barbosa 2017). Six men, representing the Levites, led the Ark to the "tabernacle," a tent erected on a large plot to reproduce the "Tabernacle of Moses."

About 20,000 people witnessed the arrival of the Ark, according to the denomination. Local officials, including the deputy governor of Luanda and the ambassador of Israel to Angola, Oren Rosemblat, were present at the event. The ambassador had a prominent role in the event and made a speech: "For me, it is a great excitement to be here with you tonight and to feel part of Jerusalem, part of Israel, here in Angola," he said, legitimizing the event.

The ambassador, speaking in English with simultaneous translation, continued:

> The event here tonight reminds me the event that happened exactly 3027 years ago, when our king David brought the Ark of the Covenant for the first time to Jerusalem. And the way he brought it is the same way you are doing it tonight, with a lot of people, with a lot of music, with a lot of excitement, exactly like tonight.

Under the slogan, "The beginning of a new history," the presence of the Ark in Angola was associated with the political situation of postwar Angola and the recent presidential elections. Jovelina Imperial, deputy governor of Luanda, said to the reporters during the event:

> It is opportune that this element that symbolizes the power of God is among us, because after all we are in need of many blessings and much prayer, because we are entering the elections and we need the spirits to be pacified so that everything works out the best way (...) and I believe Angola will be a different country from now on.

This speech can be understood in a context of appreciation of the participation of religious institutions in the process of "rebuilding the nation" in a peaceful way (Blanes 2014; Messiant 2008; Sarró 2018; Schubert 2000).

Simultaneously, the moment was promoted as the beginning of a new story for each individual worshipper. It was considered to be a ritualized rupture with the past—both personally and collectively. "When the Ark was revealed to Moses on Mount Sinai, there was a 'before' and an 'after' in the lives of those people," said the "priest of the Temple of Solomon" Luan Vilvert, during the event in Luanda. "People come here in one way and they will come out differently, with their problem solved," he continued, emphasizing the idea of the transformation of inner life for those who face the Ark.

The Ark allows many analogies. Whether in the temples, in events, or through media channels, religious agents of the Universal Church often give explanations of the meaning of the Ark, and make associations with the theological readings shared throughout the denomination. Considered a symbol of the presence of God, the Ark of the Covenant is associated in the Universal Church with the resolution of problems, a change in life, or a victory in a battle. "The Ark of the covenant brings the representation of God into the midst of the people. (...)

Where the Ark went, the spirit of the highest went and there the Hebrews won all battles," said priest Luan.

In this context, there is an emphasis on the Ark as representing the presence of God. This means that the ark is considered a divine replica, whose sole purpose is to bring one's conception of God up to date; it must therefore not be an object of worship. "It is important to remember that the Ark is not for us, the Universal Church, an object of worship. (...) It recalls only the covenant of God with his people, a covenant that was renewed by the Lord Jesus. The Lord Jesus is the central figure of our faith," highlighted Bishop João Bartolomeu, who is in charge of the IURD in Angola, during the event. In his speech, the Bishop pointed out the Universal Church's differences with Judaism, namely recognizing Jesus as Savior, and with Catholicism, namely denying the use of objects of worship; the latter is a frequent criticism made by evangelicals about Catholic practices, though in this case, we can find similarities between them.

The replica of the Ark can be seen as a "point of contact," a term used by the Universal Church for some ritual objects. The most common "points of contact" in the rituals of the Universal Church are rock salt, anointed roses, "fluidified" water, ribbons, and bracelets (cf. Campos 1997; Gomes 2011; Kramer 2001). In the Universal Church's conception, these objects do not have magic power, but they are a way of activating the faith of the worshipers (Gomes 2011). People of "mature faith" are able to understand that the "power is in the Lord Jesus Christ and in the action of the Holy Spirit," and these people are able to access Christianity in its total potential as an abstract religious practice (Gomes 2011; Mafra, Swatowiski, and Sampaio 2013). As a potent "point of contact," the Ark is the vehicle believed to awaken a "strong faith." In the context of the Universal Church, it is understood that the believer must activate and use his faith to bring about changes in his life (Swatowiski 2007). "Active faith," a term used by Kramer (2001), is the believer's action to mobilize resources in his or her present and future. This means that while the Ark is a symbol of the presence of God, it is the faith of the faithful that makes things happen. The object, in a ritual context, is capable of activating agency in the faithful.

However, the Ark is different from the objects that are distributed regularly in the temples to "activate faith"; it is a unique ritual object. Bathed in gold, the replica, which is purported to be a perfect reproduction of the original Ark of the Covenant, is sacred as Solomon's Temple is. That is why it circulates throughout the world. It should not be multiplied because it is not an ordinary object.

It is important to note that at the Universal Church's services, exercises with objects and simulations are common (see Mafra 2002). The enactments, with the participation of the audience, are used to illustrate biblical passages taken very literally. In doing so, the pastors of the Universal Church produce a kind of pedagogy that involves objects and, often, the playing of a scene in a performance that alleges to have "efficacy" (Levi-Strauss 1963). The event with the Ark seems to follow a similar pattern. The "triumphal entrance" of the Ark of the Covenant, an event that takes place in the temples which it passes through, with scenery, special clothing, and choreographed movements, creates an environment for an exceptional experience. For the clergy of Universal Church, it seems very clear that the enacting of a biblical passage with a replica of the Ark is a performance that is intended to create an experience of divine presence because of what the Ark *represents* rather than from what it *is*.

Considering the replicas of the Temple of Solomon and the Ark of the Covenant and the events surrounding them, one can note in the practices of the Universal Church an approximation of Catholic institutional practices—though there are many differences between them. We can think of the great sanctuaries that attract pilgrims in a centripetal movement and of the images of saints that circulate beyond sacred spaces for specific events, in a centrifugal flow (Rickli 2016). In a similar way, we notice flows that are configured from the Temple of Solomon and with the circulation of the Ark of the Covenant.

Additionally, this approximation of Catholic practices can also be understood within the broader context of the struggle for legitimacy and power between the Universal Church and Catholicism, but also against dominant forces inherited from colonialism. As we have already witnessed in other contexts in the Lusophone circuit (Birman 2003; Swatowiski 2013), the Universal Church establishes a competitive relationship with Catholicism, activating strategies of occupation of public space, production of major events, and reordering of centralities. This is what happens with the Temple of Solomon and the Ark of the Covenant. They are public demonstrations of the power and wealth of a denomination in search of transnational expansion and consolidation in a Christian *lusosphere*.

Concluding considerations

In this chapter, I have analyzed the role of the Universal Church's Temple of Solomon and the circulation of its Ark of the Covenant in a globally integrated

Pentecostal network. By "bringing a portion of the Holy Land to Brazil" in such a monumental temple, the Universal Church of the Kingdom of God demonstrates its power and wealth, connects the present to the past, and replicates the Christian centrality of Jerusalem in South America. The Temple of Solomon becomes a materialization of a central node of a transnational network. Its materiality and uniqueness are a demonstration of the Universal Church's consolidation. It also signals the search for stability, prestige, legitimacy, and visibility in a universe of Judeo-Christian references.

While the Temple of Solomon represents a piece of Israel in Brazil, the Ark of the Covenant is a piece of Israel that comes from São Paulo and circulates through the network of Universal temples. The Ark can recount the history of the Temple of Solomon and refer to its centrality. By promoting the circulation of the Ark, the Universal Church connects people from Angola and wherever the object passes to the Temple of Solomon in Brazil, and at the same time to Jerusalem. The Ark materially strengthens South–South circulation in the globally integrated Pentecostal network centered on Brazil. The "triumphal entrance" of the Ark, organized in Brazil and abroad, replicates the experience of an event with pomp and reinforces the place of the Temple of Solomon as the central node of this globally integrated Pentecostal network.

Part Two

Human Rights, Gender, and Sexuality

Brazilian Gay Pastorate in Mission to Cuba

Shaping a Transnational Community of Speech

Aramis Luis Silva

Introduction

By means of the limited internet network available in Cuba, religious groups scattered throughout the island have access to the electronic preaching of the Metropolitan Community Church (MCC). This is a denomination of evangelical origin, founded in Los Angeles, United States, in 1968. It is a self-proclaimed human rights church, committed to guaranteeing the religious and political "radical inclusion" of people and segregated groups in all parts of the world. Dispersed in the form of independent communities, the Cuban nuclei are exploring the possibility of becoming attached to the global network of MCC, taking into account that they still need to be officially recognized by the State. To help them in this process, a few months after the historic 2016 meeting in Cuba between then-president Barack Obama of the United States and the Cuban head of state, Raúl Castro,[1] MCC, which today projects itself as an ecumenical and transnational organization, dispatched an evangelical mission to the island. With the support of the MCC Office of Emerging Ministries, MCC Brazil was designated to accomplish this undertaking through affinities that will be examined in this paper.

MCC has become known in the religious world for attracting members who may be alienated from their original groups of belonging due to gender identities and sexual practices that diverge from the heterosexual norm.[2] Why would a church of American origin, spread over many countries, mobilize its Brazilian branch to go into action in Cuba, where an American presence is both opposed and desired? What does this church's Brazilian experience have to offer Cuban communities?

In order to answer these questions, this text will draw from information available about MCC and from fieldwork conducted from May 9th to 19th, 2016, in which I followed the MCC missionary visit to the island. By means of participant observation, I was particularly keen to notice the forms of interaction between the church's leadership at Mission and its multiple and diverse Cuban audiences as they took shape through a set of events, including services at churches, participation in LGBT pride parades (locally called Congas) in Havana and Matanzas, talks delivered at the Colleges of Law and Medicine in Matanzas, and a roundtable organized by the National Centre for Sexual Education (Cenesex) during the 7th Cuban Journey Against Homophobia and Transphobia in Havana.

The MCC delegation's timetable was interspersed with interviews and diplomatic talks with the leaders of the Martin Luther King Memorial Centre of Havana—a "macro-ecumenical organisation of Christian inspiration"[3] aligned with the government, which gave support to MCC's passage through Havana. The whole timetable was planned according to a strategy of insertion by MCC into a local religious network. MCC went to the island with the purpose of making church projects compatible, and, as we shall see next, the theological capital of its leadership would become the mediating element in this process.

For the sake of illustration, I have chosen to analyse the Pentecost service promoted by the MCC leadership in the town of Matanzas, among other pronouncements by the leaders of that church. Celebrated fifty days after Easter Sunday, the holy day is one of the most important of the Christian liturgical calendar. According to religious tradition, it commemorates initial contact between the apostles and other followers of Christ with the Holy Spirit—the moment when the first Christians allegedly received the inspiration to preach the message of Jesus. The day remains associated with the birth of the Christian Church.

The following demonstrates, by drawing on ethnographic evidence, the way in which our subject—a transnational church of polycentric institutional structure—may be described and understood as a communicational network of platforms intersected by "codes of communication" (Montero 2006), in which multiple discourses and their meanings are continuously produced and disputed by contextual and historically situated agents.

By framing the MCC's congregational nuclei as arenas of communication marked by particular logics of social associations (Cefaï 2002, 2009), the ethnographic focus turns toward the configuration of specific regimes of speech by church leaders and how they allow us to identify patterns of political activism. It is important to consider that these churches, apart from preaching what they describe as "radical inclusion," publicly project themselves as being the churches of Human Rights.

Utilizing the approach of sociolinguistics' ethnographies of speech—looking at who speaks what to whom, where, when, and in which manner and purpose (Kiesling and Paulston 2008)—we can understand MCC and its religious communities beyond their institutional framework. Our proposal, in one of its dimensions, is to outline these communities as collective loci of expression. That is to say, to understand them as communicational structures in which the members, in the process of association and bearing in mind certain common issues, define the limits of the group as a community of speech (Hymes 1974), at the same time establishing, through shared religious experiences, how they will be publicly represented. At this point in the analysis, the attention is especially drawn to the communicative action of the religious community leaders. It is they who carry out the mission of forming and maintaining their audiences.

It is also necessary to take into account that the strength of these local communities lies in their ability to articulate themselves within a transnational network that is part of and works to create a specific Lusosphere. I will demonstrate that the specific Latin-American (and especially Brazilian) connections play a particular role in the creation of a new sphere of communication in Cuba. At the same time, such a network, working to construct a religious identity across these communities, interconnects specific fields of collective experience in accordance to its promise of translatability and of rendering multiple moral meanings compatible (Cefaï 2017), as will be examined in the sections that follow. In this way, churches will be understood as technologies of assembly forming communities of speech and meaning. Let us now focus on the ethnographic data.

MCC in Cuba

The mode of arrival of MCC in Cuba replicates the way the organization has established itself in other parts of the world[4]: contact is established with local groups which have had access to MCC's ecclesiastical project through the internet or by other channels,[5] then leaders are sent to the respective countries to get acquainted with these nuclei and to check on compatibility of visions, values, and local political and theological projects with the tenets of the organization—which is proud to often be confused with a social movement. Once both parties demonstrate an interest in deepening their institutional relationship, these initial agents are put in charge of giving support to the creation of a new MCC group—a so-called "emergent community." Then the work of establishing the church begins, with the training of leaders as a top priority, a process which can analytically be described as one of communicational interaction directed at producing shared codes (Montero 2006).

Months before the mission in May, some MCC leaders had already arrived in Cuba. At the forefront were Hector Gutierrez, a gay, Mexican bishop, and general coordinator of the church in Latin America; Darlene Onita Garner, an American bishop and co-founder of the National Coalition of Black Lesbians and Gays (NCBLG); Carmen Llanos, a lesbian pastor initially attached to MCC Madrid and today living in Toronto; and Troy Deroy Perry Jr., founder of the church and a religious personality and civil rights activist who enjoys significant prestige in the American scene.[6] The seventy-six-year-old Reverend Troy (as he is called within the church), retired for almost a decade from his function as the moderator and leader of the institution and aware of the potential of bringing MCC to Cuba, decided he would be involved in this process from the beginning. This would allow him to make a double dream come true: getting to know Cuba and seeing his inclusive human rights church established on the island.[7]

On the Cuban side, some of the people interested in the possibility of strengthening the local relationship with the American church came from the group that had formed around Elaine Saralegui,[8] one of the leaders of Opening Breaches of Colours—an LGBT collective organization dedicated to fighting discrimination in ecclesiastical domains. Positioned in Matanzas, a city a little more than 100 kilometers from Havana, Elaine says she is apprehensive about the growth in number and influence of fundamentalist Pentecostal groups on the island. Funded by American churches, particularly those from the South, these new denominations, according to Elaine, have combined a theology of prosperity which criticizes the Cuban regime with traditionalist values that are soaked with homophobia and transphobia. All of this is happening at a moment when the Cuban Communist Party itself is being questioned on the inclusion of Gay rights in its so-called "revolutionary agenda." That has been made possible through the direct actions of the congresswoman and sexologist Mariela Castro Espín—director of the Cuban National Centre for Sexual Education (Cenesex), Fidel Castro's niece and Raúl Castro's daughter with the feminist Vilma Espín. In 2008, sex reassignment surgery became legal and free for transgender people once Mariela's bill was passed. Since 2007, the Cuban Journey Against Homophobia and Transphobia has been included in the official calendar and space has been reserved for an ecumenical service for designated progressive Christians.

Living in a rapidly changing country, Elaine Saralegui knows she needs to expand her scope of alliances beyond Cuban churches, with which she has already established a good relationship—such as the Ebenezer Baptist Church of Marianao. This denomination—then under the leadership of pastor and Communist Party Congressman Raúl Suárez—was one which worked to pave the way in 1984 for the meeting between Fidel Castro and the American pastor and human rights activist Jesse Jackson. The event was considered a milestone in the regime's openness to national churches.[9]

The Cuban Council of Churches (CIC), an organization acknowledged by the State that includes fifty-two Christian denominations, estimates that there are roughly 25,000 evangelical and Protestant groups on the island, according to data from the Associated Press in March 2017.[10] The CIC reckons that Cuba could be experiencing an evangelical blossoming, a phenomenon related to the current process of political opening. Some churches have allegedly found ways of acting in line with the regime. In CIC texts published in the official state media,[11] these churches are acknowledged for their community work as bodies that service the "Cuban nation and people" by promoting projects on health, community education, and social assistance in case of emergency, for example.

It is important to note that the activism of Elaine's collective, centered around conversation and debate focusing on mutual aid facilitated by the spoken word as arenas of communication, began in 2012 within her original church. "In the beginning, we had no experience on what we would do, and in the first meetings we would just tell what had happened to us, we would watch movies or debate some biblical text," she remembers, according to a report by Ivet Gonzáles released by IPS agency.[12]

According to accounts by Elaine on other forums, the inner group grew to the point that she felt it necessary to open it up to members of other denominations, trusting in the spiritual underpinning of her agenda—the general right to faith without exclusion based on gender identities or sexual practices.

But the forty-year-old pastor, with recognized theological credentials from the Ecumenical Seminary of Matanzas, wanted to radicalize the level of religious inclusion already experienced at her home church. She wanted to go even further. Elaine—who was considering artificial insemination as a way of raising a family—did not deem the space allotted to LGBT parishioners by so-called traditional churches enough anymore.

"We were apparently accepted into my church, provided we behaved in a seemly way according to a designated standard," said Elaine during a conversation we had during fieldwork. But that meant a sort of social invisibility, according to her. "People would even know you were gay or lesbian. But it was assumed that would not be an issue to deal with." As a topic of conversation, homosexuality was considered off-limits. A tipping point in the conversation about tolerance came when two young men were rebuked for having made a gesture of affection inside the church. "One of them simply placed his arm on the other's shoulder, as any other couple would do. That was enough to shock some adherents, who sought the pastor to complain that we were crossing the limits," Elaine recalls, outraged.

The word in action

In Matanzas, a town once known as the Cuban Athens for its intense intellectual and artistic activity, Elaine leads a group of about thirty people in reflection and worship. Most are young people who identify as gay or lesbian (there is one transsexual), all with the shared purpose of participating in a religious community. Coming from various denominations—mostly Protestant (Presbyterians and Baptists, for example), but also Catholic and people from Santería cults (many of whom preserve shared bonds of belonging—that is, attend two churches)—they gather regularly for activities including biblical studies and liturgical ceremonies defined by the Christian calendar.

Sunday services happen on Yvi Cruz's rooftop. She is one of the group leaders and a professional at the Kairos Centre for the Arts, Liturgy and Social Services, an ecumenical organization dedicated to social activities.[13] Perched on one of the city's high quarters, participants can see the lights spread over the coastal city at a distance rather than sitting on those green, upholstered chairs for yet another worship service characterized by liturgical ecumenism and hymn books typical of the churches influenced by the Liberation Theology—a Latin American theological current that emerged after the Second Vatican Council and hinges on the assumption that favoring the poor is the key to the Gospel.

During the delegation's visit to the rooftop on the night of May 15th, the Pentecost celebration, a makeshift altar was adorned with red fabric chosen to represent the sacred. On top of the makeshift altar was a gourd, which acted as a chalice (an important symbol within the Liberation Theology) and the container of hosts, equally notable for its simplicity. Fabric was stretched over the cement floor, where objects such as the Bible and other items of rough, simple, and organic materials were placed. A local musician played songs on guitar, bongo drums, and a flute.

That night, the members of the "terrace," as pastor Elaine calls the provisional venue of worship, were joined by the pair that made up the new MCC mission in Cuba: Cristiano Valério, a Brazilian pastor from MCC São Paulo and coordinator of the Brazilian MCC network, and Reverend Carmen Margarita Sánchez de León, a Puerto Rican bishop and member of the MCC Office of Emerging Ministries. Henceforth in this text, we will look at both clerics as examples of MCC's mission incarnate, and see how the institutional project is reflected through individual agents, each drawing on their own personal experience and histories. As their work on behalf of MCC publicly constructs these leaders as specific religious figures, so too is the project itself shaped by each of them, as we shall see.

Already acquainted with the leadership of the Cuban group involved with the mission's organization, Margarita and Cristiano were formally introduced to other members of the community at the rooftop service and called upon to share the pastoral word with Elaine during service.

Margarita, a Puerto Rican bishop and member of the MCC Office of Emerging Ministries, then fifty-nine years old, was entrusted with delivering the homily in Spanish that night. A black theologist with a degree in comparative literature, Margarita was born into a middle-class, independentist,[14] Protestant family from Costa Rica—a country which had been under American tutelage and was once comprised of a Catholic majority. A third-generation Protestant, Margarita was tied to the United Evangelical Church of Puerto Rico through her mother's side. According to her, her father was a public servant who never claimed any religious affiliation. In spite of the alleged conservatism of the United Evangelical Church of Puerto Rico (going parties, drinking, and smoking are prohibited, for example), it provided Margarita with an entry into Liberation Theology, considered a progressive theological trend by the bishop. Margarita remembers being one of the only black girls at the model public school she attended, and later being a community leader put under surveillance by the Puerto Rican police and by the FBI on account of her "libertarian and subversive" ideas.

She proceeded with the codification of the Pentecost at the "terrace," that is, she set the parameters for interpreting it and rendering its meanings up-to-date. In her sermon, she touched on a wide range of topics, from the holy day's Jewish roots to its appropriation within a Christian context when it was included in the New Testament as the moment the Holy Spirit manifested. She provided keys for the interpretation of that rite as it existed within a specific space and time, laden with mystical and historical symbols whose meanings would update themselves. The Christian church, understood at the service as a collective body that also updates itself in space and time, would also be unfolding into ever-changing future manifestations:

> Pentecost was a celebration of the first fruits of the harvest. During those feasts one would collect all the first fruits and give grace to it, because the land had been generous and plentiful to nourish them. Pentecost is also related to the escape (of the Jews) from Egypt, fifty days later, to give grace to God—a god that for forty years guided the people, its spirit, through a path across the desert. This is a feast we call peregrination. And it is also at that moment that the followers of Jesus, gathered in Jerusalem, received the spirit of God and started to speak in all the languages of the peoples that were there. For us of the Christian church, the moment of Pentecost is related to the emergence of the Church, which, from the very moment it was born, is culturally diverse. It is diverse in languages and ethnicities. It is diverse since its beginning in sexual orientations and gender. Since its beginning the spirit of God has celebrated and blown into diversity.[15]

Margarita never once left the church, not even after coming out as a lesbian, at which point she was already established as an accomplished leader. Her speech shows that such reformulation travels a continuum of shifting meanings. A speech is always embedded in biographic trajectories that are not merely a sounding board of narratives being continuously recreated and independently repeated. On the contrary, such biographic trajectories can be understood as particular processes of subjectivation and reflexivity (Butler 2015). These processes work as embodied and socially positioned loci in order for one to experience narratives and to shape meaning in the lived life—that is, "rooted in a world of men or things made by men, a world that it [the lived life] never abandons or manages to transcend" (Arendt 2010: 26)—according to the interaction with other lived lives in successive utterances and hearings of such speeches.

It is that movement of experiencing a narration in public and in oneself—that is, in an act of speech in which the orator and the audience combine a certain measure of the word-meaning-action trinomial (Searle 1969) according to a rule of utterance and hearing discovered in the interaction—that allows Margarita, as a religious woman and an activist, to put her spiritual and political struggle into cosmological terms. Before her small but attentive audience on the rooftop, she produced the equivalence between her evangelical preaching and her battle for social justice and equality. This symbolic transaction is made through what we call tryptic discourse—public speeches in which "the instances of the political, religious, and sexual coexist in order to assert a semantic unicity, although the religious communication performance reassert its independence in relation to the other functioning systems" (Montero, Silva, and Sales 2018).

The bishop had traveled to Cuba in her youth to participate in an ecumenical training, as she told audiences on more than one occasion to authenticate her ideological background. She allegedly participated in the collective cuttings of sugarcane promoted by the revolution. Her return, years later, would represent a new biographical step for Margarita, a thread of continuity and coherence in a life marked by extensive international travel on behalf of political and spiritual causes perceived as convergent.

The MCC website describes Margarita's journey this way: "Ordained in the Metropolitan Community Churches in 1998, she has been a pastor in different cultural contexts, in Puerto Rico and the UK, and also served beyond MCC in ecumenical and human rights organizations." This gives us further insight into her trajectory.[16]

Frequent transits between political and religious fields have been part of Margarita's life since her youth and were even noted in the dossier produced by the police during their investigations (the dossier now lives at her house). Ironically, it was that crossing of borders between realms usually thought of as separate that kept Margarita out of trouble. Typified as a fierce and intelligent person in information gathered from her neighbours and others, a true independentist and critical to a dictatorship of capitalist exploitation, she was also described as an extremely religious person. According to the conclusions of the report, Margarita's religious beliefs were very strong, rendering her pacifist, which led the authorities to deem she would not be a serious threat to the country.

Currently living in Mexico City with her wife and twin children, Oshadi and Siboney (the names of original peoples of Cuba), Margarita has spearheaded two successful legal campaigns in her country: the inclusion of human rights violations in the Criminal Code and a public demonstration on the obsolescence of the country's Sodomy Law—as Executive Director of the Amnesty International of Puerto Rico, she presented herself before the authorities of the State as a self-declared gay woman and demanded to be arrested for the violation of Article 103 of the Criminal Code.[17]

The event gave Margarita national prominence and the Puerto Rican legislation was put in check. Either the authorities would arrest her, or they would acknowledge the constraints of the law. In a devious way, the latter prevailed. "Authorities refused to jail Sanchez, claiming that she could not be prosecuted because she lacked a 'virile member.' Sanchez's demonstration was part of a broader civic effort led by her to have the law stricken from the criminal code as unconstitutional," informs La Fountain-Stokes (1999: 93).

Bishop Margarita, later called "the wizard" by the Cuban authorities, finished her sermon with the prayer:

> Saint Ruah,[18] for your guidance through your paths, we thank you. We thank you for your church, which from the beginning you hath founded diverse and rich. We ask you that your spirit continue to guide us, so that we continue carrying that spirit of unity in diversity; that spirit of transformation in order for the dream of God—this dream that you hath blown into our hearts, of a more just and inclusive society—to be a reality. Thank you for being amongst us. Amen.[19]

Communities of sense

Once it was his turn to speak, the bishop's traveling companion, the Brazilian Cristiano Valério, a thirty-nine-year-old pastor from MCC, São Paulo, also used the Pentecost symbology to cast light on what we might call a politics of intimacy, capable of combining religion, sexuality, and a constructionist orientation of partnership. Cristiano likes to call himself a "hillbilly" from the town of Cruzeiro while delivering his sermons in Brazil. A black theologist of Baptist origin, he uses the gay experience as a framework for understanding the place of religion in our world today.

> The Gospel of today is an invitation for us to think of the time that precedes that breath of the spirit—when the People of God were locked, isolated and fearful. We all know what that is. Isolation makes us feel alone, makes us afraid. But when Jesus made himself present amongst them and blew onto them the spirit of God, they experienced something very powerful: the communion. The "common union" provides us with the spirit's wind. It is the wind of the Holy Ghost of God that turns our loneliness, our fears into courage and strength. We are no longer alone. You and I, now, have become us, by a miracle of God. We are no longer you and I, in isolation, in fear. We are us. And when we are us, we experience the breath of the Holy Ghost.

Echoes of the work *Credere di credere* are evident in the sermon delivered at the rooftop, Cristiano being a reader of Gianni Vattimo, the gay philosopher and communist politician. The pastor is also a sympathiser of Diversidade

Tucana[20] and a regular activist within the national conversation on LGBT rights. Representing MCC Brazil, Cristiano attended the first National Conference of Gays, Lesbians, Bisexuals, Crossdressers, and Transsexuals (GLBT), held in Brasilia in June 2008. According to his account on August 18, 2011, during an interview broadcast by news channel *Mix Brasil*, directed towards a gay audience, he was there as a MCC reverend "because we understand Christianity as a position"—that is, Christianity is politics.[21]

Following the interpretative trail of Vattimo, Cristiano also supports an understanding of the historical process of secularization from a new philosophical and hermeneutical re-framing of *kenosis*, the mythological incarnation of God in Christ. According to him, this is a fundamental element in an understanding of spirituality that would open itself up to questions of the body, its practices, and its identities. In line with Vattimo's thesis, religion and the message of Christianity, understood in consonance with post-metaphysical assumptions, would abandon the severity of a transcendental God for the sake of a notion of divinity diluted in humanity, or a deified humanity. "The harshness that characterises divine justice is lost, as well as the sense of sin itself, the reality of evil, and, consequently, also the necessity of redemption" (Vattimo 1998: 87).

Anthropologist Léa Freitas Perez, another reader of Vattimo, also addresses *Credere di credere*, helping us to decipher the dense discursive inventory of Christianity, deliberately oriented to blur the boundary between religion and politics. According to her, *kenosis*, by rescuing humanity from sin with the revelation of its nullity, transforms the message of Christianity and Christian love and charity into a secular ethical language that "refers to the reduction of violence in all of its forms and imposes respect for the moral expectations of other people and of the community in which one lives" (Perez 2012: 211).

> Therefore, redemption (if redemption exists) does not come from repentance of sin as an operation of struggle against evil, but from the unconditional love as source of the organisation of coexistence. In other terms: the God of justice, frightening and violence, is dissolved by kenosis and, in its place, emerges the God of mercy. That is the liberation. The divine justice as an attribute close to the natural idea of sacred is secularised for the sake of the sole commandment of love (love as the only commandment). (Perez 2012: 211–12)

This perspective demands a merging of theological and philosophical notions, putting questions of human rights in a twilight zone between politics and religion. Cristiano's political imagination acquires a hermeneutic outline that bestows intelligibility on MCC as a body of communities engaged in the production and experimentation of civil and religious ideas. If the history of salvation is understood by Cristiano as a history of interpretation, in line with the Vattimo's position, then those communities, more than just insulated spaces of self-acceptance and shared experience, are nuclei where symbolic, intimate, and public battles are fought—spaces in which political stances take on religious significance and vice-versa. By what practical means does that occur? Through the public investigation of narratives, drawing on collective experiences to redefine concepts such as "homosexuality," "sanctity," "sin," "liberation," and "exclusion."

During the interview mentioned before, Cristiano exemplifies how such communities of sense work:

> There is no doubt that it is very important when a group of homosexual people gather and these people work out the issue of exchanging experiences in all they have in common regarding the struggle for building up an affective relationship with their own history. In that the newcomer lives with a low self-esteem and has difficulty putting in words her/his feelings and suddenly finds a religious group that has all the diversity of the LGBT community. There are people here who perform shows at night, there is a drag queen group, all overtly and peacefully. Some members gather after the service to drink draught beer at Caneca de Prata, or to go dancing at Vieira de Carvalho.[22]

As founder of MCC São Paulo, Cristiano is responsible for the presence of MCC in the biggest city in the Southern Hemisphere, and is also responsible for conducting the work of the MCC Brazilian Network, made up of churches spread over eight Brazilian states (Paraná, Rio de Janeiro, Minas Gerais, Espírito Santo, São Paulo Paraíba, Ceará, and Piauí). Although made up of small communities scattered across the continent, together these groups have developed a specific way of combining a communal religious life (based on shared religious bonds), with multiple forms of social activism, always anchored by metalinguistic means of publicizing their causes. That is to say, publicizing a cause is to put it on the stage by living it publicly (Silva, Montero, and Sales 2018), as we discuss in the following section.

Final considerations: Transnational social technologies

Following the approach suggested by Butler (2015) in her discussion of self-account technologies, as suggested previously (Silva, Montero, and Sales 2018), MCC communities can also be understood as social technologies in a circumstantiated space and time that allow their members to re-learn and practice a new rhetoric of themselves.

> It allows them, finally, to ascribe meaning to life and to their surroundings by drawing from a learning process of a new rule of enunciating themselves that is to be exercised in two overlapping scopes of experience: the intimate and the public. That is to say, it is not enough to simply discover yourself to be. It is necessary to experience that existence by being publicly recognised. This is the "coming out [the closet]" undertaken as a religious experience and, which doubles the meaning of the category of "liberation". (Montero, Silva, and Sales 2018)

For the sake of illustrating the specific technology being explored by this network in Brazil, it is worth mentioning the group's engagement in public campaigns, such as the one for "egalitarian marriage," part of the LGBT movement's agenda, which was achieved by judicial means in 2012. Public demonstrations are intended to bring communities and their agendas into the regional and national spotlight. Examples of this include participation in Gay Pride parades in cities such as São Paulo[23] and Rio de Janeiro and the promotion of outdoor queer worships in Belo Horizonte, Minas Gerais. Support is also given to leaders running for public positions, such as in the election of Deacon Dário Neto as a member of the LGBT State Council of São Paulo in 2013. Social agendas are frequently produced in partnership with the public authorities, such as the LGBT Meetings with Christ, which carried out its third iteration in Teresina, the capital of the state of Piauí. Mass media campaigns are also being explored, such as the one by Marcos Lord, leader of MCC Rio de Janeiro, who got coverage in newspapers, websites, and television programs, where he transformed himself performatively into Luanda de Perón, a drag queen and evangelical pastor who fights for the end of homophobia and transphobia, among other forms of prejudice.

Individual communities report and share activities by means of annual retreats and periodic on-site leadership courses held throughout the year by countless virtual exchanges conducted via electronic platforms such as Whatsapp. In this way, ideas are shared and sometimes adopted by disparate groups. This represents the construction of a network of agents that, in spite of geographical distance, define themselves as members of one family, and learn, regardless of their diverse social backgrounds, how to speak a common language that will render their individual experiences relatable within a shared "scheme of intelligibility" (Butler 2016).

It is this social technology—this specific manner of experiencing religion publicly, as enacted in Brazil—that pastor Cristiano can offer the new members of MCC in Cuba, who are already articulated, as we have pointed out above, into specific groups of speech. He is one of the Latin American leaders most aligned with bishop Margarita's project for the church. She has been gaining prominence within MCC for her work developing communities in Latin America. Partly benefited by the linguistic transit between English, Spanish, and Portuguese on the one hand, she also benefits from her capacity to make other projects by Latin American communities compatible and/or aligned to the MCC transnational project.[24]

With the blessing of and funding from the American headquarters, the pastor and the bishop traveled to Cuba in order to initiate the new Cuban group into a transnational network of communities that both they and the institution itself will work to expand. If the working model yielded results in Brazil, taking into account the proliferation of new nuclei, why not replicate the process in Cuba?

The Brazilian pastor saluted those members whom, he expects, are coming to enlarge his network, maybe making it ever more transnational from now on, as he wishes it.

> Before anything else, I would like to thank God for this opportunity of communion that we have had on the last days. And I am also moved to notice I have a family in Cuba. And that is what MCC makes of most precious in us. Wherever we are, we can find a piece of ourselves. And I can see myself here. To embrace myself and to meet myself in you—that communion has a transforming power.

It was with these words that the Brazilian pastor, trained in the pragmatic coordination of local churches, realized his desire to make MCC his transnational community of sense.

Identity Reconstructions of Brazilian Women in Pentecostal Spaces in Portugal

Kachia Téchio

Introduction

This chapter is a rereading of the role of the Brazilian woman within the God is Love Pentecostal Church (IPDA).[1] In the present text, I am particularly considering the forces that these women have activated or repressed in reconstructing representations of themselves as women, Brazilians, and Pentecostals. Their dynamic social dramas form a characteristic and circular strategy that's geared to create a social construction of Christian Brazilian women as "nonwomen" that is proposed or imposed by the religious group (Téchio 2011). This chapter analyzes the constructed and reconstructed identity linkages these Brazilian women produce through their incorporation or negation of the precepts of this Pentecostal evangelical religion, seeking to compare these with the current generation of religious migrants who came to Portugal between 2012 and 2017.

Machado (1996, 2003, and 2006) and Gouveia (1998) agree that gender is an ever-present variable in the study of religions, given that women always form and maintain the multitude of followers. It was found that in the IPDA, women are the pillars of the community in addition to being the majority of the church's devotees. They are daily at services and prayers: in the morning, afternoon, and evening, seven days a week. And they are at all the vigils conducted every fifteen days throughout the twelve months of the year.

The religious group remains basically unchanged in its rites, rules, and promises, promoting a religious cultural continuity in spite of the geographic displacement caused by migration, maintaining its "base membership deeply linked through repetition of performances, the use of the symbolic forms and the maintenance of the same founding doctrine" (Téchio 2011). The central question here is whether the church provides a role in the production and maintenance of representations of Brazilian Pentecostal immigrants and their host country. This would mean, on the one hand, that individuals allow themselves to conform to this religious scene in such a way as to not stand out as Brazilian or immigrant women; on the other hand, it could mean that these individuals have constructed other ways of negotiating Brazilian, female, and immigrant identities. We also intend to observe how recent Brazilian immigrants, usually family members of these women, prepare before migration to integrate themselves into Portuguese society or not, and resignify their identities based upon the experiences of these women and how they perform identity. This hypothesis is based on the assumption made by Machado and Mariz (1997) that there exists a link between religious activities and the type of role attributed to women by the hegemonic gender system in society. From this idea that a type of role is attributed to Brazilian immigrant women, we will analyze the *obreiras* (Brazilian female faith workers or sisters who assist the pastors) in the IPDA/God is Love Pentecostal Church, and identify how they move and activate forces that can generate new identity representations.

New immigrants, new identities

My idea of conducting research with the IPDA came after verifying that religious connections in Portugal propel the entire life context of Brazilian immigrants: where they work, where they live, what places they frequent, and what kind of social life they can enjoy (Téchio 2006). Being a member of the IPDA is like having a passport stamped "honesty, dedication, moral integrity, and obedience," values of interest for Portuguese employers, and transmitters of a sense of safety for Portuguese women.

The IPDA is a church that has its entire structure defined and controlled by its Internal Regulations—the IR. Each rule is accompanied by a specific punishment. For example:

> K 6—workers—malice. *Obreiras* who act maliciously, (malicious games, coarse jokes, mockery) will be punished. EF 5.4. Punishment 30 days of trials.
>
> K 7—workers—visiting other ministries. *Obreiras* or members of the IPDA who visit churches of other ministries (…) whoever does this will be punished (Rm 16,17). IIJo 1,10 and 11. Punishment: members 60 days, *obreiras* 180 days. (Internal Regulation, s/d, p. 52)

F22—Sisters' hair. Cutting the hair or trimming its ends. Punishment: members 3 months, *obreiras* 6 months. IC10 11, 10.15

G13—makeup, eyebrow, nails—not allowed (…) Punishment: members 30 days, *obreiras* 90 days. IPe 3.2 to 5

G1—inappropriate clothing. Sisters: mini sweaters, sleeveless sweaters, skirts or dresses that do not cover the knees (…) Punishment: sisters 30 days, *obreiras* 60 days. (Téchio 2011: 115)

Because of this structure and its many punishments, getting into the IPDA's world was something of a challenge. I started contact through a friend of my family in Brazil, who prepared me a bit as to how to dress and to behave. When I arrived in Portugal, I already knew the basic codes necessary to enter the group. For almost four years, I remained within the world of the IPDA and its rules; it would not have been possible to conduct my research otherwise. In the end, I made several good friendships with many *obreiras* and, in an incredible gesture of courage and rebellion during a period of transition between pastors, when the church was without formal leadership, these women included me in the prayer group of the sisters and gave me the pink uniform of an *obreira*. From that moment on, there were no more secrets between us. The older women wanted to carry out my complete conversion. On the other hand, the younger ones (the under fifty-year-olds) felt happy to have someone who could say that which they could not.

In the analyses I carried out in 2011, I verified that Pentecostal representations and performances permitted the diffusion of a Brazilian religious identity that is very useful for Brazilian women's processes of integration into Portuguese society, especially with regards to access to work and housing. This is a representation of a Brazilian woman who is "family-oriented," "respectable," "selfless," and who renounces herself and hides her body; a nonwoman, an almost invisible woman who despises her own body and desires in the face of greater things, that is, the salvation of her soul and those of others, in direct opposition to culturally inculcated ideas that promulgate the stereotype of carefree and sensual Brazilian women (Machado 2006).

Women need to distance themselves from these "symbolic prisons" that are expressed in the reconstruction of Portuguese stereotypes about Brazilians and Brazilian stereotypes about the Portuguese. These are loaded with determinisms about what it is to be a woman and to be Brazilian in a migratory context. This Brazilian "nonwoman" admirably serves the Pentecostal religious discourse exported by the IPDA and maintained up to the present day through extreme attempts at preservation.

In the same period that I was doing my research, Bahia (2015a, b, this volume) developed her studies on Brazilian prostitution in Portugal and its linkages to Afro-Brazilian religions in that country. This context of different religious possibilities, with the presence of different Brazilian identity representations, becomes a bustling center of forces and dynamics that sometimes passionately confront each other or seek to ignore each other's existence, but are connected at the root by rhizomes that are almost impossible to separate (Deleuze and Guattari 2004), as will become clear throughout this chapter.

Thus, the *obreiras* of the IPDA, the *mãe de santo travestis*[2] of the *terreiros* (Afro-Brazilian temple; Bahia, this volume), the Brazilian women who change their ways of speaking to make themselves sound more Portuguese, the young prostitutes who frequent both Pentecostal churches and Afro-Brazilian *terreiros*—all have a common nucleus which revolves around several goals. Two of these are the search for a more sustainable way of life and a way of maintaining different identities. Here we find both the immaculate identity of the daughter who migrated and works in a café or cares for the elderly, maintained for her family through photos on social networks showing her participation in religious groups, and the identity of the professional, sensual Brazilian who possesses all the charms Portuguese men dream of.

Whether they are Pentecostals or not, Brazilian women day laborers and who do not want to see themselves reflected in any of these stereotypes, who work cleaning houses and offices, who raise their children on their own, who participate in different social nuclei besides the religious (such as the Afro-Brazilian martial art Capoeira), who try to project an image of themselves as fighters, frame themselves as exceptions to other Brazilian types because they need their employers' confidence in their honesty.

Obreiras, travestis, and all the various other ways of being women—all these identity representations connect, blend, and surround themselves with a characteristic energy that helps these women survive by producing micro social nets that are nurtured with tips for jobs, access to documents, dates and marriages, shared housing, and other activities based on the roots of Brazilian identities. In other words, at times and according to their convenience, these subjects emphasize different nuances or wear different masks that are all produced based on a single root: Brazilian identity, which never can be completely erased or removed.

On the one hand, these women express different ways of seeing themselves and being seen as Brazilian. On the other hand, the Pentecostal identity in some ways shapes perceptions of these women, making them more acceptable in terms of social integration. Unlike Brazilian *travestis* and prostitutes, Pentecostal women who deny their bodies and desires are perceived as not having the necessary sexual and physical capital "to steal husbands from Portuguese women." And because these women seek to speak the Portuguese of Portugal, they attempt to immerse themselves in the local landscape as a way of being better accepted in the labor market—especially as cleaners and in commerce.

Pentecostal collective identity representations establish symbolic bridges used by individuals to insert themselves into the immigrant-receiving society (Téchio 2006). Brazilian members of the IPDA are recognized everywhere—in the streets, shopping malls, in commerce in general—through their unchanging personal image: uncut long hair, skirts below the knees, lack of accessories, and no makeup.

In the same way, *travestis, mãe de santos*, and prostitutes are perceived and recognized in the streets and in all places where they go, whether through their clothes, language, gestures, exuberant makeup, or other bodily identifiers (toned and perfect bodies) that are impossible to hide. In many cases, these Brazilians do not want to hide these markers, but rather to emphasize them, since this differential identity linked to the body can be a powerful product, especially in the sexual market. If the power that emanates from these Brazilians comes from the *exus* and *pombagiras*[3] (Bahia, this volume), the power of the *obreiras* comes from their ostentatious purification.

Obreiras gain symbolic capital from the "denial" of their bodies: exactly the opposite of the *pais* and *mães de santo* whose symbolic capital is rooted in sensuality. Each body obtains and maintains its power of presence and negotiation only in the places where it is established. Outside those places, the same body totally loses its value: in the *terreiro* or Afro-Brazilian temple the *obreira* is not recognized as legitimate; in the church the *pai de santo* is equally rejected.

The central question that arises among all of these Brazilian identities and Brazilian bodies that inhabit Portuguese imaginaries and the spaces is that the symbolic bridges that these individuals dream of constructing between their country of origin and Portugal are revised, reconsidered, and reconstructed as they meet Brazilian groups that recognize, approximate, or harass them in Portuguese territory. The romantic image of the migratory process that these groups hold before moving is quickly erased. Often before a young woman emigrates, she will have an almost fairy tale–like perception of Portugal. She dreams of the status of living abroad, of having access to beautiful clothes, of visiting places she's never seen before, and, perhaps, of marrying a prince sent by God. But the realities these Pentecostal migrants encounter when they reach their destination do not allow coexistence with fairy tales: for them, life in Portugal is dry, cold, and rigid.

Barth (1976: 188) points out that "cultural differences may remain, despite interethnic contact and group interdependence." In this way, the main identity representations of the IPDA women are connected to a community that is strongly imagined as based on Pentecostal performances and linked to them by an umbilical cord, despite the seas that separate the church's headquarters and its diverse branches throughout Portugal and the world. When one imagines a possible interruption of these performances, of the cutting of this umbilical cord, one needs to imagine a degradation or destruction of these representations of identity, which is certainly not a situation desired by the women of the IPDA. In the Portuguese context, their Pentecostal representations of themselves as self-denying hard workers allow them to enjoy a religious bricolage that provides them with a new identity. This thus (re-)nourishes a circle of dependency between these women, the church, and the maintenance of that privileged identity. An example of this can be seen in the rigid and physically demanding quotidian existence that these women voluntarily face.

This new identity demands and emerges from the act of purifying oneself. It is built through arduous injuries to the body. The "gratification" these *obreiras* receive is the audience's applause during worship, the increase in the numbers of people seeking out their religious works (healing prayers, casting out demons, prayer drives to achieve a desired goal). Public demonstration of the gift of casting out devils, the gift of tongues, the gift of healing, makes the worker known throughout the entire country and even abroad. This brings with it a feeling of importance for the *obreira*. Seeing one's name on posters or hearing one's name on the radio promotes visibility and a sense of having one's "15 minutes of fame" that in other contexts might seem too small a reward compared to the size of the effort required. But in the space formed by Brazilian Pentecostal immigration in Portugal, it is a status that is greatly desired.

> I leave home at 5 AM. I clean offices until nine o'clock, then I come to the church to clean here before the afternoon service. I stay here to open the afternoon service and only leave the church around ten [PM]. I leave food already prepared at home. I do this from Monday to Sunday. (Maria Esperança, field notes, Lisbon: May, 2007)

When asked about how they care for their house, children, and husbands, the *obreiras* often respond in ways similar to this:

God's mission comes first. They get used to it. When they do not get used to it … we try, pray, try to bring them to church, but if it is not God's will … then the choice is always to obey God first. The children go to school and then take the bus and come meet me at church. They do their homework here in the church and then go home with me. At first they did not like it: they wanted to watch TV. But then when they saw me in the pulpit, when they see people looking for me to bless their food, their clothes, to pray for them, and when they see me singing or preaching, they become proud. They tell their friends that their mother is a Pastor (…) But I am not a Pastor. I am only a *obreira*, but without bricks, the house can't be built. (Maria Helena, field notes, Lisbon: May 2005)

In this bricolage, it is difficult to identify the levels of dependency between these women and the church at some moments. On the one hand, domestic lives, children's education, affective and social life, and in fact everything, is mixed in with the church. On the other, the church has no reason to exist and is only a cold and empty room without the presence of these women.

The forces of attraction and repulsion that exist among the various Brazilian groups present in Portuguese space are visible in the speeches heard during the IPDA's rituals, especially during exorcism cults when the main figures of the Afro-Brazilian religions are summoned and invited to "withdraw" from the bodies that they have "invaded."[4] *Pombagira*[5] is very often invoked by the *obreiras*, who emphasize her powers and influence in granting wishes to those who ask them. She is the entity most feared by the *obreiras*: their number one enemy. The women warn that to "expel" *pombagira* takes much prayer and fasting and that novice ministers should not try to do this because it can have disastrous consequences.

As denial of the body is the basis of the *obreira*'s "purification," it is thus possible to understand her desire to "escape" from all possibilities of the "appearance of evil," which could be taken as evidence of *pombagira* "possessing" the woman's body. An extreme and dangerous turn for the Pentecostal image would be an *obreira* becoming "lost" and "falling into *pombagira*'s coils." This could happen through something as simple as the *obreira* being seen wearing lipstick.

The Pastors also cite other entities such as the *exu Caveira*,[6] *Zé Pilintra*, *preto velho*, *Cosme*, *Damião*, and many others. In many cases, the first time the audience hears about these entities is during worship in the church. Some people actually become intrigued by this information and, urgent to solve their own problems, begin to frequent *terreiros*. In these moments, the imbricated Brazilian religious scene in Portugal becomes immersed in itself. At different levels of depth, where nationality is the axial point of trust between individuals, it represents a small space of immigrant resistance against national traditions and prejudices. A Brazilian immigrant may seek out a Pentecostal church or a *terreiro* or even both spaces at the same time, but will not seek out a Portuguese *terreiro* or a Portuguese Pentecostal church. The trust in religious power is rooted primarily in the fact that a given religious house's Pastor or *pai de santo* is Brazilian.

Feminine migration and religious attractions

Due to its regimented control and harsh punishments, the IPDA attracts a different kind of Brazilian woman. The immigrant Brazilian woman who is a member of these religious groups experiences her identity differently from other Brazilian women from other social classes, both in Brazil and abroad. Her socialization process is based on different results (SALEM 1981) and emphasizes a maximal perception of the feminine condition and a perception that "the course of her existence is escaping her control, being, in this sense, external to herself" (SALEM 1981: 93).

In the migration space (which is in and of itself isolating), and also with nation of origin and gender, there is a tendency to "fill this gap with indeterminacy. That is, the space that is already wide by virtue of its conditioning factors of class is enlarged" (SALEM 1981: 93). There is a characteristic profile for Brazilian women abroad who are part of the "Pentecostal model." This profile exposes limits that make these women doubly conditioned to connect with religious life and spaces, because of the great difficulties they encounter upon arriving in the immigrant receiving country. There are divorced women who have left children in Brazil which they must support. There are women over forty or fifty years old who have been abandoned by their husbands and need to financially aid their family. There are women with low levels of education, who have mostly migrated alone because they knew someone who was in the church (in Brazil). For these women, the church becomes their main home, their main place. Brazilian Pentecostal women are extremely vulnerable, and in many cases this profile began to be sketched out in childhood in their families in their country of origin.

In this way, when they are helped by a member of the church to find a place to live and a job (a main concern of everyone upon arrival), they initially feel compelled to reciprocate by attending church. Over time, they realize that their entire social life has become formed around and within this religious core. However, it would be wrong to read the Brazilian women who are members of the IPDA as only vulnerable, only needy. They negotiate their identity representations, their understanding of their corporeality, and the construction of the feminine identities of their descendants in a much more complex way. We will now take a look at how these relations develop between those women who are *obreiras* and other Brazilian Pentecostal women.

Women as *obreiras*: What does this mean?

The construction of identity representations is translated through and integrated with migration processes and the integration of migrants into the receiving society. In the case of Pentecostal Brazilian women in Portugal, the reconstruction of their identity involves choosing which elements they want to perpetuate and which they seek to hide. Within this context, the preservation of religious elements highlights the visibility of the women's group, distinguishing as much as possible the religion from its culture of origin. This is due to the characteristics of the Brazilian women who attend the IPDA, who are looked down upon even by members of other Brazilian churches, such as the Christian Congregation, where women wear full, embroidered white veils and become organists, or other neo-Pentecostal churches where women wear modern clothing, trousers, and even makeup.

Makeup seems to be one of the most fearsome items that women *obreiras* must resist. Pastors claim that vanity enters the woman's body through makeup, and they believe that the use of a simple lip gloss can quickly become the use of a red lipstick, a visible symbol that *pombagira* resides in a woman's body. There are other issues, however, like not shaving one's armpits and legs, not using nail polish, or not employing anything that produces "beauty or sensuality." *Obreiras* are only allowed to cut their nails and keep themselves clean.

The secret of the *obreira*'s "power" is the "sanctification of the body" created by her denial of sexuality. The loss of purity generates a need for punishment, which can range from not being allowed to sing, begin a service, or wear the pink robe that makes it possible to identify an *obreira* from afar, etc. The length of punishment may also vary between days or months, as decided by the pastor—the man who guides the church.

In terms of migratory patterns, being a Brazilian woman *obreira* in the IPDA is built upon the constitution of new bodily identity marks and in the rigid observation of community structures. In this place, the woman performs through singing, rituals, and performances that constitute her desired identity. She lets her hair grow and all the hairs of her body become a source of divine strength, initiating the restructuring of a new woman. This construction of a new desired identity slowly proceeds within the context of Brazilian migration in Portuguese society, often facing challenges of everyday life such as the lack of housing or employment. This woman is no longer Brazilian in her view of the world. She rejects this identity in favor of that of a woman *obreira*, a Pentecostal woman. Some subjectivities of this new identity are only perceived by other Brazilian women and men. However, the most evident characteristics are intended to be perceived by Portuguese society, and they are.

The Brazilian Pentecostal religious field in Portugal began its existence by employing many symbols brought over from the country of origin, including the idea of eternal joy. Over the years, however, it has been distancing itself from emphasizing Brazilian ethnicity (Barth 1976), choosing instead to link itself to sacred symbols closest to the "original source": in this case, Jerusalem.[7]

Geertz (1978) points out that sacred symbols function to synthesize a group's lifestyle, moral disposition, and worldview. Some Brazilian religious groups in Portugal utilize these symbols to reshape their identity, reinforcing religious belief and practice in order to create a group ethos that is more understandable and which, in their worldview, represents an ideal type of life, making this vision emotionally persuasive.[8]

The IPDA is the most traditional Pentecostal group with regards to the use of objects. They even use yellow envelopes stamped with the words "vow of freedom [from worldly things]." But the church's strongest and most radical visible brand is its use of the bodies of its women members. This is the IPDAs symbol of greatest power. The women who join this church discover, cooperate with, and can enjoy the same power by marking themselves with certain corporal identifiers: hair that is more than a meter long or which even reaches to their feet, a body purposely erased with pale-colored clothes that completely cover it, and lack of makeup and perfume. The woman's body, displayed in this fashion, is the church's strongest symbol, representing its vision of the world and life.

On the other hand, Pentecostal Brazilian women, in spite of being fully capable of differentiating Brazilian culture from that of the Pentecostal religion in which they are inserted, constantly relate religious elements to Brazilian social rules, taboos, and stereotypes. Although it is not possible for them to completely separate their national identity from their religious identity, due to the existence of a dynamic and organic relationship between all the dimensions of being "woman," "Brazilian," and "immigrant," *obreiras* struggle on a daily basis to physically and emotionally create this separation. They demonstrate this through hours of kneeling in prayer (counted in the member's notebook); through their hours of vigils; through their strict following of all the rules created and imposed by the founder of the church; through the long, daily, and tiring journeys to work at night services. But mostly they demonstrate this desire through their daily presence, for as many hours as possible, in arduous and uproarious ceremonies in a basement church, seeking to be regenerated or reborn in that overheated, closed basement, almost as if it were a uterus. This uterus of the church in downtown Lisbon, in which these expanded interrelations between the sacred and the secular take place, is precisely and ironically housed in a building that previously contained a porn cinema (Téchio 2011).

In any case, since the sacred space or religious field is also socially constructed by the actors who give meaning to and receive meaning from it, a certain power is what is especially attractive to this sort of immigrant from Angola, Mozambique, Cape Verde, but most emphatically to women from Brazil. As these women discover or experience revelations of the sacred, however, they acquire an existential value that motivates their ever-deeper immersion both in the church's sacred spaces and to the commitments that their identity representation must assume in other spaces. It is as if by arriving at the break of dawn and frantically washing the church floor (where the consumers of porn once walked) they are washing away the demons of sinful lives. By loudly intoning prayers and songs throughout the day and also during the night vigils, they seem to be purifying themselves: exorcizing these same demons from their own bodies and killing them. There is something of an ironic, circular, and continuous paradox in this process, which might be seen as tragic, if not hysterical, were it not for several issues:

1. without demons, there would be no need for purification;
2. the church has enough money to rent any space it wants, but specifically chooses to stay in a basement in a small commercial building in the center of Lisbon, hard to access, almost imperceptible to anyone walking by on the sidewalk. The church consciously chose this location, as various interviewees emphasized, taking the place of the old porn cinema.

Other factors also contribute to the construction of these new female Brazilian Pentecostal identities. One is linked to the redefinition of power that Galbraith (1986) takes from Weber, the claim that power is the "possibility someone has of imposing their will on the behavior of other people" (1986: 2). The performance of Pentecostal religious identity by Brazilian women (most particularly in the IPDA, known throughout Brazil as the most rigid and traditional church), is due to the distinction given to the instruments used by *obreiras* as women and which sets them apart and above other women as well as men. One of these is the pink uniform, which symbolizes a declaration of worthiness that brings with it threats of punishment and suffering. When an *obreira* receives her mantle, she becomes a leader capable of imposing her will upon others by making use of her oratorical and moral qualities. This image is linked to an objective kind of power: those who accept the will of others (or of God through another person) are conscious of doing so and those who exercise power also do so consciously (Galbraith 1986).

The *obreira*'s uniform and her untouchable hair[9] are two of the strongest symbols of a woman's strength and purity in the IPDA. These symbols express an essentialized character to which other church members must submit. With persuasion as an instrument and the church's organization as a source, what matters here is the maintenance of belief. *Obreiras* as women are always striving to keep the faith. Their discourse is about "true doctrines," conditioned education, and the mechanisms of defense and discipline of the Pentecostal organization. This makes it possible to safeguard correct language and the people who accept the church's dominion. Younger women who are beginners in the faith are closely monitored and undergo a kind of tutoring initiation, whose final diploma is to be named an *obreira*. Disputes for this position of status within the church, the person who "raises up new *obreiras*," are highly competitive, given that this is a position of great importance in the organization, involving the right to exercise power. As a result of these disputes, the women not chosen may even undergo a reverse process, not surviving the process of identity construction that they have engaged upon. In other words, their self esteem may become quite impaired and they might come to see themselves as "simply women" who were unable to purify themselves enough to be allowed into the religious group's elite.

In many cases, these immigrant women return to secular life and may even dive into self-destructive processes, working in brothels for example, which they might begin to understand as their due place in Portuguese society. One of Pontes's interviewees says that "she does not think that prostitution is a case of lack of choice: it is often the product of a 'weak mind', 'shamelessness', and 'spiritual weakness'" (Pontes 2006: 268).

In these women's imaginations, when they cannot become *obreiras*, all that remains is the acceptance of the body: the Brazilian body that, in Portugal, is still very much linked to the idea of Brazilians as "the hottest women in the world" (Pontes 2006: 268). Regarding this sexualization of Brazilian women and the concomitant desexualization of Portuguese women, it is worth remembering the case of the "mothers of Bragança,"[10] which was even highlighted on cover of the *Time* magazine's European edition. In Bragança in 2003, Portuguese women launched a protest against the presence of Brazilian women in the city, adopting the symbols of motherhood, child care, and domestic life in order to repudiate the supposed attributes of the Brazilian women who, at the time, were working in a local bawdy house. The Brazilians were described as vain, sexually voracious, corrupters of the social order, con artists, and husband thieves. Here, the symbol of Brazilians-as-prostitutes was cast in sharp contrast to the image of Portuguese-as-mothers. Although this event occurred more than a decade ago, it is still very much in the memory of Brazilians in Portugal and especially of Brazilian Pentecostal women who feel that, over the last twelve years, the media has not substantially changed their pejorative portrayals of Brazilian women in Portugal.

Reconstructing lives

In analyzing Brazilian feminine roles in the expansion of the Pentecostal religion in Portugal, we have taken as our basis the configurations of the prevailing Pentecostal religious field of 1960s and 1970s, when the IPDA established the rules that continue to be important until today. This preached a radical rupture with the religious models previously employed by the individuals, and proposed new patterns of socialization that followers should adopt. The radical changes that Pentecostalism brought to Brazil were similarly exported by the IPDA, imposing a kind of dualistic conversion and creating a radical separation between the secular world and the customs practiced within the group. The process of religious transformation and rupture preached by this kind of Pentecostalism finds in the imaginations of Brazilian immigrants territorial and identity references. By leaving their country of origin, these women opt to break family, social, and economic ties in search of a reconstruction or resignification of their lives, their roles in the world and—in the final analysis—their identities.

By thinking of religion as symbolic systems through which each society represents the main themes of its worldview and by understanding that "this view is permeated by memory, which, at the same time it is re-signified by and helps order the present" (Geertz 1978), one can understand the process of adherence to Pentecostalism as "an intricate set of re-significations and re-arrangements between local and institutional, social and individual memories" (Téchio 2011). In this way the Pentecostal space, constituted by a relatively simple bureaucracy and a free interpretation of the bible, is presented for these Brazilian women as a means of and a place for reorganizing their identity representations.

Halbwachs (1990) points out that the past is not only constructed through social conventions, but is continually rebuilt, denying the influence of the past on the present. In this view of things, memory presupposes a constructive and rational organization of the present, in which aspects of the past are adjusted and recalled through social and collective conventions. In this way, the past is continually remade according to the pressures and interests of the present. Brazilian Pentecostal women selectively appropriate their memories and negotiate among each other with "outside" society, and with other Brazilian women, to create invisible circles that demarcate the territories of identity to which each individual belongs.

By analyzing Pentecostalism in Lisbon between 2006 and 2011, I found that a significant portion of the Brazilian migrant population converted to Pentecostalism in the first months after their arrival; the majority of these converts were women. At the time, I understood this according to the theory proposed by Mariz (1996), that "Pentecostalism makes its believers see themselves as 'individuals', with a certain degree of autonomy and choice." In the years that followed (2012–17), in contacts with the same interlocutors I had interviewed between 2007 and 2011, I observed in them an even more voracious and perfected reaffirmation of Pentecostal faith. Except for one interlocutor who died alone in a taxi on the way to the hospital, everyone kept their posts and strengthened their central positions in the church. They recount their stories from the moment of their baptism in Portugal as rebirths, as victories in a process of magical articulation granted to them by Pentecostalism. This magic power allows direct communication with God and makes these women special, in a way they couldn't conceive of before migration. Low esteem, cultural marginalization, insecurity, and fear have been minimized to the point where these women have almost forgotten about them. In their present view, this is a direct effect of the kinds of experiences they have had in the Pentecostal religious space. What was before understood as negative in the lives of these women has, in their view, been minimized or even eliminated by their experiences in the church. This, they feel, has allowed them to re-establish a sense of dignity and coherence and to engage in a reorganization of their lives that they never before have experienced.

These experiences are transmitted to new migratory generations that have other dreams of achieving a reborn life in an imagined Europe, with beautiful and attractive landscapes seen through images shared in social networks, but which is quite different from the realities with which Brazilian migrants live. The forces of attraction for migration and Pentecostal conversion are thus still very much alive.

As Brazil passes through a politically and economically delicate moment, these family and religious networks of influence make promises to adolescent and young women who dream of migration as the promise of a better material future achievable through a divine plan in which one of their relatives is already included.

Final considerations

The IPDA is administratively and financially well structured (Freston 1993), creating a safe and stable basis for Brazilian immigrants who decide to make the church their home and the church's codes the basis of their representations of identity. The church continues to prohibit theological study. The women who enter and immerse themselves in the cellar where the IPDA is headquartered in Lisbon feel safe, as if the basement were a womb—a "bubble" or bounded sphere (Sloterdijk 2011)—within which they can generate a new identity infused with Pentecostal warmth and the strength of a continuous flow of new immigrants who arrive and depart. The security of these women's choices lasts for as long as they can withstand the church's doctrinal codes.

Understanding the processes at work in the construction of Pentecostal female identities within the Brazilian migration flows in the IPDA means reflecting upon the multiple opportunities that these women have, and the type of forces and movements that make them choose one or another kind of religious tradition. Some possibilities become temporary transits between churches without, however, distancing oneself too much from a certain Brazilian Pentecostal core that has enough power to reproduce itself, attract followers, and expand in a foreign land overseas.

Some churches believe that their umbilical matrix will be faithfully recreated in other countries. Current research on religions in migratory contexts, however, demonstrates that different religious possibilities are born every day (see also Bahia, this volume). These demonstrate complex and plural dynamics, structured around convergent and divergent spaces, and providing new religious options for Brazilian migrants who find themselves on the frontier between confrontation and attraction, thus building multiple Brazilian religious identities abroad.[11]

Where Do the Prostitutes Pray? On *Travestis, Mães de Santo, Pombagiras,* and Postcolonial Desires

Joana Bahia

Introduction

This article looks at how Brazilian prostitution in Portugal merges with Afro-Brazilian religious practices and ideologies. I analyze the complex trajectory of Afro-Brazilian spirits and those who incorporate them, looking at the interface between prostitution and Afro-Brazilian religions, while taking into consideration the sexualities at play and seeking to explore the new meanings these intersections produce in transnational contexts.

In order to contextualize the correlation between migration, prostitution, and the Afro-Brazilian religious field in a transnational context, the present article concentrates on migratory flows between Brazil and Portugal, and on the ambiguities that are present in these relationships. More concretely, I look at the relationships between Brazilians and Portuguese that are exposed by a case study of a *travesti* and her *pombagira*[1] in the context of an Afro-Brazilian Candomblé *terreiro* (temple).[2] The image of *pombagira* serves as a sexual and religious metaphor with which to explore tensions between Brazilians and Portuguese. *Pombagira* is Iberian in origin (sixteenth century), but her spirit has been brought back to the peninsula by Brazilian migrants involved in African Brazilian religions and she now possesses Portuguese bodies. She also has the power to transform the body of a *travesti* into a *mãe de santo* (mother of saint/ Afro-Brazilian religious leader). In all of these trajectories and transits, *pombagira* makes possible logical shifts that invert postcolonial relations. *Pombagira* invests a *travesti* with sacred power and, this woman moves through different social spaces in turns, dominating spheres that take in colonial desires for the Other, spiritually and carnally penetrating Europeans. To be a *travesti* and transform oneself into a *mãe de santo* implies a subtle, postcolonial penetration that inverts genders and powers.

My ethnographic work was carried out in Candomblé temples, between 2011 and 2013 in Caparica and in cities located between Lisbon and Porto, Portugal. In sharing time with my informants, we also shared meals and knowledge about religious activities, creating a different atmosphere from the distrust that generally prevails in prostitution. While many sex workers attend Afro-Brazilian *terreiros* in order to resolve quotidian problems involving work, money, love affairs with Europeans, or immigration, in the present article I am dealing in large part with the narratives of the *travestis* who, during incorporation of *pombagiras* and *exus*, demonstrate relationships that touch on transnational religious connections, the migratory field, sexuality, and postcolonial relations.

All of the authors who analyze sexual markets, especially those involving *travestis* (Benedetti 2005; Kulick 2008; Pelúcio 2009; Vartabedian 2018) conduct research in prostitution venues. None these authors treat religion as an important component in the lives of the people they study, however. The devotion present in the language of sex workers only enters as a minor part of the scenario in some of these ethnographies (Perlongher 2008). Yet, many (if not most) brothels—both in Brazil and Portugal—have altars to *pombagiras* and *exus,* and these spirits are very much present in the sexual markets of these countries.[3] Living religious experience sets bodies, colonial relations, and migratory realities in motion, according to the narrative of the spirits that my interviewees worship and incorporate.

The idea here is to construct a new perspective regarding the relationships between religious assemblages (Latour 2005), migration, and postcolonial sexuality. The Orixás and/or spirits that manifest in *travesti* bodies are mediators. They are entities that participate in the construction of content that shifts, transforms, and is translated in the process of establishing transnational relations with other actors, in this case, the Portuguese. These meanings are produced in inseparable form in bodies and spirits (Lambek 2014), as the actions of the spirits reshape postcolonial relationships through the sexualities that are at play, particularly those of *travestis*. I present the sexualized and erotic components (Mcclintock 1995 and 2003; Stoller 2002) of the lusosphere in question and I examine how religious diasporas interface with transnational migrations.

A sexual and religious lusosphere

Brazil was once an immigrant-receiving country, the main destination for Portuguese immigrants in the nineteenth and early twentieth centuries. From the 1980s on, however, Portugal (now a member of the European Union) began to receive significant numbers of immigrants from its ex-colonies, including Brazil. Initially, the Brazilians arriving in Portugal were highly qualified professionals who participated in the large-scale infrastructure projects that accompanied Portugal's integration into the European economic bloc. Economic crises in Brazil led to new migratory flows, however. The new Brazilian migrants found jobs in the service economy, largely in bars and restaurants. Portugal also began to attract ever more disadvantaged social groups, people unwanted by the Portuguese state, who became involved in drug trafficking and prostitution networks. Then the flow reversed once again in the 1990s, becoming known as "the return of the caravels (old ships)" (Feldman-Bianco 2010: 65). In search of new transnational markets, many Portuguese investors turned to Brazil and migrants followed suit.

The ambiguity of the relationship between Brazil and Portugal involves different conflicts and negotiations that are manifest in the Portuguese community in Brazil and the Brazilian community in Portugal. These have a long history characterized by an ambiguous relationship of "false brotherhood and linguistic union," that is full of commercial and diplomatic conflicts and marked by a colonial past. To "turn away from or face the Atlantic," an eternal dilemma for the Portuguese State, has also implied solutions for the internationalization of the Portuguese economy, which turns to (or away from) its former colonies, understanding them to be the "supranational territories of the Portuguese language" (Feldman-Bianco 2010). At some points in recent history, Portugal faced the Atlantic in order to attempt to re-conquer its colonies as part of the international market. At other moments, such as during the country's entry into the European bloc in 1981, this was not possible.

The images conveyed about Brazil in *telenovelas* (Brazilian soap operas which circulate in more than twenty countries) and tourist advertisements corroborate the idea that sexual licentiousness is common in that country. This, in turn, implies a sort of "free pass" in terms of personal relations, which reinforces the idea of *malandragem*[4] as part of Brazilians' personal and professional strategies of social ascension (Machado 2009).

The Portuguese interpret Brazilians according to this sex-*malandragem* framework. In everyday life, these stereotypes not only delimit the spaces reserved for Brazilians, but also extend to other planes of social life. The tropicalization and racialization of the femininity associated with Latin America sets Latin women under the sign of abundant love and sexual passion and molds engendered opportunities for work, mobility, and citizenship. In this way, Latinas (and also Latina *travestis*) are understood as having "ethnic sex appeal," being supposedly happy, sexy, and nice. This gives them visibility in transnational sexual and matrimonial markets (Machado 2009; Piscitelli 2008). An interesting perspective regarding these stereotypes and the conflicts between Brazilians and Portuguese can be found in the metaphorical world of religion, in which sex workers speak of stigmas and annoyances through their spirits. Religious metaphors recreate postcolonial discussion from a corporeal and sexual point of view (Bahia 2015). If Brazilian female, queer, and *travesti* bodies have historically been penetrated and occupied by the Portuguese, the postcolonial map offers other nuances when we turn to its spiritual embodiments.

The power the Portuguese colonizer tries to exert over the Brazilian body is constantly subverted in a postcolonial logic exposed by the incorporation of spirits of *Umbanda*[5] (Bahia 2015). This inverts the colonial process and postulates a reality in which Portugal is discovered by Brazilian *caboclos*,[6] where spirits show how deeply they can subvert the order of the colonial map. If more than 500 years ago, colonizers invaded the body of the colonized, today's immigrants invade Portugal, transforming the Portuguese into "whores" and "faggots," inverting the exact same stigma that are attached by Portuguese to Brazilians, especially those of the latter migratory waves (Bahia 2015). According to McClintock (1995), the map found in the colonial narratives shows that genitalia are understood to be three witches. In other words, the body of the Other in Western imperialism is also a place of bewitchment and danger: it is a degenerated body, prostituted and also dangerous, for in the colonial map of the world, sex is the realm of the uncontrolled.

Sex is also part of a market in which things and desires are exchanged. Sexual contracts are not explicit and not all who make them are prostitutes. The relationships formed by sexual intercourse comprise a large heterogeneous market in which many things are involved, including love and affection (Agustín 2005; Piscitelli 2008, 2011). In this case, the spirits look at these contracts and often favor those who need a visa, an extra trick with better clients, or who want "that one guy who helps me out" to continue to be prosperous and generous. They may even favor a marriage with a Portuguese person. Enchanted baths to attract tourists and clients for programs and material objects such as belts and charms that can be used to tie someone to oneself also tie the Portuguese into this sexual and commercial game.

Europeans complain of immigrants' "low level of culture," of their "culture of origin," and their "superstitions" (Agustín 2005). Magic and religion are always present in Brazilian immigrants' lives, however, and these elements provide them with means of survival. Such survival might even involve exploitation (i.e., working without documents), as long as it guarantees an illegal immigrant a means of making their way in the world as a low salary worker in a very competitive European market. Survival might also mean gaining a "European passport" through a "good marriage." Many immigrants deal with magicians as a means of protection and as a way of enchanting society, constructing strategies to deal with and bypass rules that tend to classify them as "ignorant Latinos." In this way, the postcolonial map can shift positions, depending on one's point of view (McClintock 1995).

Desires are involved in this game: competition in the religious field and market exchanges and "penetrations" on both sides. If, on the one hand, the Portuguese "ate" the Brazilian Indians during the conquest of Brazil, on the other hand, in the incorporation of the *caboclos* by the Brazilians, the Indians take hold of Portugal and invade the bodies of the Portuguese in both the sexual and spiritual sense, transforming the country (Bahia 2015). Understanding this postcolonial game as a sexual metaphor, the *travestis* turn the Portuguese into "faggots."

In one of the meetings I witnessed between Portuguese and Brazilian fathers of saints, one of the Portuguese present verbally skewered the *travesti* Sandra, claiming that her sexuality impeded the recognition of Afro-Brazilian religious practices as legitimate. A Brazilian father of saints leapt to her defense, recalling that the Portuguese man in question was sexually involved with his own *pai pequeno*[7] and that, at the end of the day, everyone present at the meeting was "faggot," whether they were in the closet or not. In order to delegitimize Brazilian religious power in this field—for in religious transnationalization, Brazilians are often considered to be more qualified to maintain the "purity" of African–Brazilian religious practices when these occur overseas—many Portuguese employ sexuality and, in particular, sexual preference. The Brazilians, in turn, accuse the Portuguese of being hypocrites, given that the Portuguese desire the Other and everything he or she represents but do not publicly out themselves as gay—or at least not as often as Brazilians do. The Brazilians also feel that the Portuguese do not tolerate *travesti* beauty or success in migration.

In this sense, McClintock's map contains a paradox. If, on the one hand, it shows a path for men to follow, when inverted, it shows a female body

(McClintock 1995). The map delineates the colonizer's route to the colony, but when turned upside down, it shows the colonizer being swallowed by a vagina. Genital power thus inverts the relationship between colonizer and colonized, with the colonized often gaining the upper hand. Female genitalia signal the presence of alternative feminine powers and, in parallel, in the Afro-Brazilian religious realm, African notions of time and knowledge, and elements that defy imperial power, negating them by inversion and control (Bahia 2015: 270).

The association of Brazilians with the idea of *malandragem* and *mulatinhas* (brown or mixed-race women—a pejorative term, here) supposed control over bodies dates from the period of Brazil's independence struggle. "Con men," "*mulatinhas*", and "hordes of black monkeys" are Portuguese expressions that were used to describe Brazilians between Brazil's independence and the founding of its First Republic (Ribeiro 2010). These insults are taken up again in today's competition in the Portuguese labor market. Gender stereotypes affect the ways in which Brazilians are classified, transforming *brasucas* (pejorative term used by Portuguese to call the Brazilians) into *mulatas* (a person of mixed white and black ancestry). This intensified after 1981, when Portugal entered the "whiter and more civilized" European community.

If Brazilians take their religions with them when they migrate, they also carry Brazilian social differentiations. In Portugal, many Brazilians do not belong to Afro-Brazilian religions and many Portuguese participate in these religions. Other Brazilians frequent neo-Pentecostal churches and have been responsible for the expansion of these religions in Portugal (Mafra 2002; Téchio this volume). These immigrants do not want to be associated with religions that are part of the African and slave past, nor do they want to be further stigmatized, which they believe would be the case were they to identify with Afro-Brazilian religions. Many of these Brazilian immigrants are members of those social strata that are considered to be the most suspect in the migration process, and they really do not want to be associated with religious groups that make them even more *exotic* than they already are. In their bodily practices, this type of Brazilians (Pentecostals—especially if they are women) "desexualize" themselves so as not to be recognized as having the body and the accent of a Brazilian (Téchio this volume).

It is worth remembering, however, that not all Brazilians—not even those of the lower classes—are neo-Pentecostal or evangelical Christians. Many do not follow these religions. And among these are Brazilians who are relatively numerous in recent migrations to Portugal: prostitutes, *travestís*, and *michês*. Unlike the Brazilian Pentecostals (Téchio this volume), the people whom I observed during my fieldwork expose their bodies to the sex market as part of their work routine. But they also take great care of their bodies, eschewing sexual activities when they need to do spiritual work in which sex is polluting, and employing their bodies according to the advice of *pombagira* so that they can obtain advantages in the very competitive sex work market. This is especially true when this involves competition among the Brazilians themselves. *Pombagira* does not only possess sex workers, however: she also gives advice to other types of Brazilians, especially those who share the same sexual market and transnational realities.

Dealing with migrants who are sexual workers and are often socially marginalized, is not only difficult for many Brazilian migrants (who do not want to be associated with the members of these groups), but also for many Portuguese. Even those who share the spiritual beliefs of these migrants do not identify with the habits and customs of those who do not have a place in the formal job market (prostitutes) or who are sexually ambiguous (*travestis*). At the same time, many Portuguese are attracted to the relative tolerance of the Afro-Brazilian religions with regard to homosexuals and *travestis*, given that the evangelical and neo-Pentecostal churches condemn these sexual and gender practices.

Faced with these stereotypes about Brazilians, we can catch a glimpse of how migrants who actually work in prostitution are treated and to what gods these Brazilians, unwanted by the Portuguese State, might pray to. How is this interface between migration, religion, sexual choices, and prostitution composed? At what moments does *pombagira* erupt into these worlds?

A *pombagira* transforms her daughter into a *mãe de santo*[8]

During my research, I observed some *travestis* who were professional *mães de santo*, giving consultations, reading the *búzios*,[9] and circulating among the cities of Portugal, as well as among other European countries such as France, Spain, Italy, and Switzerland. The presence of various forms of prostitution was part of the everyday life of Candomblé practitioners in Portugal, whether they were currently sex workers or had abandoned sex work to marry or to devote themselves to the religion as a job or a vocation, occupying a higher position in the hierarchy of their *terreiro*. I discuss below one of the cases that I followed during the course of my research, which shows how a person can exit prostitution in order to become a mother of saints. (It should be noted that I could not find any cases of transsexuals doing this, only *travesties*.)

In most of Brazil, there is a strong prejudice against transsexual heads of *terreiros*. Few are recognized as religious authorities and many do not assume the religious life as temple leaders, since they are stigmatized. Western Europe has a more open attitude toward sexual behavior. Additionally, Brazil enjoys great prestige in the transnational religious field for having preserved mythical Africa in Brazilian religious practices. Transsexuals and *travestis* can thus transform this religious market into work and, despite suffering from prejudice, may have more prestige than many of the Portuguese who practice the same religion.

It is worth remembering that for *travestis*, migrating to Europe has been an option since 1970, at least. Traditionally, this has meant obtaining greater financial and bodily resources, strategically taking advantage of Europeans' ideas regarding Brazilian sexuality, transforming their bodies, moving about more safely than in Brazil, and just generally improving their lives (Pelúcio 2009, 2010; Vartabedian 2018: 193). A trip to Europe gives a given person prestige and empowers the *travestis* who have been "successful" in these voyages and thus have been able to take a step forward in their career of becoming *travestis*. Many *travestis* go from the red-light districts of Lisbon to the *terreiro*, seeking solutions to their spiritual problems and aid in dealing with the sexual and affective exchanges that are a part of their working and personal lives.

In the *terreiro* that I analyze here, there are adepts and clients of all types, including Portuguese. Many are cisgendered men and women, *travestis,* or *michês* (name used for the man who practices prostitution), with significant numbers of Brazilian and African clients. Many of the adepts and clients that frequent the temple work in various manners in the sex trade. I saw more Africans and Brazilians in the temple, but many fathers and mothers of saints received Portuguese clients, including especially the female owners and managers of brothels. In a variety of ways, this diversified market of sexual-affective contracts and exchanges circulates in the *terreiros* in general. In this particular *terreiro*, there was a significant number of *travestis* who had been part of the old sexual circuit of the current mother of saints.

To better understand this circulation of labor and sex as part of religion, we must now turn to the life story of Sandra and her relationship with Maria Padilha, the spirit. Sandra is thirty-three years old, a *travesti* and is currently a *mãe de santo* in Europe. She circulates between Italy, Portugal, and Switzerland. Her case is interesting, because before she became a mother of saints, she worked as a prostitute in Italy.[10] Her transformation into a *travesti* began in Brazil at the age of 16, almost at the same time that she began her spiritual path, being initiated into Candomblé in Brazil.

Sandra's *orixá* and her *pombagiras,* especially Maria Padilha, compelled her to withdraw from prostitution. Her spirits (Iansã in particular) confirmed her spiritual gifts and opened up new possibilities to Sandra, possibilities that deny masculine and feminine binaries and which allow her to simultaneously be a *travesti* and a *mãe* and to gain a recognized position in Europe. Many in Candomblé believe that the *orixá* has no color, sex, or nationality: they go and stay where they want. On the other hand, however, there are *orixás* who abandon their children when their devotees change their sex, with other *orixás* taking over when this occurs.

After seven years in the faith, at a moment in her religious career when a Candomblé devotee is considered to be knowledgeable enough to open their own *casa do santo,* Sandra had doubts. She stated that her "story proves very well how the *orixá* can change a person's life." But the *Orixás* do not look at one's exterior: they perceive one's essence. At the moment, Sandra's Iansã confirmed to her that she should be a *mãe de santo.* One of the proofs of this, according to Sandra, is that during her four years of prostitution, she did not contract AIDS, because the *orixá* protected her and "closed" her body to the disease. Sandra believes that it is almost a miracle that she has not been contaminated by HIV and she is very concerned with the issue of health as a whole, and especially with regards to thinking of health as an important part of social issues. Sandra thus speaks often of Omolu, the bringer of both disease and cures (and through this, related to sexually transmitted diseases), with whom her *orixá* has great affinity.

If Iansã and Omolu confer a sanctified body upon Sandra, despite her past as a prostitute, then we must look at some new implications this brings to the fore. If, on the one hand, the association between disease and prostitution is built into Sandra's narrative as inevitable, thus stigmatizing the act of prostitution, on the other hand all that heals also kills. In myths regarding Obaluaiê, ugly becomes beautiful and vice versa, associating the image of the doctor with that of the sorcerer. What kills inevitably heals, as a circular principle. In this sense, prostitution and disease are part of the history of Sandra's body, and of the many evils that were necessary in order to make it a body.

The relationships between mediums and entities are complex (Hayes 2011: 411). Entities are autonomous and beyond the control of their mediums. And, of course, the management of this autonomy is yet another complex question when dealing with wider kinship and social relations. What happens when these spiritual entities transform *travestis* into *mães de santo*? The construction of the role of the medium through possession engenders transformations in the person and in their social roles. Possession builds new agencies (Lambek 2014).

Many *travestis* refer to womanhood in terms of physical appearance, behavior, and relationships with men (Kulick 2008: 109). They do not talk about women in biological terms. Some *travestis* never speak of feelings of motherhood; many, indeed, may want to be fathers rather than mothers. However, in the Candomblé family—which is socially constructed based upon an internal hierarchy, initiation, and religious identity—this becomes possible. Here, religion presents a vocation that is both religious and maternal, occupying the top of a hierarchy imagined as a matrilineal family: the *mãe de santo*. In a family of saints (that is not biological), being a mother of saints opens up the possibility of playing the role of a mother, even to *travestis*. This is because the Candomblé family is not related to biological sex, but based on social roles. Despite the fact that prejudices exist in the Afro-Brazilian religious field, there are *travestis* who are *mães de santo*, occupying the highest place in the religious hierarchy and constituting a family of which (s)he is the head.

Kulick (2008: 111) shows that in *travesti* views of the world, "femininity appears as something that is within the reach of anyone who really wants it. In order to feel like women, *travestis* do not have to live the lives of real women. All they need is to acquire the proper attributes and appropriate relationships." More than asses and skirts (building the feminine in masculine bodies), they need to relate to men. In the case of Afro-Brazilian religion, they need to relate with the whole religious family and with the gods. This is not a simple task, when it comes to constructing the role of the mother.

Contrasting Kulick, Pelúcio (2009: 93) shows that "while [*travestis*] destabilize gender binaries with their experiences, they remain submerged in a normalizing heterosexuality. It is only through this paradox that they can express their conflict with the prevailing gender norms." Even when paradoxical, however, holy families exist. A house of the saints demands a family. But a house is also a fixed place, which alters the mobility present in *travesti* life, in which gender and body are constantly changing and movement between countries is normal. In this life, change is a constitutive part of body and identity (Pelúcio 2009).

Travestis' transformation into *mães de santo* is dramatic: they have to deal with codes regarding tolerance, forgiveness, and others' emotions in a new affective apprenticeship. Despite being imbued with power in the religious hierarchy, *travesti mães de santo* may still have to deal with the prejudices of their children, clients, and other *pais* and *mães de santo*, who associate them with prostitution. Because Sandra is Brazilian, this stigmatization is also built into relations between Brazilians and Portuguese and has been for some time. Some adepts identify with Sandra as they did the same job, see prostitution as work, and have suffered from discrimination, both in religious and social terms. Few *terreiros* in Brazil accept *travestis* as *pais* or *mães de santo*, and many adepts would never accept a leader who carries this stigma.

In order to ensure a fair balance of forces in the disputes in the religious field between Candomblé groups in Portugal, Sandra's Brazilian *pai* comes to Portugal whenever he can to help maintain Sandra's authority. He is Sandra's father of saints and, although he is a homosexual, his authority is considered to be more masculine than that of a *travesti*. Although Portuguese *pais de santo* are often gay, homosexuality has been cause for discrimination against Brazilians, who never fail to remind the Portuguese that they are also gay. *Travestis* are heavily discriminated against in Candomblé, both in Brazil and in the groups I have observed in Europe. However, despite being discriminated against, the possibility of having a vocation other than being hairdresser and/or prostitute (professions still common among *travestis*) appeals to many. Adding to this is the possibility of social ascension, brought about by a gift for the religion, in a transnational market in which religions are valued. In other words, becoming a *mãe de santo* can open up many new life possibilities for a *travesti*, in spite of persistent prejudice.

Although the street is a place where identities, affections, and desires (themes that cover the most varied emotional and corporeal aspects of human feeling) can constitute knowledge that aids in both the formation of a professional religious vocation (and certainly in the constitution of one's *pombagira* in the exercise of said vocation), this knowledge also constructs stigma in the eyes of other participants in the religious field. In their past lives, *pombagiras* have generally had contact with the most stigmatized of social conditions: female prostitution. These entities deal with cases of love by relating proverbs, sayings, and jokes with sarcasm and irreverent humor. Sex and various forms of loving behavior are the domain of the *pombagiras*, who also protect women who seek out sex and love. These entities are able to provoke any kind of sexual/affective union. *Exus* and *pombagiras* dominate crossroads and they transit freely through the streets, being entities that are close to mortal human beings and their doings.

Beyond the image of protection and reception, the image of confidant and self-taught "psychologist" is often alluded to when people speak of *mães de santo*. The *pombagira*, who protects and supports prostitutes, protects Sandra from her pimp. He is Brazilian, homosexual, and from the same city in Brazil where Sandra was born. Both have the same neighbors back home. Sandra's pimp witnesses the problems she experiences with her *pombagira* Maria Padilha and he describes this entity as a powerful spirit whom he greatly fears and who gave Sandra the path she should follow. The spirit protected Sandra at many moments in her life as a prostitute and especially protected her against her pimp, imposing upon him a certain devotion borne of fear. Although her *pombagira* places her in a more "respectable" position in society as a *mãe de santo*, Sandra's relationship with the entity has several nuances, levels of tension, and contradictions.

By submitting oneself to the power of the spirit during possession, the medium also becomes powerful (Lambek 2014). This is what makes Sandra's Brazilian pimp fear her. Possession can take on many different types of relationships (slave/owner, for example, and many others) in a complex chronotopical polyphony (Lambek 2014). Sandra's *pombagira* has often protected her from the police by telling her when they were coming. On the other hand, however, she has used the police, customers, and the money earned in prostitution in order to convince Sandra to transform herself from prostitute to *mãe*. The *pombagira* has full control over Sandra, who related to me what happened when once she disobeyed Maria Padilha and went back to prostitution.

The spirit of her *pombagira* came to Sandra and said she would take her out of prostitution if Sandra would serve her. Sandra wanted to get out, but she had a hard time making a living earning less money than she did in prostitution (Sandra portrays this "being addicted" to the money she made in sex work). Once after her Maria Padilha possessed her, she drank a lot of whiskey and champagne and almost left Sandra in an alcoholic coma. She also gave Sandra a message that would change her life. On this day, Sandra almost died. She understands the message to mean that she needed to leave her life as a prostitute behind and that Maria Padilha would help her in this, but put her to the test.

Maria Padilha said that she would be ready to confront Sandra if she sold sex again, but Sandra disobeyed when money got tight and she went out with a client. Out of the blue, the client accused her of stealing his wallet and cell phone, making Sandra's life hell. After an entire day of the client threatening her, Sandra apologized to her *pombagira*. An hour later the client called and apologized, saying that he had found his wallet and cell phone.

On another occasion, after two nights of prostitution in Italy in which she earned 2,000 Euros, Sandra lost her wallet with all the money as soon as she arrived at the bank. She was left with only her passport in her purse. That same week, she traveled to Portugal without any money aside from the 100 euros that her friend had loaned her in order to travel. And there in Italy, before embarking, Sandra was possessed by the *pombagira* Maria Padilha. The spirit laughed said that Sandra could sleep with as many men as she wanted, as long as it was for free: no more sex for money. The spirit also said that Padilha now controlled her life and that Sandra should obey the *pombagira;* that if she did not obey, she would pay with her life.

Many stories are told about the *pombagiras* by those who incorporate them. *Travestis* often joke that their colleagues only pretend to be possessed while still selling sex to their clients. The congruence of sexuality with spirituality often appears in these stories, making a connection to the idea of sacred prostitution (Qualls-Corbett 2005). Leal de Barros (2013: 517) claims that during his fieldwork "there have been reports of mediums invoking the 'vibration' of their *pombagiras* before initiating a sexual relationship, or even when trying to seduce someone." This is a sexuality that can hardly be described as sanitized and which is conveyed in the form of jokes and jests before beginning rituals in the *terreiro.*

The same sort of story is used to report cases of how the Portuguese do not understand how to worship the spirits of *Umbanda,* ignoring the codes of dress and behavior of *exus* and *pombagiras.* In these cases, the same sorts of accusations regarding false possession are recounted, however this time in a negative and accusatory sense. They are forms of social control and competition with regards to the dispute for power in the transnational Afro-religious field, where Brazilians dominate the religion in terms of prestige and its main codes. Even though the Portuguese question her sexuality, Sandra has greater religious and symbolic power than any European. She dominates both religious and sexual codes with confidence, given that she once took part in the sexual market and attends migrants who still do. In the quotidian world of possession by *pombagiras* and *exus,* this exchange of accusations highlights the nuances of a postcolonial discourse that is reproduced in the religious field, although with some inversions. We can see that Brazilian *pais de santos* need Brazilian legitimacy in order to practice a form of religion that is understood to be close to Africa. To submit oneself to the symbolic efficacy of a Brazilian *travesti* in the transnational Afro-religious field is something that seems to be quite paradoxical and complex in a postcolonial reality. Both the *pombagira* and Sandra, sexually and spiritually transgressive, mediate this postcolonial reality where Portuguese and Brazilians compete and enter into conflict, both in the religious field and in terms of their postcolonial memories.

Even though *travestis* and their spirits may be prostitutes, there are spaces and codes of conduct that are separate and quite important in the exercise of possession. According to some Brazilians I interviewed, the Portuguese do not understand these codes, exaggerating their perception of what a *pombagira* is and eliminating all subtlety from their worship and possession. *Pombagiras* seduce, play, amuse and warn: according to Brazilian accusations, these sorts of nuances are lost to the Portuguese. The Brazilians accuse the Portuguese of practicing religion incorrectly. They claim that the Portuguese do not know that *pombagiras* do not dress in panties and bra, or that the people who receive them must interact with the spirits, building an educational relationship with these spirits (Hayes 2011). In this view of things, it is not enough to incorporate a spirit: possession is built upon the nuances performed between the person who incorporates and their spirits. *Pombagiras* are the best example of this sort of relationship.

Conclusion: *Pombagira*, a spirit between worlds

Pombagiras have been circulating for centuries between the Iberian Peninsula and colonial Brazil, exchanging new meanings as Afro-Brazilian religions came to Portugal carried by Brazilian migrants (Bethencourt 2004; Espírito Santo 1988; Souza 1986). Espírito Santo (1988: 216, 1993) and Bethencourt (2004) show how, until the mid-sixteenth century, Spanish and Portuguese Catholicism (which was brought to Brazil) was permeated by an ancestral culture that included the worship of the sun, of the "divine Holy Spirit" (a dove), and of the "Mother," Christianized as "Mary." Paradoxically, Barros (2013) reports that of the many names attributed to *pombagiras*, Maria is the most common. Both authors show how the *pombagiras* descend from ancient cults of the great goddesses who became "the mother" (Maria) in Catholicism and its syncretic popular variants, inheriting some of the earlier goddesses' attributes. Maria Padilha of the Umbanda *terreiros* possibly originates in the thirteenth century in a homonymous woman who was reportedly a lover of the King of Castile (Meyer 1993). Ironically, then, it seems that the Brazilians and the Portuguese invoke a *pombagira* who is both Iberian and Brazilian. The name of Maria Padilha was invoked by many sorceresses in love spells and many of these women were sent to colonial Brazil as punishment during the Inquisition (Augras 2009; Meyer 1993). The name of Maria Padilha was recurrent in the transcriptions of spells filed in Inquisitorial processes. Souza (1986) reports that a sorceress named Maria Joana learned prayers from the Brazilian Indians and translated them into Portuguese, adapting Iberian expressions to her new local reality.

Maria Padilha can refer to sexuality and to a way of thinking about the world, but it does not necessarily reference prostitution at all times. *Pombagiras* are not defined only in prostitution or by prostitution, but above all by their free and independent attitude. On the other hand, however, this entity also carries with her marks of sensuality, eroticization, and lust. She is commonly understood as a "sacred prostitute" (Qualls-Corbett 2005). Her image evokes a female transgressor who was present in historical times, when prostitution was not always as stigmatized as it is today. This is the case of ancient Babylon, where sacred prostitutes stood on an equal footing with male priests (Barros 2013: 510 and 516). In this sense, *pombagira* speaks of the past and its rereading in the present time links the spirit to modern women. *Pombagira* projects into the present day this divine and transgressive female spirit who lived in primordial times in equality with men.

For a *travesti* to become a *mãe de santo* means taking on new forms of agency that are not connected to prostitution, at least not all the time. Taking on this hierarchical position also means that she must understand the universe as well as she understands prostitution, and this is a level of knowledge that few people possess. It can also help her aid those who are still enmeshed in the universe of prostitution, which she herself now stands partially outside of. If, on the one hand, it serves the publics that consume sex in prostitution because it dominates the codes of commercial sex, it also can protect a holy body that cannot be all the time disposed to sex, since many of the bodily practices of religion do not allow for this. It masters the body for fetish (in both senses of the word), and fetish for the body. But what about the *pombagira*? How is she re-semantized in the transnational context?

With regards to sexuality, Afro-Brazilian religions are still even more ambiguous. In this sense, *pombagira* brings unpredictability and a disrespect to the social conventions of construction of the feminine (Contins 1983), representing a danger and a reforming of legitimized gender relations in domestic space and in the broader social sphere. In the case analyzed above, she dramatizes and performatizes gender inversions, transforming a *travesti* into a mother and connecting differentiated worlds. Her spirit sagaciously crosses through the worlds of prostitution, religion, and (post-)colonial desires and transgresses gender roles, particularly when we speak of *travestis*.

Travestis are fascinating because they can strategically combine performance with the desire to be penetrated and at the same time to penetrate, "incorporating" (in body and spirit) their own modes of understanding femininity and creating a kind of game in which the symbols of masculinity and femininity are appropriated, rejected, and sometimes accepted in shifting contexts of social and sexual interaction (Vartabedian 2018). While subverting gender, they paradoxically emphasize the submission that lies beneath the cult of normality, such as heteronormativity, or the ideal standards of body and beauty (Pelúcio 2009: 35, 184).

Femininity can also be constructed as a model and one model could be the mother of saints that can be added to the other modes of construction of the feminine (or other nonbinary constructions) that are accumulated in the religious experience of the subject. The *travesti* learns to be a mother of a saint, for example, and to belong to a female *orixá* that gives her a reference to an autonomous feminine image that is, in turn, a warrior. In these experiences, various bodily postures, behaviors, techniques, and emotions are triggered by the subject, recreating ways of constructing the *travesti* in different femininities. There are several possible ways of constructing *travesti* identities by living in the various subjectivities that these subjects create in interactions with their spirits—Iansã, mother of saints, *pombagira*, Maria Padilha—and with their clients, in prostitution or in the religious field. Sandra has a body and emotions that are both under construction. Her spirituality accompanies these processes, involving the other actors that are part of this field. Both her mediating presence and that of her spirits form a dynamic, transformative field of relations in which people, places, and things intertwine. Her mediation reverses colonial relations at some points and shows that gods, men, and *travestis* find themselves in these intersections and dialogical references between different social fields, genders, and sexual and religious markets at the transnational level.

Brazilian *travestis* transform their bodies in texts that are capable of provoking colonial desires in which "hybridism is associated with wild nature." This gives them a leg up in transnational sex markets (Pelúcio 2010: 211) and brings even more ambiguities into the postcolonial scenario, since in the game of desire the power of *pombagira* can incorporate, possess, and penetrate the Old World.

Moving Homes

Transnational Meanings and Practices of the Brazilian Catholic Charismatic Renewal Movement in the Netherlands

Andrea Damacena Martins

Introduction

Brazilian transnational religious movements are spaces where migrants have an opportunity to make new relationships, to get to know the host society, and to exchange experiences and information about daily life (Levitt 2001; Sheringham 2010, 2013; Vásquez and Alves 2013). On the one hand, these movements or churches offer a symbolic and material space for social adaptation. On the other hand, it is possible in this context to establish a dynamic of production, and reproduction of religious and symbolic forms, which link the homeland to the new land. These are religious practices shaped by transnational ties. In this way, the movement of religious practices shapes a luso-Catholic form in the domain of Dutch Catholicism. In this chapter, I examine one particular manifestation of this by looking at the religious activism of Brazilian Catholic charismatics in the Netherlands.

In this chapter, I propose to connect the practices and discourses of Catholic women who are involved in Charismatic Catholicism to their positionality as migrants and religious activists, to find out how they build a sense of belonging in Dutch society. Although much research focuses on the functional role that Brazilian religions play in the integration processes of migrants in their host societies (Euser et al. 2006; Martins 2012; Vásquez and Marquardt 2003), less attention has been paid to how these groups or individuals elaborate meanings of home and belonging and an experience of locality. Therefore, I focus on the micro level of everyday life, where Brazilian Catholic women in the Netherlands actively mobilize symbolic and cultural repertoires in the religious sphere. I seek to show how the dynamism of the transnational relocation of cultural–religious forms elaborates new mixtures or allows the production of new spaces and connections. Appadurai (1996: 31) has pointed out that imagination is important for cultural processes, conceptualized as social practices. Imagination thus represents a form of work in both senses of the term—labor and culturally organized practice—as well as a form of negotiation between sites of agency, i.e., individuals, and globally defined fields of possibility. I borrow this concept of "work of imagination" to explore the religious practices of Brazilian women. The mobility of images or the circulation of ideas and people with their stories, projects, and agency contributes to a break with the idea of isolated spheres such as the global and local. In particular, Appadurai (1996) underlines that ordinary people, through their "work of the imagination," create a space of possibilities based on their own individual or group agency, which enables them to reconfigure their social life. The stories of the Brazilian Catholic women in the Portuguese-speaking Parish in The Hague will illustrate how in this social ethnosphere material and symbolic dimensions are mobilized, such as devotions to saints and forms of worship. These create new modes of cultural interaction that shape a particular lusophere, which affects the sense of belonging of the women in Dutch society. It is a sphere where new cultural interactions take place that, although not without conflict or tension, allow new mixtures of (Dutch–Portuguese–Brazilian) forms and practices that are related to different geographical and sociopolitical contexts.

The religious group that I discuss in this chapter consists of Brazilian Catholic women; they play the most important role in shaping the religious activities within the parish. I have decided to focus on their practices and discourses because this empirical context offers insight into their leadership and the way they, as migrants, put transnational ties in motion to create a sense of belonging in the Netherlands. This builds on the work of Sheringham (2010), who shows that a sense of feeling "at home" or belonging is both a real and a symbolic conception. I try to reveal a phenomenon that is far from a static reality, but rather, as she puts it, "a dynamic process, involving the acts of imagining, creating, unmaking, changing, losing and moving 'homes'" (Sheringham 2010: 64). In this sense, the focus is not on the gendered role of these women in the institutional religious field; instead I am considering that their geographical and cultural mobility informs us about their agency and their role in transnational religious spaces. As Van de Kamp (2016: 21) argues, due to their experience of mobility and establishing new connections and relations, the "pioneering" of

Brazilian Pentecostal women in Mozambique leads them to actively engage in new forms and meanings of family and (wo)manhood. I see a similarity with the discourses and practices of my informants when they aspire to feel at home in a host society. They are also influenced by moving between spaces, which not only helps them to establish their own sense of identity, but also makes them introduce new religiosities into local Catholicism. In fact, the construction of belonging within religious movements and churches has a functional aspect because, in this context, collective representations support a moral order and give a sense of integration into daily life. Nevertheless, they are also spaces where a creative process of agency and mobilization of cultural capital and repertoires takes place, as I learned while listening to the experiences of my informants and participating with them in religious activities.

I start by considering the background of Brazilian migrant women and the central question of belonging. Then I draw on the results of my ethnographic research on the place-making discourses and practices of Catholic Brazilian women in the Netherlands. I will show how the religious practices of the Brazilian Catholic Charismatic Renewal Movement, represented by prayer groups of the *Servos do Amor* ("Servants of Love") in Amsterdam and The Hague, connect transnational images, rituals, and symbols. This represents a "work of the imagination" based on the connection between Brazilian religiosities and a sense of belonging on the part of the Brazilian migrant women. In the conclusion, I will use my findings to highlight the importance of ritual and religiosity for the debate about migrants' belonging and integration and how they affect Catholicism in the Netherlands.

Brazilian migrant women in the Netherlands

Women are becoming increasingly more involved in migration flows, which characterizes the recent development of globalization. They are migrating as recruited domestic workers or nurses, as in the case of Filipino women (Brettel 2003); as sex workers linked to sex tourism (Piscitelli 2007); or due to family reunion or individual choice. In the Netherlands, the presence of female Brazilians is significant. They correspond to 60.6 percent of the registered Brazilian population living in the country (CBS 2014).[1] Regardless of the gender of the respondent,[2] the survey indicates a couple of reasons for the immigration of this population, namely the formation of families (*gezinsmigratie*), and education (*studie*) and employment (*arbeid*). Almeida's (2008: 63–83) research on Brazilian women in the Netherlands found similar reasons for migration: marriage, prostitution, human trafficking, work, and study. She observes that the inclusion of a gendered perspective into migration studies has deconstructed the classical approach where women were described as passive actors or were invisible. Miranda (2009) points out that the presence of women is higher among undocumented Brazilians. During fieldwork, it has always caught my attention that Brazilian men are usually a minority or are completely absent in places like churches, parties, bars, or informal gatherings (Martins 2012).

The literature indeed suggests an increase in female participation in international migration. Women are involved in transnational relationships, elaborating interconnections between the local and global as well as creating transnational economic, political, and religious practices (Margolis 1994; Levitt 2001). The long-distance activities of these women have been influencing national and global issues, as well as their position in the local context, e.g., "transmigrant" (Glick-Schiller and Fouron 2001: 3). However, migration also includes the creation of experience and meaning connected to the new place of residence. Salman and de Theije (2011: 08) call attention to the reconstruction of local and transnational ties, which can be seen as a "social morphology," serving as key evidence that the perception about local cultural forms needs to be stretched. Local defense of interests or values—by migrants or minorities—may impact international relations between countries or religious groups. Hence, there is no analytical validity to starting from a binary local–global point of view, which means that the reconstruction of "locality" or "belonging" creates new realities and combines new "translocal" material and symbolic dimensions. By observing the social practices of Brazilian women, it becomes clear that they are linking and reconstructing local Catholicisms, because these women actively situate themselves in multiple contexts. The local level becomes a relevant axis that has an influence on their everyday life and provides context for understanding experiences, actions, practices, and conflicts in Dutch society. It is also the basis from which they are creating possibilities of expression, building new networks, and making use of their transnational mobility.

Belonging and senses of "home" and "house"

The increasing ethnic diversity in Dutch society has changed the social and cultural homogeneity of popular neighborhoods in large cities (Duyvendak 2011). As a result, local residents are challenged to find new forms of interaction and bonding. In this context, an intense debate about national identity and integration of immigrants has fed into a powerful political discourse influencing the way people look at "the other." A vision has grown inside society favorable to mandatory integration of immigrants, employing the Dutch language as an instrument. Nationalist groups and politicians have also emerged, who nourish a nostalgic political vision of restoring the "nation" as a "house" or "home" and salvaging "Dutch identity," which refers to an essentialization of reality that is seen as homogeneous and unchangeable (Duyvendak 2011: 28; WRR 2007: 24). Their notions are centered on a cultural representation that portrays reality as a mythical homogeneity, which has never existed in society. My ethnographic analysis shows that the notion of "house" is associated with social well-being and security experienced by the migrant women in a well-organized Dutch society, but it does not provide them with a sense of "home" and belonging. Besides these discourses that want to restore an "authentic" Dutch identity, there has also been a flowering of resistance groups and people that mobilize social initiatives in the neighborhoods toward connection and communication. They are searching for a new inclusive social identity, a new "we," in which immigrants are recognized as an integral and active part of Dutch society. This affirmative discourse has mobilized several NGOs, Christian churches, and progressive Islamic sectors (Hart 2013: 33; Kalsky 2013: 17), based on a relational approach of individuals and groups instead of the dichotomy of "us" and "them."

Both positions within the debate on integration should be considered in relation to one another in order to provide a context wherein discourses of "feeling at home" or "belonging" gain a central place in the academic and public debates (Duyvendak 2011; Kalsky 2013). The focus on "home" and "belonging" in my research was motivated by the declaration of an informant who said during an interview, "In the Netherlands, we have a house but not a home." This strong notion that the country is just a roof or a house and that there is a lack of identity or emotional attachment interested me, and I became curious to know how Catholic women cope with this situation.

Taking the migration experience as a central point, I reflect on "place-making" in everyday life practices, particularly addressing the role that religious practices have (or do not have) in locally based attachment and integration (Sheringham 2010: 62). How do the women position themselves transnationally and how are they reworking symbolic and social practices? How does religion shape "belonging" from the point of view of a particular Brazilian group?

Research and methods

Between 2014 and 2017, I did fieldwork among Catholic women in the Portuguese-speaking Catholic Church in The Hague. Usually, after mass, they talked about their daily lives and their difficulties with feeling part of Dutch society and learning the language. They made constant comparisons with the Brazilian way of engaging in friendships and social relations. Immersing myself in those social gatherings, I became interested to learn more about what kind of life these women were living in The Hague. Jasmin was the first woman I listened to in September 2014, and starting from her I applied a snowball sampling technique. A remarkable characteristic of the group is that most of the women belong to the Charismatic group *"Servos do Amor"* inside the parish, which I will address later on.

The use of a snowballing technique has not always worked. Two of my informants had agreed to recommend someone for a subsequent interview, but they did not put me in further contact with people from their network. I insisted a couple of times by email or by phone to reach out to new contacts, but they did not reply. I interpreted their silence as a desire to withdraw from collaboration. I could not find out why this resistance occurred, but I sensed that they were not willing to tell their personal stories to a researcher. Therefore, I found new contacts, which means that I have used different resources and entrances during my fieldwork, such as participant observation inside the parish and conversations with women who do not regularly attend the parish. Reflecting on practices and discourses from these Catholic women who are connected to different networks brought some diversity to the research group. I conducted seven in-depth interviews; in addition, I included field notes from events, casual conversation, and participant observation in gatherings of the Charismatic group, informal conversations after the Catholic Mass, or in social gatherings among Brazilians.

Moving between "home" and "house": Freedom, consumption, and rights

The Brazilian women that I interviewed come from the states of Bahia, Maranhão, Fortaleza, Belém, and São Paulo, but the majority lived in cities in the northeast of Brazil before moving to The Hague.[3] They have immigrated to the Netherlands due to marriage or partnership and have legal status. In my research population, it was the search for a prospective partner to marry, an individual project, that has encouraged the migration experience rather than established network ties in the receiving country; all the women informed me that they were active in online social media looking for a partner. As Oosterbaan (2010: 295) points out, Brazil has the largest population of internet users in Latin America, and Brazilians are very active in different virtual communities, which, in the case of his research, were used to help people who are moving from Brazil to Barcelona or from Barcelona to Amsterdam to become embedded in the city. In my findings, I observed similar online activity that helped women to move. Furthermore, I noticed that many Brazilian women were taking strategic steps through online dating, although their narrative about meeting their partners expressed a search for "romantic love or marriage."

When living in Brazil, the women who participated in my research were mostly working in the service sector and were between thirty-two and fifty-five years old. Two of them revealed that they had suffered discrimination and had been considered "old" for marriage once they were approaching forty years of age, especially being single mothers. Here we note a strong confrontation with Brazilian traditionalism, with which they found a way to cope using the unbounded potential of internet dating. As Rosa (2000:163) remarks in her study of Brazilian women looking to marry European or American men, this corresponds to a clear project of individualization of these women. She identifies that they elaborate a project of change for their lives in which their self-esteem grows while they are aiming for an upward step on the social ladder. In my findings, I see a rupture with a traditional vision in which they would have to accept that they were old and no longer capable of finding a local partner. Instead, these women have developed a modern attitude of dating online and looking for opportunities of marriage with foreigners.

Nevertheless, considering the circumstances after the migration, these women trespass cultural and symbolic boundaries imposed by Brazilian society. They took the risk of starting a new life, being critical of Brazilian male behavior or what the social structure imposed as suitable for "old" women. At the same time, many women have pointed out that, due to unexpected difficulties in finding work and learning Dutch, they have found themselves in a more dependent social position than in Brazil, especially having lost their previous economic independence. Most of them became housewives and had to elaborate new adaptations in their life projects, dealing with the structures and constraints of gender relations in the Netherlands.

My informants used the word "freedom" frequently and in several contexts when they described how they felt living in The Hague: the freedom to cycle in the city; to come and go at night without being worried; or to take children to and from school. According to them, the public services, facilities, and good functioning of the city promote a feeling of "well-being." Some women referenced freedom when discussing the ability to behave or wear clothes without being controlled. "In the Netherlands, nobody cares wat you are wearing. People do not mind or even look at you," said Jasmin, forty years old. Other women mentioned their personal development, e.g., acquiring new practical abilities. For example, Daisy told me that she never thought she would be able to learn to ride a bicycle, being fifty years old already. Once she learned it, she could become more independent from her partner and move freely about the city from home to work, to church, and other activities. Sara related the notion of freedom to transformations in herself, becoming aware of her own life and her own choices, distancing herself from the traditional patterns of her relatives in Brazil. Paths of personal growth and self-cultivation were opened after moving from Fortaleza.

Another important meaning associated with freedom is the consumption of products. Almost all interviewees have improved their living standards and they are able to consume products or services which are exclusive to upper middle classes in Brazil. As Jasmin reported "(…) here I have the life I always wanted and buy clothes or toys for my children that I was not able to in Brazil. I was used to very little or nothing there. Even though I do not speak Dutch, I work, and my life is much better here."

On this topic, we identify in their discourse an exaltation of basic rights and services to which they were afforded access in the Netherlands. This could be understood, on the one hand, as reflecting the upward mobility that they are experiencing now, and the lack of full citizenship experienced before in Brazil. On the other hand, this group presents an uncritical discourse about their own integration as citizens in Dutch society, where they are unable to participate in all domains of public life since they have still not mastered the Dutch language. The women, however, do not see this as unfavorable because they maintain their sociability, positioning themselves within the local Brazilian networks and transnational ties. In Brazil they could not achieve a comfortable standard of living, but in the Netherlands, even doing manual labor enables them to fulfill their consumer expectations. Here I want to point out that although they have built at least a sense of "house" in the Netherlands, the feeling of "home" seems to emerge only through participation in a religious community.

Attachments and feelings of belonging

Forty-year-old Iris uses an interesting metaphor to describe Dutch society that reveals another ambiguity and conflict experienced by Brazilian women. "Living in the Netherlands is like living in a private condominium. It has everything: security; tranquility; the apartments all look the same. But there is a lack of social mixing and the mess of street life."

Regarding social rights, the structure, organization, and proper functioning of Dutch society, as indicated above, are praised and appreciated. However, those same phenomena are considered impersonal and mark a distinction between them and Dutch people; for example, Brazilians are open and "the Dutch are very closed." Iris's discourse, for example, reveals an interconnection between physical place and her social process of integration (Harvey 1973:24), which in turn affects her sense of feeling at home. Feeling at home in The Hague makes palpable the absence of "street," which in Brazil corresponds to both a geographical space and a sphere of social interaction or public order that offers opportunities such as work. Mareels (2016:170–74) points out in her study about Brazilians in Brussels that contrary to Brazilian cities, many Brazilians experience the street as a "nonplace" in Brussels, limiting their options for social interaction. Niches such as the street, which Mareels defines as lusophone niches, link Brazilians in Brussels to opportunities for work and housing; however, these often involve "social drama," consisting of insular networks, risk, bickering stemming from differences in regional identities, and distrust arising therefrom. The distrust of one another in this setting incites insecurity and prejudice among them. In terms of the reinvention of the social morphology of Brazilian migrants in a transnational context, Mareels emphasizes the reshaping of the Brazilian social hierarchies in a new context. Here, it is important to note that Mareels's research focuses on disclosing the internal dynamic of Brazilian networks, mostly formed by people from a specific region in Brazil—Goiânia—who, in contrast to the women discussed here, have a lower level of education, a working-class background, and who have immigrated with the goal of improving their lives. In my own fieldwork, I see more ambivalence about how the women consider the "street."

On the one hand, these women experience a sense of freedom and security due to the material, social and cultural conditions they enjoy as citizens in the city of The Hague, as in the case of Dália, who gives particular importance to her subjective transformation during our interview. Her feelings about the "street" in The Hague enable her to realize something new in her life: "a real sense of my individuality, no more under the social control of family ties," like she experienced in Fortaleza, Brazil. On the other hand, representations of "street" are attached to an emphasis on the women's Brazilian background. Returning to the discourse of Iris, I have already noted that she felt the absence of "street life" in The Hague because it does not resemble the street life in Brazil. It is clear that she gives preference to her own cultural values, such as the Brazilian way of social mixing, "mess," and intense and affectionate relationships, which could be interpreted as cultural forms of authentic attachment with the country on her part (Reis and Sales 1999; Ribeiro 1999). The other form of recreating closeness and social belonging is through religion, which reveals the "work of the imagination" that I mentioned at the beginning of this chapter. The Brazilian Catholic Charismatic Renewal Movement (MRCC), with its diffusion of Brazilian religiosity and devotion, can be seen as one of the most important imagined spaces of belonging for the Catholic migrants that I interviewed.[4]

The Servants of Love—home and belonging in a Catholic Charismatic Renewal Movement

The Servants of Love is a Charismatic prayer group first organized inside the Portuguese-speaking Catholic parish of Amsterdam. Later it formed a sister group in the Portuguese-speaking Catholic parish in The Hague. Mary, a charismatic Brazilian woman, is the leader, organizer, and founder of this group. Before she migrated to the Netherlands, she took part in the Charismatic Community "Boa Nova" in the city of Jaboatão dos Guararapes, Recife, Brazil. Telling me about how the prayer group in Amsterdam was born in 2009, she recalled the support she received from the Boa Nova community: they helped her with material and instructions for becoming a leader. Her interpretation of the foundation of the Servants of Love is that it is an offshoot from the Catholic Charismatic Movement in Brazil that has settled in the Netherlands. To put it in her own words: "I see myself as a seed from that group; I am a seed from that community. God has touched me over there to come flourish here. I really understand it like this."[5]

The Servants of Love group is well known among Catholic Brazilians through announcements of prayer meetings or activities in Amsterdam.[6] In this way, they also attract Catholic Charismatics from other places in the country like Den Bosch, Handel, and Enschede to their gatherings and events. They have been spreading out their mission connecting Brazilians from big and small cities, especially through the missionary and vocational work of Mary and participants of the group. Another important impulse for the missionary agenda was the collaboration received from Friar John of God, a Brazilian Carmelite priest who came to live in the city of Handel, the Netherlands, with the mission to give a new impetus to his own religious order, The Discalced Carmelites, which was suffering a very large decrease in members.

Carranza and Mariz (2013) have already pointed out that the style of Charismatic Catholicism has been used as an export product, spreading out through missionary service and migrants. The missionary agenda of Catholicism is nothing new. However, the novelty nowadays is that Charismatic Catholic groups from Brazil are organizing communities and groups in Europe. They carry on the idea of being chosen to revitalize Christianity in the European countries through which they mean to fulfill the mission of converting people and bringing them back to the church. Freston (2010: 155) calls attention to the idea that this "reverse mission"[7] is a movement *from below;* in other words, it represents grassroots groups and activism of leaders, missionaries, and immigrants. The leaders involved in the Servant of Love group correspond to this definition. They exemplify the ambition to change Dutch Catholicism and "make it more spiritual," due to a strong emphasis on the intimate relationship with Jesus and the gifts of the Holy Spirit.

Catholic Charismatic Renewal represents a movement inside the Catholic Church that seeks a religious restoration and imposes an ideological discourse based on traditional values (Carranza 2011; Mariz 2006). Important characteristics of this religious form are being "reborn in the faith" through "baptism in the Holy Spirit," giving the participant divine power and spiritual gifts such as glossolalia (speaking in tongues), faith healing, and the ability to make prophecies. Although the Catholic Charismatic Renewal Movement sustains a broad campaign of changing rituals, practices, and discourses within the global Catholic Church (de Theije 1999), looking at a local diasporic prayer group allows us to identify that there are limitations to their discourse vis-à-vis sustaining the aims of their "reverse mission." Language barrier and contents of the group's specific Catholic religiosity might make crossing ethnic boundaries difficult. However, the reasons that this ambition might not come to fruition will not be explored in the present discussion. What is most important to understand is that the group must be able to expand within the lusophone networks that exist in the Netherlands, because its members elaborate their religiosity, intertwined with transnational Catholic ties and practices (Reesink 2013). Still under the spiritual guidance of Friar John, who now lives in Rio de Janeiro, Mary has traveled from Amsterdam to The Hague once a week to set up the Servants of Love in The Hague. The new group was nurtured by these connections with charismatic leaders from Rio de Janeiro and Amsterdam.

Attending a couple of gatherings of the prayer group Servants of Love, I noticed that the Brazilian Catholic Charismatics use saints and devotional objects as a way of reinforcing their religious and cultural identity in the Netherlands. Visiting the celebration of the eight-year anniversary of the group, which took place in Amsterdam in September 2017, two images occupied a special place during the mass: Our Lady of Aparecida and the Archangel Michael. Both were displayed in front of the altar and they were worshipped with prayers and songs during the Eucharist celebration. I want to explore here that the presence of those figures in the ritual signifies their role as guardians of the group's missionary work, thus combining a sense of belonging and religious transnationalism.

The devotion to Our Lady of Aparecida is a spiritual reality from Brazil that defines the religious identity of many Brazilian Catholics in lusophone spaces.[8] This is similar to the position of the Lady of Fatima in the collective imagination of Portuguese people. One can recognize cultural boundaries related to these images in a lusophone church. The image of Our Lady of Aparecida has traveled to the Netherlands to play the role of protector of Brazilians abroad, but it has also been used as an instrument of cultural differentiation inside the Portuguese-speaking parish in The Hague. Indeed, the Portuguese majority group mostly defines the religious life in the parish as characterized by a devotional and traditional Catholic religiosity. The Brazilians criticize and gossip regularly about the behavior of the Portuguese members of the parish, describing them as "owners of the Church" and being "closed." On the other hand, Portuguese members declare that "Brazilians do not take the church seriously." The Portuguese see the Brazilians as people who do not get much involved in the parish life. Similarly, Violet, forty-five years old, commented that the Portuguese organize the mass without inspiration and spiritual depth. In addition, she reveals that she would like to feel the "fire" or "passion for the faith" as she felt it in Brazil. For this reason, in part, some Brazilian women have taken the initiative to organize the Servant of Love inside the parish as a way of experiencing an imagined Brazilianness in their Catholic faith. This emphasis on Brazilian identity, namely being relational, spiritual, open, and emotional, are strong elements in Violet's discourse and can be seen as a way of sustaining the Brazilian position inside a lusophone parish, where tensions, conflicts, and negotiations are usually present among the groups.

In this context, I have frequently observed that the images of Mary embody cultural disputes between Brazilian and Portuguese immigrants, which priests or pastoral workers who are involved in the pastoral care of these groups try to temper. Each year, the members of the Portuguese-speaking Catholic parish hold a special festivity: the *festa* of Our Lady of Fatima and Our Lady of Aparecida together, though many parishioners refer to the *festa* of Our Lady of Aparecida as the Brazilian *festa* (*festa dos brasileiros*). The crux of said dispute is that the Portuguese members of the parish set up this church in the 1960s to rekindle their cultural roots, as I have discussed earlier (Martins 2012: 148–50). Despite the ethnic diversification of the church in the last decades with the incorporation of Brazilians and people from Guinea-Bissau and Angola, some Portuguese consider themselves to be the "guardians of tradition." They prefer to preserve certain conventional elements of Catholicism to the extent that this may be seen as a subjective expression of superiority, based on a "traditional" morality and combined with the working-class background and ethos of the Portuguese members of the parish. In contrast, the Brazilian women in my research achieve innovation by the agency of reinforcing transnational ties through Charismatic Catholic rituals. These are not common forms of Catholicism, especially from the point of view of the Portuguese migrants.

Another spiritual figure is the Archangel Michael who has been incorporated into the discourses of the Charismatic women as a resource for transmitting protection and belonging. The Archangel Michael was presented as a devotional gift to the Servos do Amor prayer group by Friar John of God. As I heard from a participant of the Servants' prayer group in The Hague: "The Archangel Michael helps us in the struggles (*lutas*) and protects our existence as prayer group." She relates this to conflicts within the parish with the Portuguese members: "when they have conflict among them it means that it is necessary to intensify the prayer to the Angel, because he is the supreme commander who protects [the group/the people] from dangerous threats." Perhaps the Archangel Michael has also been as a spiritual power to mediate real conflicts between the Portuguese and the Brazilians inside the parish. In this sense, the circulation of this devotion around the Archangel Michael, relocated from Brazil to the Netherlands, represents a way to obtain extraordinary power and more recognition for Brazilians. The devotion to the Archangel is now also very much appreciated by Portuguese members of the church.

The introduction of this popular devotion has been part of the missionary project of the Carmelite Friars. These friars came from Brazil to revitalize their religious congregation in 2009.[9] It was a missionary project with the objective of finding new candidates to continue the Congregation in the Netherlands. In the beginning of 2017, they had to return to Brazil because they did not attract new members to join the Carmelite Congregation.

Nevertheless, during the period that they lived and worked in the Netherlands, they added new objectives to their mission. They chose to promote the Charismatic religiosity, supporting the Servants of Love prayer group in Amsterdam. During these few years, the Servants of Love group came to incorporate a Brazilian Charismatic network, which includes people from different cities, as I have already mentioned. The second most important "sister" of the Servants of Love (i.e., the way that Mary refers to these local groups) is now located in The Hague, where it has been since 2015. The group in The Hague is a concrete outcome of the work of the Servants of Love. As the friars represent institutional power, they were able to be accepted without resistance by the Portuguese members of the parish, at the same time that they reinforced and spread the Charismatic religiosity. The engagement of the group of local women and the missionary agenda of the friars came together and facilitated the creation of the group "Servant of Love" in The Hague.

The final point concerns that the incorporation of the Lady of Aparecida and Archangel Michael, two material and symbolic signals of popular Catholic religiosity from Brazil, have been utilized by the Charismatic Catholic women as a way to strengthen their missionary work in other cities in the Netherlands. Moreover, they use their charismatic religiosity to construct a sense of belonging. In each gathering of the charismatic prayer group, through a special prayer for the Archangel Michael, who is invoked as a spiritual reality to face spiritual and material struggles (*lutas materiais e espirituais*), these women link the real difficulties from their daily lives in the Netherlands with the extraordinary spiritual power of the Archangel. I consider this cultural form of worship in the prayer groups a co-creation of spheres of belonging to which I will now turn.

Final considerations

To put the empirical findings in a broader perspective, I want to connect them to the concepts of home and belonging in order to show how these are framed as a "work of the imagination" (Appadurai 1996), as suggested in the beginning of this article, to create new spheres of belonging.

The group of Brazilian women who I have interviewed and continue to follow maintains their connection to the Portuguese-speaking Catholic church in The

Hague. They consider that this church gives them social and spiritual support. In this religious space, they build friendships, develop networks, and create a sense of belonging through their participation. The use of their native language is also an important aspect of their choice to affiliate themselves with the lusophone parish. Nevertheless, the religious experience in the parish is imbued with battles between differing forms of Catholicism: between a traditional and a Charismatic form, for example.

During my research, I found that most of my informants mentioned their engagement in the Catholic Charismatic group "Servants of Love" (Servos do Amor) in terms of a space in which they are "at home." Through their Charismatic Catholic religious practices, they invoke this sense of home by mobilizing a Brazilian cultural repertoire within a transnational "social morphology" (Salman and Theije 2011) to create a distinct cultural place in the sense suggested by Sheringham (2010).

This cultural emplacement is intertwined with various transnational resources and repertoires that enable the women to exert agency in an innovative way. First, the group translates Charismatic Catholicism into the reinforcement of an ethnic (or Brazilian) identity. This offers a distinct space of belonging through their participation in their local (The Hague) lusophone transnational Catholic parish. Vasquez and Marquardt (2003) have highlighted that, for migrants, the sense of ethnic identity constructed inside two religious communities in Atlanta was also very important to understanding how Latino migrants dealt with globalization. The imagining and performing of a distinct Brazilian space for Charismatic Catholicism also enabled the women from The Hague to connect to a new and evolving network of Brazilian Charismatics in the Netherlands: the Servants of Love. The support rendered by the Carmelite priest as part of his "reverse mission" (Freston 2010) adds a particular dimension to the role of transnational religiosity in re-creating such an ethno-national sphere, linking "Brazilian" Charismatic forms of devotion and materiality (objects and images) to the globalized agenda of a particular Brazilian Catholic institution, in this case the Carmelite Discalced Order.

Second, the network of the Servants of Love creates a specific space of belonging, when related to the sense of being home in Dutch urban society. Although the women acknowledge the value of freedom and the relative comfort of their livelihoods,[10] these material conditions are not the only factor that give a sense of integration in the Netherlands. From their discourses and religious practices follow that participating actively in the Charismatic group not only provides them with an ethnic (Brazilian) sense of "home away from home," but also opens up a repertoire of meaning that is experienced in terms of spirituality, emotion, and, eventually, protection. The religious agency of migrant women and their ability to mobilize and create dynamically a transnational "Brazilian" Catholic lusophere could critically enrich the debate on "integration" by adding the aspect of multicultural belonging. This is generated by their "work of the imagination," which creatively shapes a new sphere of belonging while the women navigate the uncertainties and constraints of their lives in the host country.

Part Three

Heritage, Embodiment, and Spirituality

Between Brazil and Spain

Structure and *Butinage* in the Trajectories of Santo Daime and União do Vegetal

Jessica Greganich

Introduction

União do Vegetal (UDV) and Santo Daime (SD) are Brazilian *ayahuasca* religions. Both religions base their services on the religious use of *ayahuasca*,[1] though they have different mythical narratives and rituals. In this chapter I intend to understand the transnationalization process of these religions both to and from Spain. On the one hand, transnationalization denotes the expansion and integration of these two Brazilian religions in Spain; namely, the process of relocating the rituals and doctrines of SD and UDV from the Brazilian context to a Spanish one. On the other hand, the spread of SD and UDV in Spain is not only the result of circulating Brazilian migrants taking their *ayahuasca* religions with them, but is also a resulting effect of the travels of spiritual seekers to and from Brazil. Instead of examining the "global" expansion of the Brazilian *ayahuasca* religions as a "cultural boundary negotiation in multicultural contexts" like Groisman (2013: 363) has done, I argue that we should examine the multidirectional flow of *ayahuasca* Brazilian religions between Brazil and Spain from the perspective of assemblages and *butinage*.

I define *butinage* as an intrinsic experience in religious practices where something escapes from a preceding tradition, system or structure, based on desire, and assemblages in a skein of interwoven lines that produces new connections. According to Gilles Deleuze (in Tonkonoff 2017: 100), the relations of force which make up the social field are indeed relations between lines or flows of belief and desire, and every dispositive/assemblage is "a tangle, a multilinear ensemble." The concept of butinage, in relation to transnational religion, offers us a broader way to comprehend global religious spread and its transformation since it shifts the focus from "re-ritualization" (Groisman 2013) to flows. This leads us to view transnational religion as a way of organizing experience, of building or "avoiding" assemblages, of articulating values and formulating enunciations of identity, ideology, and/or politics. The ways in which people organize their experience has consequences for religions. When SD and UDV are transnationalized, power constructions are displayed and formed: the power that the state exercises over these religions, i.e., biopower (Foucault 1979), and, the internal power of religious groups that arises otherwise. These power constructions are a component of assemblages, which historically, are always notable. According to Deleuze, desire, via the inventions, escapes, and sublimations it motivates, is opening up forms of subjectivity and territorializations of power. Analyses of the trajectories of people and their religious practices, ideas, objects, and media, allow us to capture the desires that stand at the heart of the construction of assemblages. "The trajectory merges not only with the subjectivity of those who travel through a milieu, but also with the subjectivity of the milieu itself, insofar as it is reflected in those who travel through it" (Deleuze, 1997: 61).

Butinage emphasizes the primacy of desire over power. In a continuous process, the structure constructs the agency of the religious practitioners, and these agents realize and transform this structure. The desire constructs agents from assemblages, only then can it break the structure and construct new power structures (butinage). Butinage is visible in relation to the power constructions that shape the way SD and UDV are reterritorialized in Spain. For example, UDV and SD traditions when reterritorialized, did not circumscribe the experience of practitioners within the limits formed by tradition. Butinage helps to define "the form of creativity specific to that assemblage, the particular ways in which it can effect transformation in other assemblages or in itself" (Deleuze & Guattari 1987: 531).

Therefore, transnationalization implies deterritorialization and reterritorialization, which Deleuze and Guattari (1987: 508) define as the movement whereby something escapes or departs from a given territory, to reterritorialize in another form, in a different territory, a "new earth" to come. This implies the transference of practices from one geographic place to another, between Brazil and Spain, for example, but it is not only about this geographical delimitation. Deterritorialization constitutes the cutting edge of an assemblage (Deleuze and Guattari 1987: 88). Every assemblage is territorial in that it sustains connections that define it, but every assemblage is also composed of lines of deterritorialization that run through it and carry it away from its current form (Deleuze and Guattari 1987: 503–04). The deterritorialization of SD and UDV emerges from connections between humans and nonhumans, people and their life paths, finding lines that inform their interactions with the world; of governmentality, of history, of definitions of religion, and of religious structure.

This chapter is based on ethnographic fieldwork that was carried out between 2008 and 2009 in Brazil and Spain, and which consisted mostly of participant observation and interviews with SD and UDV practitioners in Porto Alegre and Madrid. I begin this chapter by contextualizing the religions in relation to the respective countries and governmentalities, bringing out the power constructions that are part of the transnationalization processes. Then, I describe the flows of SD and UDV between Brazil and Spain, based on the religious trajectories and desires that construct "agents" in assemblages. Subsequently, I analyze how the churches of SD and UDV are structurally organized in Brazil, and the implication of these structures in terms of the agency of religious practitioners (agency in relation to structure). I finalize the chapter showing how these systems can then be disturbed, attacked, and rebuilt (agency that escapes structure) between Brazil and Spain.

Histories of religions, social political contexts, and power constructions

Brazil is known for its various spiritual traditions. Until the late nineteenth century, there was no "disenchantment of the world" in the Protestant style, or even a strict Catholic control over religiosity, as was the case in Latin Europe. Brazil's so-called luso-Brazilian Catholicism was characterized by a low degree of ecclesiastical control over religiosity practiced on the margins of the church. There was a multifaceted process of cultural encounters, crossings, and syncretism between beliefs in deities and *eguns* (gods) of African religions brought by slaves, and the shamanic spirituality of indigenous peoples, as well as the Catholic popular beliefs in saints, guardian angels, and wandering souls (Souza 1987). This variety of spiritual traditions is continued in new ways by SD and UDV.

CEBUDV, Centro Espírita Beneficente União do Vegetal (Spiritist Center of the Beneficent União do Vegetal), known as União do Vegetal (UDV), was founded by Mestre Gabriel in 1961. His doctrine is transmitted orally and secretly to disciples, according to the level they occupy within the religion's hierarchy. Santo Daime (SD) was founded by Mestre Irieneu in the 1930s and his doctrine is transmitted through musical hymns. After the death of Mestre Irineu, *Padrinho* (Godfather), Sebastião founded the Santo Daime community known as CEFLURIS, Centro Eclético da Fluente Luz Universal Raimundo Irineu Serra (Raimundo Irineu Serra Eclectic Center of the Universal Flowing Light).

In both religions the doctrine is always transmitted during the *burracheira* (strange force) or *força* (force), which are the emic terms for the experience of being under the overwhelming influence of *ayahuasca*. This experience is associated with healing or with the personal transformation from a learning process or spiritual evolution. According to Labate (2004: 92), both religions originated from contact with the Andean shamanic universe, a tradition that they have in common. In other words, although coming from the same tradition, they have developed in different ways.

SD expanded to Spain in 1989. Though Spain is formally a secular country, it still bears the marks from the strict control of Catholic religiosity. Article 16.3 of the Spanish Constitution defines the country as a state without confession; "No confession will have a state character." Freedom of religiosity and individual worship is guaranteed, and a cooperative relationship between the government and all faiths is assured. However, the *ayahuasca* religions are facing the burden of legal processes in legitimation, and other state regulations, anchored on issues involving the use of a psychoactive substance.

When SD and UDV transnationalized, the process of deterritorialization and reterritorialization displayed and formed power constructions that could best be analyzed according to the following four elements:

The first element is about the problematic, that Foucault (1979) calls, "governmentality," the art to govern, and tactics, the "conduct of behavior" in the population and the subject. These are the tactics of government that allow one to constantly define what should or should not be the state's business, what is public and what is private, what is state-owned and what is not. The *ayahuasca* religions, in their survival and in their limits in Spain, should also be understood from the notion of the tactics in/used by governmentality.

Health and public safety are considered by the Spanish state to be factors that limit the free practice of religion in the country. Spanish criminal law, however, is primarily focused on the impacts of drug trafficking on health and public safety, and not on possession and personal use, which are considered protected under the right to privacy (Spanish Constitution, Article 18). In this sense, the religious ban on *ayahuasca* in Spain was assured by the state through a particular mode of biopower. The state framed *ayahuasca* as "toxic" to exercise its power, since there is no criterion or rule to declare whether *ayahuasca* is in fact harmful. In 2000 the National Institute of Toxicology released a report in which the low toxicity of *ayahuasca* found in the samples was shown.

Secondly, the specific historical moment and social setting co-define how religions are being framed. Spain has a strong history of dictatorship and inquisition that is currently associated with human rights and ecumenism by expanding the rights of religious freedom and interreligious dialogue. In this sense, the Daimists,[2] in facing lawsuits over the right to consecrate *ayahuasca* in Spain, still feel that they are living in a form of dictatorship and inquisition without religious freedom and thus, their religious projects have moral, religious, and political meaning.

The third element refers to the definitions of religion within governmental procedures. As stated by Labate and Feeney (2012), definitions of religion that have been sustained in the legalization process of the *ayahuasca* religions in Europe are substantially influenced by Western Judeo-Christian concepts, and thus, exclude rules related to *ayahuasca* shamanism, a practice deeply rooted among the Indigenous and mestizos in the Amazon. As these religions expand outside of their traditional regional and cultural contexts, they come to be viewed through a Western framework, as seen in the "War on Drugs," and are therefore classified as criminal enterprises. "If the groups want legislative support, the ceremonies must be done in a Christian-inspired manner or they will not be legally recognized.[3] Conducting *ayahuasca* ceremonies in an Indigenous framework is not enough to gain legal acceptance" (Kaufman 2015: 194).

The analysis of structure within these religious groups and the power relations between them, form the fourth element. I will demonstrate that the specific "figurations" in religious societies and communities of SD and UDV, provide their disciples with the possibility to build agency and subsequent structures in different ways.

These power constructions are lines/flows that inform the deterritorialization and reterritorialization of SD and UDV. I will explore these lines further in the following, first examining how modes of governmentality create assemblages from the two religions in Spain and second, how the internal power structures reinforce the agencies and structures of these religious communities and their subjects. And finally, I will determine how the agents from desire can break and rebuild these power structures (butinage).

Bringing SD and UDV to Spain: Flows, trajectories, and assemblages

The reterritorialization of SD in Spain began with the trajectory of a spiritual seeker, Francisco de la Cal (Known Paco) in Brazil; from there we can map the network of agencies that were formed among people with an interest in New Age[4] alternative medicine and psychedelics, as well as their practices, ideas, objects, and media. Within this network, two women had a chance to encounter UDV in Brazil which then established its own place in Spain.

Paco was a "hippie journalist" interested in shamanism. He met Padrinho Sebastião in the "Colônia 5000"[5] in Acre, 1983. There he had his first transcendent experience and became a SD believer, living for some years in the SD community while simultaneously writing for Spanish magazines. At the end of 1985 he returned to Spain carrying a bottle of Daime, with which he conducted occasional informal sessions with relatives, among them his brother, Juan Carlos de la Cal[6] and his friends.

In 1988, Juan Carlos visited Céu do Mapiá and met Padrinho Sebastião. During that year, Paulo Roberto, the godfather of the Céu do Mar Church (in Rio de Janeiro) met the gestalt Chilean psychologist, Claudio Naranjo. Claudio Naranjo's research was aimed at refining the Gestalt Therapy training program known as SAT (Seekers after Truth), of which the Enneagram[7] of personality, interpersonal meditation, and various therapeutic resources were key components. He also directed research with psychopharmacology, exploring individual therapy with psychedelics (psychedelic therapy). Naranjo offered workshops in Europe until 1987 when he presented his program of Gestalt Therapy in a property called Babia, near the province of Almeria in Spain. The SAT Program for personal and professional development was then reborn in Spain under the name "SAT Babia." Thus in 1988, there was a meeting in Babia to which Naranjo, through a friend, invited a Brazilian Daimist to come with *ayahuasca*, in order to perform meetings in Spain. After participating in rituals in Céu do Mar, Claudio Naranjo invited believers to coordinate SD sessions. Thus in 1989, a group of five people came to Babia from Céu do Mar, led by Paulo Roberto. This event is formally considered the first official work of CEFLURIS in Europe. There were two sessions on two consecutive days with over one hundred people in attendance, all of them related to the field of health sciences.

In 1991, the owner of SAT Babia visited Brazil. In 1992, Padrinho Alfredo traveled to Spain for the first time, leading sessions in Babia and then moving to the province of Guadalajara. In 1993, Padrinho Alfredo visited Catalonia, founding the first permanent group in Spain with fifteen members. After Catalonia, Padrinho Alfredo traveled to Madrid, Seville, and Ibiza, and, in all of these places, people became *ayahuasca* users.

Until 2000, the Spanish Daime church has functioned without legal support, and a specialized department in the Spanish police has been tasked with investigating them. According to the conversation I had with Fernando Ribeiro, Godfather of Céu das Estrelas Church in Juiz de Fora (Minas Gerais, Brazil), who was leading the work that I participated in at the Church of Madrid, this investigation was highly extensive and even included wiretapping. The investigation culminated in the arrest of two Brazilian Daimists, Fernando Ribeiro and Chico Corrente, at Barajas airport on April 5, 2000, along with Juan Carlos. They had landed in Spain carrying ten liters of *ayahuasca* from Brazil. Juan Carlos was released on bail, but he was also sued, along with Fernando and Chico, who were contained in prison for fifty-four days.

After this arrest, the Spanish police filed a case against the Daime church, in which six members were sued. According to Daimists, during the operation about sixty policemen entered the Church of Madrid with dogs, searched it thoroughly, and sent six police officers to the residence of every *ayahuasca* believer. The case had worldwide repercussions on the Spanish church, and the two Brazilian prisoners began to receive support from a number of people in the international community. In Brazil, for example, senators wrote a document on behalf of the Brazilian parliament, explaining that the use of *ayahuasca* had an ancient origin in Indigenous traditions, and was syncretically linked with Catholic tradition brought by Northeastern immigrants, eventually generating the manifestation of SD. They claimed that the two Brazilians could not be confused with international drug traffickers. Furthermore, several Brazilian Catholic bishops and two Spanish bishops signed a supporting document.

After 54 days in prison, Fernando and Chico were released on probation and after two-and-a-half months following their release, they regained their passports. The case, including the prosecution of the six charged Spanish Daimists, went to the National Court, the highest legal court in Spain, but was closed and filed without trial on the basis of a document signed by the presiding judge, which stated, "The perpetration of the crime has not been justified." This was the first time that a case had been filed at the National Court without going to trial.

The arrests and legal threats prompted the Spanish Daimist church to restart the legalization process at the Department of Religious Affairs, related to the Ministry of Justice. Registration was granted on October 7, 2003, under the name "Iglesia del Santo Daime de España (CEFLURISE)." Nevertheless, the *ayahuasca* churches still faced an uncertain legal standing; while the churches were recognized as religious organizations in Spain, they could not freely import *ayahuasca* since the ecological conditions are inappropriate for the development of the plants in Spain (instead they must be imported from Brazil). Starting in 2006, SD began requesting that the Spanish Agency of Medicine and Health Products grant them a permit to import *ayahuasca*, stating that it is only used as a sacrament. After two denials from the agency, the church appealed to the Administrative Court without success. After losing on two occasions, they finally won the legal right to import *ayahuasca* due to a decision from the National Court in 2008.

Juan Carlos says that the decisive victory of SD's legalization is proof that *ayahuasca* is not toxic, especially considering the report from the UN Commission on Narcotics in Vienna, which affirmed that *ayahuasca* and the plants that compose it, have no need for inspection. The prohibition on drug trafficking is outlined in the Vienna Convention on the Law of Treaties, which is thirty years old and signed by almost every country in the world, including Brazil. This was the reason for the international prohibition of DMT (dimethyltryptamine, the active psychedelic molecule in *ayahuasca*), although ranges of tolerance are not yet defined since it is very difficult to establish figures on toxicity. International laws stipulate that where there is no tolerance table, DMT is considered hazardous for health when a preparation contains more than 2 percent of the alkaloid. The Spanish court that started proceedings against the Daimists, believed that the Daime drink contained between 20 percent and 70 percent DMT. When the toxicological analysis determined that the proportion of DMT in all of the bottles of Daime collected by the police did not exceed 0.08 percent, they therefore had to release Fernando and Chico and close the case. The official expert certified that *ayahuasca* is not harmful to health. The judgment stated that, in addition, the use of the substance in a religious context is not a crime. This was the basis of the later success of the Daimist Church against the Spanish Government.

Currently, there are four nuclei of SD in Spain, but the top position has passed to the group in Madrid, which bought a piece of land and built a church with the aim of following the community model proposed by CEFLURIS. The Church of Madrid is over ten years old and usually gathers around a 100 people for the big work (hymnals), according to Juan Carlos.

UDV arrived in Spain in 1992. This year was the centenary of Mestre Irineu and due to this, a group from SAT Babia traveled to Brazil. Two women who were looking for *ayahuasca,* established a casual relationship with a member of UDV who put them in touch with UDV, which then opened its doors for masters of UDV to visit Spain. The first session of UDV in Spain was conducted on October 2, 1994. Initially, the sessions were only organized when masters and counselors came from Brazil. In 2000, CEBUDV requested enrollment in the register of religious organizations and it was installed by the Pré-Núcleo[8] Inmaculada Concepción. The request was denied by the Ministry of Justice of Spain. Then, UDV hired a lawyer specializing in religious issues in order to apply again in 2005. The request was denied once again. In 2006, UDV appealed to the National Court and in 2007, obtained a favorable judgment. In 2008, the State Attorney accepted the sentence and UDV was enrolled in the register of religious organizations as an association. Currently, UDV has an administrative unit in Spain (the only one in Europe), located in the province of Madrid and Valencia, where there is a small group for the "*distribuição autorizada* [authorized distribution] *do Vegetal.*"[9] In total, UDV has approximately eighty members in several countries across Europe.

Thus, from trajectories and flows, SD and UDV deterritorialized and reterritorialized bringing out power constructions; the power that the state exercises over these religions, biopower, and the internal power of religious groups and the agency of religious actors that arise otherwise. These power constructions are a component of assemblages that produce new connections that shape a new sphere for SD and UDV as will be examined in the following section.

Structure and agency in SD and UDV in Brazil

Contrary to Spain, in Brazil, there are more followers of UDV than SD CEFLURIS line: currently, there are about forty-two churches affiliated to CEFLURIS and approximately 4,000 official members, while UDV has approximately 15,000 official members. But there is a greater movement of people who go to SD to experience it or, who remain for a while but do not become official members.

Both UDV and SD have eclectic doctrines. But SD has a flexibility and openness that allows members to continue to incorporate other traditions that may contribute to its enrichment, with the prospect of a "living, mutable doctrine," which Groisman (1999: 233) has called *Ecletismo Evolutivo* (Evolutionary Eclecticism). UDV has an immutable doctrine, which aims to maintain a set standard and follow only the teachings of Mestre Gabriel; something that I have called *Ecletismo Involutivo* (Involutionary Eclecticism) (Greganich 2010). SD does not require a radical departure of its associates from their religious pasts. Thus, one can find in a group, for example, Daimists that are also Umbandists, Buddhists, or followers of Kardecist spiritual centers.

The eclectic "involutionary doctrine" of UDV, its organization, rituals, and myth of origin, point to a "society of religious court" (Elias 2001). According to Elias (2001), the court must be regarded as a society, a social formation in which the relations between social citizens are defined in a specific way and where reciprocal dependencies that link individuals to each other engender codes and unique behaviors. Moreover, a court society should be understood as a society endowed with a (real or princely) court, which is fully organized from it. UDV is considered a "religious society with [an] origin of nobility," based originally on a myth about the origin of kingship (with king, council, liege, and disciples). This royalty is being recreated in UDV (in the form of Master, Counselor, Instructive Body, and Associates), and thus as a religious society founded on this hierarchy in order to perform a "personal transformation" aimed at spiritual evolution.

UDV has a religious social structure centered on a strong hierarchy, with rigid discipline and a strict control of emotions. This shows an aspect of rationalization in a Weberian sense, as contained in the religious experience, which marks the "rational religious ethic" with a much more controlled and smoother ecstatic trance than that of SD. This rationalization is facing a "civilizing process" (Elias 1994), understood as the pacification of behavior and control of effect based on the social distinction of *hoasqueiros* (hoasca users) and non-*hoasqueiros*, a dynamic reminiscent of Elias' "society of religious court."

Therefore, the disciple must have great self-control, for this is necessary to be shaped according to the doctrine which claims the ideals, e.g., to be married, to have children, not to drink or smoke, not to use any kind of drugs, to work hard, be honest, not to lie, to be courteous and obliging, and to attend all sessions of UDV. According to the doctrine, UDV has to be a "protected" environment with a "perfect" harmony between followers. They should not scream, for example, rather they have to treat each other kindly, and demonstrate affection, friendship, respect, love, and trust for one another. Participants must undergo an individual civilizing process according to the rigid ideal of a new/better society that UDV has configured. And, according to the masters, one's behavior outside of UDV also appears in the *burracheira* where the master exercises extremely gentle, polished, and attentive tendency to correct someone.

In contrast, SD with its eclectic evolutionary doctrine, organization, rituals, and myth of origin, points to an "apocalyptic religious community." SD presents an apocalyptic community structure (alluding to the work of Hervieu and Léger 1983) with a messianic character. They believe that the Daimist doctrine can save and guide the battalion for the New Age that will emerge following mass global environmental disasters. SD religious community appears therefore as the necessary mediating place of initiation into the knowledge and customs that will be the "remnants" by which humanity will be perpetuated beyond the apocalypse. It is a grouping network centered on the charismatic leader, the godfather, as understood from a Weberian perspective based on the "routinization of charisma," with a flexible and tolerant discipline emphasizing the autonomy and freedom of the subject from the point of view that divinity is within each of us. In SD, one's behavior outside of SD appears in the force, in the consciousness of the individual.

UDV religious society centered on a hierarchical rise of "court" and the Daimist religious community centered on the "charismatic leader" (the godfather) are linked in a didactic principle that occurs by different logics. In UDV, it is through a self-taught process where God and the master manifest in the *burracheira,* and with the incarnate masters that represent the knowledge of Mestre Gabriel and comprise the highest level of hierarchical structure. In SD, it is through learning by itself, by "force," where God and the master are manifested and therefore, the consciousness of the individual becomes its own guidance pointing to the idea of "agency" (Ortner 2007).

To Ortner (2007), the notion of agency has two fields of meaning. In one, agency has to do with intentionality and with the fact of pursuing projects that are culturally defined. In the other, agency has to do with power, with the fact of acting in the context of relations to inequality, asymmetry, and social forces. In fact, however, agency is never merely one or the other. It has two sides; as (following) "projects" or as (the fact of having or being against) the "power"; or it mixes/transfuses in a Moebius-type relationship. Moreover, power itself is a double-edged sword, working from the top down as domination and from the bottom up as resistance (Ortner 2007: 58).

In the specific "figurations" (Elias 2001: 158) that are set in the religious communities of UDV and SD, disciples have built "agencies" that are distributed differently. In UDV, the master is the interpreter, the one who has the duty to interpret. The disciple is in the position of the apprentice, in a place of not knowing or understanding. The knowledge is within the master and the master plant (*ayahuasca*); in other words, it is in the "other." The master is the one who knows, the one in the place of mastery, knowledge, and/or power. Understanding occurs through indoctrination, through interpretation of the master as well as the "master" within oneself as you intake the tea. There is a reference to knowing, which is placed structurally, as an agent for the production of *hoasqueiros*. The speech of a master is the discourse presented to the other (the disciple), as the knowledge of the true masters. The training of a disciple into a master is thus based on the ideal of gaining access to knowledge, through which one attains a degree of knowledge about how to control and act.

In the ritual of UDV, the disciple operates according to his/her own issues in a ritual centered on questions and answers, and thus causes the other master to produce knowledge. To the master, what matters is making things work/flow. The disciple knows from the *burracheira* and he works to transfer this knowledge to the master, who produces knowledge in speech; he is the master because the disciple grants him knowledge and hopes that he will produce.

In SD, the godfather has knowledge but does not stand as the one who possesses it. Knowledge is shifted to the position of the agent's speech: Jesus, Mestre Irineu, Padrinho Sebastião. The godfather teaches as someone who has no knowledge; it comes to him from the master, the astral, and this causes his disciples to produce knowledge themselves based on his leadership. The godfather operates based on his own issues and aims to reach the other, in his relationship to the signifier, so that the disciple may produce from the teaching through hymns and "force" a knowing that belongs to him. The truth at stake in the godfather's speech is his own relationship to the impossibility of saying (with the lack of knowledge). In other words, it is a discourse that questions the human knowledge and mastery that is clearly represented in the "Juramidam Empire."[10] For example, the teachings in SD are transmitted through the hymns. The hymnal is received directly from the astral and all Daimist members can potentially receive hymns, though not all do.

In this sense, when it comes to agency as a form of power that people have at their disposal, their ability to act on their own behalf, to influence other people and events, and to keep some kind of control over their own lives; it can be concluded that Daimists have much more agency than Udevists, since in UDV, what dominates is the law of the center, while in SD the knowledge produced by each individual is the dominating factor.

As for the agency to pursue culturally defined projects, which in both religions would be spiritual evolution as defined by the local logic of the good and desirable and how to pursue them, it can be concluded that both UDV and SD are guided by the experience of transformation brought about by *ayahuasca* as a basis for the process of butinage. The experience of trance is a butinage where the body opens up to new connections in a "wandering learning" to be represented. However, it is mixed with agency in the sense of power, and therefore the UDV disciple has the project of "climbing" the grades to get to the master's level, while in SD the project of agency is "open" to the choice and creation of each individual. This distinction is quite possibly one of the factors that leads to UDV having many more members than SD, even though there are more people who have visited SD than UDV, as the statistics cited above indicate. These different ways of organizing experience in SD and UDV play an important role in their transnationalization, to which I will now turn.

The UDV and SD between Brazil and Spain: Structure, desire and butinage

Nowadays, unlike Europe, religions such as UDV that exercise control over religiosity are successful in Brazil. I have found an opposite pattern within the *ayahuasca* religious field in Spain in comparison to Brazil. In Spain, there are more members of SD than UDV: there are approximately 200 members of SD in Spain alone, compared to approximately 80 members of UDV spread across Europe; furthermore, beyond Spain, there are more SD believers in other European countries such as the Netherlands, Italy, Germany, and France. The only Daimist church in Europe is in Madrid, but the works of SD are carried out all over Spain and other European countries, in gardens, rented rooms, and even in the leaders' homes. There are about 100 believers scattered across the nuclei of Madrid, Catalonia, Andalusia, and Balearic. Thus Spain, according to Juan Carlos, has approximately 200 Daimists, with most of the participants (estimated at 95 percent) being Spanish. Juan Carlos told me that new people are increasingly appearing in search of SD. According to a Spanish master, UDV has about eighty registered members living in several European countries; since UDV sessions are only held in Portugal and Spain (with the exception of some distributions elsewhere when there is a qualified person present), residents in other countries such as Germany and Italy sometimes attend sessions of UDV in Spain. Of these eighty members, about twenty-five are European and the remainder are Brazilian citizens residing in Europe.

UDV is concerned with the fact that most of its members are Brazilian immigrants and, that there are barriers to Spaniards joining the UDV. In order to attract more Spaniards to UDV, some changes in the rituals had to be made, such as amending the reading of the statute governing the CEBUDV, which is always read at the beginning of sessions; in order not to bore and exclude the Spaniards who do not understand Portuguese, it was amended so that questions could be asked and answered in Spanish. This being so, the masters are also preferably Spanish, so that it is not nationality or origin that determines members' mobility or the possibility of hierarchical ascension, but rather their "degree of memory" and their display of "practice" befitting the doctrine.

UDV has internal divisions and its own hierarchy, with different degrees of commitment from its agents. The Masters Board acts as an "elite" and the aim of hierarchical ascension mobilizes the whole group's functioning, directly influencing people's behavior. In this sense, the care taken in the utterance of certain words in the "Udevist language," a distinctive language used between *hoasqueiros*, and which according to UDV is related to the "mysteries of the word," is rigidly followed in Brazil, but is not evidenced in Spain since much of it does not make sense to Spanish people. For example, according to Udevist language used in Brazil, one cannot say "thank you" but rather "grateful," because thank you (*obrigada*) in Portuguese comes from obligation, and in UDV no one has any obligation to anyone or anything.

In Brazil, members of UDV call themselves firstly by their hierarchical level and then by their name. What differentiates them is the hierarchical level that represents their level of spiritual development, the personal transformation achieved by the person; this is the case, although "all are the same" and "everyone has a chance" or opportunity to ascend in the scale. In Spain, members rarely call themselves by their hierarchical level, only by their name, even when they are a master. The hierarchical ascension does not mobilize the whole functioning of the religious group. In the session that I participated in, the Brazilian master, in a moment of collective effort in the nucleus, reminded us that everyone could call each other by their title in the context of UDV, and that this had nothing to do with authoritarianism. However, no one acted upon this instruction.

If a partner does not commit to the doctrine, before being dismissed, he/she will be properly "indoctrinated" by the master and "demanded." The "demands" are given by the master in a fair, attentive, and polite way to "improve his/her attitude." This is done during the ritual, under the effect of *burracheira*, and thus they acquire a character of indoctrination. This too does not occur in Spain; at least, during the sessions there is no indoctrination since Spanish and Brazilian immigrants alike do not tolerate this kind of behavior even if it comes from a master. I witnessed the case of a Brazilian woman who had an argument with the master during a session because she disagreed with his position. This would never happen in Brazil, where the word of the master is law, since the master represents Mestre Gabriel. In Brazil, members are required to attend all scheduled sessions that occur on the first and third Saturday of each month. In Spain, this also does not occur, since it is the only church in Europe and many members cannot always afford to travel. Despite this "loosening" of religious orthodoxy, I nevertheless perceived in the Spanish Udevist members, the appreciation of and the importance they gave to "good actions" and to the teachings of Mestre Gabriel.

UDV plays a role of support and protection for its members, establishing the great family of UDV. This also occurs in Spain; for example, I observed the case of a Brazilian immigrant who had a child with a Spanish man who kicked her out of the house after the birth of the child. She was unemployed and homeless, but was fully received into the house of one of the masters where she remained for a year before her reestablishment.

Brazilian UDV, based on its strong hierarchical and moral structure, exerts control over emotions and acts as a civilizing process on its members. Spanish people engaged in New Age practices seem not to need a religious group to perform this "civilizing" and "family" role. Rather, what the Spanish desire is an "uncivilized" way expressed through freedom, flexibility, and autonomy, as offered by SD. This becomes clear when one[11] observes that UDV in Spain is composed mostly of Brazilians, i.e., it is in an immigration situation where families help each other. So UDV religious structure appears to make less sense to Spanish people who have a strong history of dictatorship and inquisition, and therefore it seems to go against the problems and interests of Spanish people engaged in "New Age." The popularity of SD in relation to UDV in the Spanish context is related to the version of "Believing without belonging" developed by Hervieu-Léger (1999) grasping this individual and intimate religiosity which is growing, as opposed to classical and institutional forms of religiosity.

UDV, unlike SD, does not accept homosexuality, recommends no sex before marriage, prizes marital fidelity, and rejects divorce. UDV proscribes the use of cigarettes, alcohol, and other "plants of power" such as cannabis sativa, the latter of which is used by Daimists. Furthermore, once one becomes a member of UDV, one has to commit to no longer belonging to or attending other religious services.

UDV has had to be more flexible with orthodox rules in order to bring Spanish members in which has caused a break in its original engine. This did not occur in SD which has an eclectic evolutionary doctrine that by itself allows for openness and flexibility, and which admits the incorporation of other practices and beliefs that contribute to the "enrichment" of the doctrine anywhere.

The "Evolutionary Eclecticism," according to Groisman (1999), enables the coexistence of various cosmological systems such as Umbanda, Spiritism, and Christianity, and it is thus a whole system that encompasses all aspects of life. Therefore, SD in Spain has a strong intersection with alternative therapies and the use of various psychoactive substances, as well as other fields of interest for those that come to the religion.

UDV does not approve of its members attending other religious services after they commit adherence to the doctrine and become a member, especially *ayahuasca* religions. For UDV, the true master, the highest master, is Mestre Gabriel; the rest are called "masters of curiosity."[12] Thus UDV is the "real science."[13]

In Spain, this does not exist, or "cannot exist" as one Daimist member said—a Brazilian immigrant whom I interviewed. He is currently a member of SD in Spain (where he lives), but he also visits UDV in Spain. He says that UDV had to join SD since the latter was leading the lawsuit that benefited both religions, and that it is very common in Spain (unlike Brazil) for members and believers to be in touch with each other; they walk between the two religions, and there is a crossover in several other therapeutic uses of *ayahuasca* found in Spain according to the ecumenical perspective of union and religious liberty.

UDV refers to something of an intransigent Catholicism that is, articulating with Hervieu and Léger (1983), resetting the antimodernism of the Roman Curia (such as the "religious court" society of UDV) in the resumption of doctrinal stability without committing to the demands of modern rationality and the assertion of primacy of the Papal Authority (in this case the Master). Although this discourse brings in the idea that all of its members can achieve the degree of master, it seems that this idea does not capture Spanish people from New Age who are oriented toward the use of entheogens (generating the divine within). This approaches the description of Hervieu-Léger (1999), of pilgrims crossing spaces and boundaries in their individual religious path, the idea of reflexivity and hyperindividualization, the radical freedom of self-questioning, and choice of paradigms (D'Andrea 1996). The Spaniards from New Age desire an agency project that is "open" to the choices and creation of each individual.

Conclusion

Building on the work of Deleuze and Guatari, I have demonstrated that we should comprehend the process of religious transnationalization as deterritorialization and reterritorialization and that religious transnationalization is produced by multidirectional flows and lines. Lines are co-produced by desire and belief and they inform interactions with the world. Analyzing the trajectories of people and their religious practices captures the lines and the desires that stand at the heart of constructing assemblages. Desire can thus break existing structures and construct new power structures. As I argue, this process can be captured well with the notion of butinage and, in this chapter, I have demonstrated that butinage is visible in the power constructions that shape the way SD and UDV are reterritorialized in Spain.

Power constructions are lines that inform the deterritorialization and reterritorialization of SD and UDV according to the following key dynamics that interact in a specific historical moment and social setting: 1) The tactics of governmentality, in which the religious ban on *ayahuasca* in Spain was assured by the state through a particular mode of biopower; 2) The definitions of religion within governmental procedures that classified the *ayahuasca* religions as criminal enterprises; 3) The structure of the *ayahuasca* religions and the power relations within these religions.

The specific "figurations" of UDV and SD provide their disciples with the possibility to build agency and subsequent structures in different ways. UDV has a religious social structure centered on a strong hierarchy with rigid discipline and a strict control on the emotions within an eclectic "involutionary doctrine." SD has an apocalyptic religious community structure with a flexible and tolerant discipline emphasizing the autonomy and freedom of the subject within an eclectic "evolutionary doctrine." However, the *ayahuasca* users also have agency informed by desire; a desire for freedom, flexibility, autonomy, and individual and intimate religiosity related to New Age spirituality. Agency informed by desire confronts the existing traditional structure and the process of butinage rebuilds the religions traditions and systems in Spain creating new power formations. We could thus best view the transnationalization of SD and UDV as ways of organizing experience, of building and avoiding assemblages, of articulating values, and formulating enunciations from multidirectional flows.

"Pray Looking North"

Change and Continuity of Transnational Umbanda in Uruguay

Andrés Serralta Massonnier

Introduction: The ways of conceiving the arrival and diffusion of Umbanda in Uruguay

The analysis of studies on the transnationalization of "La Umbanda"[1] and its development in Uruguay shows that some of them, such as María Pallavicino (1988) and Horacio Solla (1992), have understood this process as the diffusion of a religious phenomenon that, after spreading through Brazil, crossed borders and was implanted in Uruguay. This conception is based on the assumption that the passage of religion across the border of both countries occurred almost as a natural or foreseeable fact, derived from the Umbandist expansion through the Brazilian territory. Other studies that have analyzed the transnationalization of this religion in the border region between Uruguay and Brazil, such as Alejandro Frigerio (1998), Rita Segato (1996), and Ari Oro (2002), have pointed out some of its particularities. However, their attention have not been focused predominantly on the Uruguayan case, but on its treatment as part of the transnationalization of Afro-Brazilian religions toward the Rio de la Plata region, especially toward Argentina.

This chapter examines the particular transnationalization process of Umbanda in Uruguay, since it has characteristics that distinguish it from other transnationalization processes, and explains the appearance of this religious phenomenon and its settlement in Uruguay prior to its settlement in other countries. In this regard, the following builds on Renzo Pi Hugarte (1997:212), a Uruguayan anthropologist who has specifically addressed the case of the expansion of Afro-Brazilian religions into Uruguay:

> The presence in Uruguay of religious expressions that have emerged in Brazil is not the result of any globalization: it is caused by the growing influence of Rio Grande do Sul on this country, which certainly expresses the greater demographic weight of that State and also of its economic development. Of course, this influence is also particularly strong in border areas.[2]

Regarding the process of transnationalization toward Uruguay, Pi Hugarte (1998: 23) also points out that "there was never an institutional action," or any temple, Umbandist federation, or other cult of possession,[3] that carried out plans to propitiate the arrival of Umbanda. The beginning of Umbandist practices and the establishment of *terreiros* (temples) in the country took place in the early 1940s (Segato 1996; Serralta Massonnier 2015), although its consolidation in the border zone happened from the 1950s.

Whereas Umbanda has a Brazilian origin and its expansion in the State of Rio Grande do Sul favored its arrival in Uruguay (Oro 2002) as part of the border zone between Uruguay and Brazil (Hugarte 1997), I consider that the border space between Uruguay and Brazil should not be understood as two culturally different spaces on either side of the border. Culturally, they constitute an integrated, unique, cross-border, and transnational space. Once formed, the Umbandist religious phenomenon arrived and spread out to the rest of the Uruguayan territory. For this reason, I argue that it is a specific form of transnationalization, different from the other cases that occurred in America and Europe. This hypothesis maintains that, when the Umbanda diffusion process within Brazil reached the border zone, there was an introduction and diffusion of the cult in both sides of the border, where a high level of integration and cultural hybridization had already created a unique cultural space, differentiated from the rest of the territory of both countries; the border cultural space. The existence of this cultural phenomenon would explain the earlier arrival of Umbanda to Uruguay compared to the rest of South American countries that also have a land border with Brazil.

Likewise, the transboundary and transcultural origins of Umbanda in Uruguay were historically determined by the perception that i) being initiated into the Umbandist practices, or even better, ii) being initiated by recognized Umbandist practitioners confers religious prestige to the members of Umbanda in the border region. This is consolidated within this religious community. However, since the 1960s, the majority of the Uruguayan Umbandist community and its temples are in the city of Montevideo and surroundings, not in the border area. The geographical disposition of Montevideo, with respect to this cross-border region, implies that the Montevideans refer to this geographical space as "the North" or "the border." That is why this chapter is titled "Pray Looking

North." "The North," or the border, has special characteristics that make it a dynamic frontier (Clemente 2010) in permanent movement and change. The border area with Brazil, especially in the north of Uruguay, is a "frontier in movement" (Albuquerque 2008): a territory in which people, ideas and cultural elements flow from one place to another and amalgamate within each other. Thus, frontier zones, such as the Brazilian–Uruguayan one, consist of "social spaces of tensions, contradictions, and intersections. Frontier zones are fields of force and of political and symbolic confrontations, but also of varied cultural mixtures and forms of integration" (Albuquerque 2008: 56).

The following sections explain how the transnationalization of Umbanda developed as a "frontier in movement"; its expansion into Uruguay from Brazil; the changes that have occurred in the last thirty years with respect to the presence of Umbanda in the public space; and the search for legitimacy by its leaders. Finally, this chapter will discuss how religious transnationalization has moved new frontiers that shape the current dispute between the religious leaders and its other members as well as the presence of Umbanda in the public sphere.

Cultural identity of the region bordering Brazil

The hypothesis is based on the existence of a space with its own cultural characteristics, which allowed the earliest arrival of Umbanda in Uruguay, and then its diffusion from there to the rest of the country. Being called "La Frontera" (the border) in Uruguay, this transnational space[4] has some characteristics that provide the region with its own cultural identity that clearly differentiates it from the rest of Uruguayan and Brazilian territories. The area with the greatest cultural hybridization[5] and integration is within the cities of Rivera and Santana do Livramento. Similar effects can also occur in other "twin cities"[6] in the Uruguayan-Brazilian border.

The cities of Rivera (northern Uruguay) and Santana do Livramento (southern Brazil) are part of a conurbation,[7] whose political boundaries tend to fade away in the daily tasks and cultural practices of the residents of the area. As Adriana Persia (2010: 4) says, in the border region, "continuous flows of people and things, visible or hidden, pass through the real border without any problem. Those who live on the border can decide in which state to work, study, shop, open a business, go for a walk."

In this case, analyzing the phenomenon from a Uruguayan perspective, it can be noted that not only Rivera or other cities bordering Brazil are identified as part of a distinguished space from the rest of the countries. As expressed by Arocena and Gamboa (2011: 403), the entire northern region of Uruguay is characterized by "the distance from Montevideo," and that "a feeling of cultural isolation and the intense cross-border impact with Brazil mark a strong identity of this region, which clearly differentiates it from other regions of the country."

Examples of cultural hybridization can be seen in the celebration of joint festivities, which has become traditional, such as the International Carnival. The festival is characterized by the presence of elements from both countries, integrated into a unique culture – specific to that territory: the border culture. The contributions of both cities are integrated as part of a unique whole and are perceived as natural to that region and its local tradition, in which the division between the cities operates almost solely for administrative and political purposes.

The influence of Portuguese language and creation of its own linguistic codes

The widespread use of the Portuguese language across the Uruguayan border seems to have been a factor that facilitated the spread of Umbandism in Uruguay, as well as the presence of that language was an element that fostered the expansion of Afro-Brazilian religions in the case of Portugal, as argue Carlos Silva and María Vasconcellos (2012). One of the main elements of cultural hybridization on Uruguay's border with Brazil has been the language. This factor has reached such a magnitude that it has led to the creation of its own form of communication: the Portuñol Riverense dialect, one of the variations of Portuñol spoken in the border area between Uruguay and Brazil.[8]

This language code, typical of the border region between Uruguay and Brazil and derived from the interaction of people who speak Portuguese and Spanish, shows the degree of influence that the Portuguese language has on Uruguayan border culture. The inhabitants of the Uruguayan border do not perceive Portuguese as a foreign language, but rather a language which is part of their daily cultural universe. In general, the use of Portuguese as a sacred language in Umbandist rituals does not impede access to the religion for those who are native to the border or have lived there for a long time. Therefore, an opposite process occurs in other countries where Umbandist transnationalization has recently occurred, such as France and Germany, in which the use of a foreign language as a ritual element may constitute a difficulty in accessing positions of hierarchy within the temple (Bahia 2015). The understanding of the ritual and the meaning of the chants can be deciphered without great inconvenience by the border population.

In this sense, as Pi Hugarte (1998) points out, the original Portuguese terms, although widely used at the border, have been "adapted" to reach a pronunciation closer to Spanish or Portuñol – the local languages spoken at the border. In fact, it is possible to find places of worship in which terms can be applied in both ways (Portuguese or one of the languages of the border). As examples, we can cite the case of Mãe (mother), that becomes mai, and terreiro, that becomes terrera.[9]

On the other hand, Umbanda, as a minority religion that for a long time lacked public legitimacy (especially during its first decades in Uruguay), had a propitious space on the border for its diffusion, in which language was also a vehicle for the expansion of minority cultural options. As Jorge Locane (2015) points out, this dialect, due to its constitution, by the absence of regulation and norms, is a space for the emergence of dissident projects, where the dominant order is absorbed and put into question.

Being a member of Umbanda was one of the cultural expressions of strong local roots on the border which, during its first decades of expansion in Uruguay and Argentina, as Segato (1996) maintains, was associated with people of low acquisitive power, and with a certain degree of social marginalization. Umbanda was settled almost exclusively on the border, where the use of Portuñol creates a Uruguay that is different from its official or dominant national image, with very little expansion into the rest of the Uruguayan territory for two decades (the 1940s and 1950s). In this sense, according to Antje Hübel (2011: 5), language plays an important role in cross-border relations between Uruguay and Brazil, and contributes to maintain "an exceptional transnational culture."

It is a "dynamic frontier"

The border between Uruguay and Brazil has been called a dynamic frontier. This type of boundary between these countries has been characterized as:

> Large areas, with intense economic and social interdependence, multiple cross-border interactions between populations established along the border, migratory movements of a labour nature and asymmetries of diverse weight. In these regions, the movement of people is constant in both directions. Trade relations, joint ventures, communication channels, a shared culture, are all factors of interaction between border communities with great potential for the development of integration. (Clemente 2010: 169)

Rivera and Santana do Livramento have been geographically categorized as "the city with two sovereignties" (Copstein 1989), to convey the existing degree of complementation and union between the societies that inhabit this area.

The ethnic composition of the northern region of Uruguay

The northern Uruguay, which includes part of the border area with Brazil, is the region with the highest proportion of population that recognizes themselves as indigenous (5.1 percent) and Afro-descendants (16.5 percent), according to data from 2006 (Cristiano 2011).

This would seem to ratify the discourse of the current Umbandist leaders who see themselves as defenders of the African and Uruguayan indigenous heritage. However, as Daniel Vidart (2012) points out, "there are no Indians in Uruguay," that is, they do not exist as indigenous communities that preserve the cultural legacy of their ancestors or live in the traditional way. Though there are those who practice what Pi Hugarte (2003) called *Charruism* – to characterize those groups or individuals who, for various reasons, exalt the Charrúa[10] culture and legacy in an uncritical and unscientific way –, there is very little evidence to show the survival of Afro-Uruguayan religious practices in Uruguayan territory. The survival of Afro-religious practices by generational transmission to their descendants in Uruguay is unlikely and there is no scientific evidence to support it

Uruguayan authors dedicated to the study and preservation of the legacy of the Afro-Uruguayan ethnic group, such as Ildefonso Pereda Valdés (1965), stated that the Africans established in the territory of the Banda Oriental[11] did not possess a legacy rich in myths and legends, and even if they had, this collection of legends and myths did not survive them but died with them, since they did not pass it on to their descendants.

> They did not create religious cults independent of Christian practices, nor did they pretend to impose the cult of their native gods, and if this existed it was for a short time, because their cults, if they existed, were evicted by devotion to Christian saints. (Pereda Valdés 1965: 97)

This is consistent with Ari Oro's (2002: 363) claim that there has been no historical African religious practice in Uruguay. Based on Vidart (2012), Pera Valdés (1965), and Pi Hugarte (2003), it would be a mistake to consider that there was a transmission of the indigenous or Afro religious phenomenon in Uruguay through historically settled populations in Uruguay. The original religious culture from indigenous people and Afro-descendants did not survive until the 20th century in Uruguay.[12] However, in recent decades, there has been a boom in *Charruísmo*.[13] This implies that some social organizations integrated by individuals who consider themselves as heirs of the Charrúa culture are linked to religious phenomena that claim to have indigenous influences.

The revaluation of the concept of African-descendance in Uruguay is associated with a vindictive discourse of the national minority with ancestry of that origin, which defends its legitimate right to nondiscrimination and to the defense of its cultural contribution to Uruguayan culture. In this sense, Umbanda is related to African descendants resistance against the dominant culture imposed on them during colonization and conquest of the territory which is now Uruguay by the Europeans and their descendants. This intended association, for the Uruguayan case, is not historically verifiable.

Umbanda is a twentieth century phenomenon that has been present in Uruguay since the 1940s. Therefore, there is no historical basis to affirm that the Afro-Uruguayan population preserved a religious system with African or indigenous roots until the twentieth century, which would have resurfaced with the arrival of Afro-Brazilian religions. What seems to have happened is a cultural phenomenon, similar to that described by Beatriz Dantas (1982) in Brazil, in which certain groups reproduce a discourse linked to religion and their identification in order to defend their own individual or group interests. This is a relevant transnational element in which strategies for the defense of rights and political activism that are developed in other countries, such as in the Brazilian case cited, were transferred to the local sphere.

The Secular State in Uruguay

The Uruguayan secular state was established by the definitive separation of the Catholic Church in 1919, and was reinforced while religion was confined to the private sphere through the decades, especially from the 1920s until 1985 (Caetano and Geymonat 1997). Secularization created the necessary conditions for Umbanda to reach the border territory without being persecuted by the authorities Uruguayan authorities.

In fact, the settlement of Umbanda in Uruguay, as Pi Hugarte (1998) points out, had already occurred during the 1950s, then began to expand to outside the border area in the following decade, especially to Montevideo. Even the harassment suffered during the military dictatorship (1973-85) did not prevent Umbanda to constensouly expand through the country. In opposite to what happened in other South American countries, there were no religious campaigns against Umbanda during its arrival and consolidation in the country. Waves of attacks on Umbanda, although on a small scale, occurred after the establishment of the religion in the country.

It appears that a set of elements, such as a common identity of the Uruguayan–Brazilian border, its own linguistic code, distinctive ethnic characteristics, the existence of a dynamic border, and the existence of a secular state in Uruguay, give specificity to the transnationalization process. The arrival of Umbanda in Uruguay took place in a space that was already transnational, occurring almost simultaneously at the points of greater integration of the border with Brazil. This explains the earlier emergence of Umbanda in Uruguay compared to other Spanish-speaking countries bordering Brazil. Therefore, the advent of this religion in other parts of Uruguay was a consequence of an internal transfer within the country, from the border region with Brazil to the rest of the territory, as part of a "frontier in movement" (Albuquerque 2008).[14]

The transnationalization of Umbanda in Uruguay in comparative perspective

The fact that a country borders Brazil, per se, is not a guarantee of the transfer of the Umbanda culture through Brazilian migrants. A case in point is the transnationalization toward Venezuela. According to Elizabeth Pollak-Eltz (1993), Umbanda arrived in that country through the Uruguayan citizen Heber Ureta, who had practiced Umbandist rituals since 1976 in Maracaibo while working in other activities. In 1985, he established a terreiro in Caracas, and in the 1990s he founded the Temple of Oxalá in the same city.

In other cases, such as the transnationalization of Umbanda in Argentina, bonds with neighboring countries have been decisive for the introduction and development of religion in that country, with the first temples opened by Brazilians and Uruguayans, while the members were iniciated and trained in the Umbandist traditions developed in those countries, even if they have another nationality (Frigerio 1998). In any case, the arrival and establishment of Umbanda in Argentina are subsequent to its consolidation in Uruguay, as Frigerio (2002: 131) points out in this respect:

In contrast to the temporary trips made by the Brazilian countries, there are several of Uruguayan origin who are based in Buenos Aires and who will play an important role in the development of religion in the city—the Umbanda and the Batuque arrived in Uruguay in the late 1950s, and their expansion took place in that country before Argentina.

Alejandro Frigerio (2013) places the arrival of Afro-Brazilian religions in Argentina in the 1960s. He also points out that the expansion of religion in that country was due to the short-term visits of Brazilian *pais* and *mais,* male and female Umbandist leaders, to Argentina and vice versa,[15] as well as the establishment of Umbanda pratictioners from Uruguay, specifically *pais* and *mais.* This emphasizes that it was a process that was not primarily due to migration.

In this sense, I build on what Oro (2013) points out the existence of a transnationalization without migration from Umbanda to Uruguay.[16] The configuration of the transnational space as described above and the cultural hybridization in the border region were factors that allowed Uruguay to be the first country reached by the transnationalization of Umbanda and also the country in which Umbanda was first consolidated among other South American countries. In any case, it is important to emphasize the fact that the existence of a cultural hybridization does not, per se, guarantee the diffusion of this religious phenomenon. On the Bolivian–Brazilian border, despite a certain degree of cultural hybridization, there were no land settlements on the Bolivian area border with Corumbá (Brazil) and the cities of Puerto Quijarro and Puerto Suárez (Bolivia). In this border area, Bolivian clients,[17] faithful, and even those who could be in a position to open their own terreiro in Bolivia, continue to attend Brazilian temples (Viegas and Martins 2015).

Other cases of transnationalization that have taken place as a result of a significant Brazilian migration, such as the migration from Brazilian citizens to Portugal studied by Ferreira (2011), show clear differences with respect to the Uruguayan case, once Uruguay is a clear example of transnationalization without having a massive Brazilian migration to promote the process.

Although the Uruguayan case has relevant differences compared to the process of transnationalization occurred in Argentina, some of which were pointed out above, both processes share some characteristics, such as the lack of institutional planning for transnationalization and the fact that the first members of Umbanda in both countries belonged to the lower classes. For this reason, both cases are, as Frigerio (2013) maintains, transnationalizations carried out "from below."

The adaptation of Umbanda to the local context: Change and permanence

As Renzo Pi Hugarte (1998) points out, African–Brazilian religions have ceased to be an exogenous phenomenon and are now part of Uruguay's endogenous reality: "Uruguay's Umbanda, Quimbanda[18] and Batuque[19] are a phenomenon [...], which has become part of the national popular culture considered as a whole" (Pi Hugarte 1998: 26). Pi Hugarte (1992) affirmed that in the areas of "religion," that is to say, among those who attend Afro-Brazilian cults, receiving the religious teachings in Brazil is considered a factor of prestige, something that confers better religious foundations, and greater magical -religious capacities. While this is still true, the importance of having training at that origin has diminished.[20]

This has become notorious among the Umbandist leadership figures as well as perceived by the rest of society. For the religious leaders, being trained as Umbandists in Brazil is still a matter of legitimacy. Since the death of Armando Ayala (2004) and under the new leadership of Susana Andrade, the importance of this factor has declined.

Since 2005, the most notorious figure of Umbanda in Uruguay has been Mai Susana Andrade. Her religious trajectory shows a change in the forms of access to hierarchical positions within the community. She did not join the Umbandist practice through contact with border regions, nor did she come from them, but after meeting her husband, Julio Kronberg, who is also Uruguayan, she was initiated into Umbanda by him.[21]

This new religious leadership corresponds to a new lineage of Uruguayans initiated into Umbanda by other Uruguayans. Although the reference to initiation in Brazil or by prestigious Brazilians in the Umbandist sphere countinues to be a source of legitimacy and prestige, it has now been challenged with other local references.

In turn, as the transnationalization expanded, networks have turned Afro-Brazilian religions into international religions (Frigerio 1998). In this sense, the existence of links between the temples in Argentina, Brazil, and Uruguay, have tightened. However, the influence of religious practices carried out in other countries not only generates networks for cooperation and communication, but also creates conflict. The latter has embroiled Pai Donatto, a new figure with media presence who uses to preach on the street with posters with his name. He claims to have received training in Argentina and declares that his own religious practices are a way of making money. Donatto aparently considers his behavior and speech as legitimate. he openly accepts and reinforces a kind of "religious capitalization". As a result, there has been a confrontation and public debate between Pai Donatto's way of understanding religion and the understanding of the most visible Uruguayan Umbandist leaders consider as acceptable. While the struggles with and among leaders are endemic to Afro-Brazilian religions and also the mutual disqualification of those "competitors" (Pi Hugarte 1998), it is novel for Uruguay that these disputes are beyond the reach of the religious community and, moreover, that they are transferred to the mass media.

A case of resistance and dissent: Pai Donatto of Oxúm

Twenty years ago, Renzo Pi Hugarte (1998) stated that conflict between religious leaders is endemic in Afro-Brazilian religions. At the same time, factors such as the acquisition of religious knowledge in Brazil, and dedication to worship as a "vocation" or "call" – not only as a way of earning money exclusively –, were factors of prestige and merit.

While this has not completely changed, it is clear that there have been changes over the last two decades. The accusation of religious commodification as a way of discrediting another *pai* or *mai*, which Pi Hugarte (1998) describes as a frequent practice, seems to have lost some effectiveness. This is demonstrated through the construction of a public image in open contradiction with these values, such as that of Pai Donatto of Oxúm, which summons without hiding it, to those who are willing to attend Afro-Brazilian cults to achieve ethically or morally questionable ends.

Pai Donatto of Oxúm presents himself publicly as an Umbandist, says that he acquired his religious knowledge in Argentina, and advertises in posters in the city of Montevideo that he makes "Black Magic."[22] In some of the interviews carried out with him, he does not hesitate to affirm that his religious activity is destined to provide him with economic benefits, even if this means complying with actions that can be seen as negative from an ethical or moral point of view. Likewise, he is manifestly resistant to disassociating himself from negative practices or concepts toward Afro-Brazilian religions in general, contradicting the discourse of the most visible Umbanadist leaders in Uruguay in the last thirty years, Armando Ayala and Susana Andrade.

The disputes that have been transferred to the public sphere and are now between neo-Pentecostals and representatives of Afro-Brazilian religions. These disputes mostly concern issues on evil forces, a phenomenon that has been transnationalized from Brazil to Argentina and Uruguay (Frigerio 2007), and are not only being prosecuted among these actors through the media and the Judiciary courts, but this logic has also been reproduced in the conflict between the main leader of Umbanda in Uruguay and her husband, Susana Andrade, and Julio Kronberg against the Pai Donatto of Oxúm. The newspaper La República (see below), in which Susana Andrade frequently participates as a columnist referred to the Pai Donatto as a "false pai", while the Umbandist newspaper ATABAQUE (2005–6), directed by Julio Kronberg, expressed that Donatto lies about Umband and its doctrine.

On the other hand, the notoriety and media exposure of Pai Donatto did not decline, but, on the contrary, increased. Pai Donatto continues to be interviewed by other media outlets, including FM del Sol de Montevideo, a radio station in which Susana Andrade was also interviewed. Andrade, through an article of her own in the newspaper La República, publicly criticized Donatto for being interviewed in a program in which he participated without her knowledge. She referred to the practices of the Pai Donatto in the following terms:

> Those who offer black magic are not *pais*, they are criminals. And those who advertise them in the media are inevitably complicit. Tired of explaining it, I repeat: black magic does not belong to the ambit of the Umbanda religion or to any of the Afro cults such as Batuque, Kimbanda or Candomblé.[23]

The public stance taken by Mai Susana contains several relevant aspects to analyze when involving a vision that attempts, from a position of religious leadership, to establish or set limits to what constitutes a crime in relation to religious practices. For Andrade (2006), black magic would not be part of the cults of African–American cults, nor therefore of Umbanda. She maintains that "it is a celebrated ignorance to associate the *Pais* and *Mães* with that."

In the following paragraphs her intention was even more explicit:

> A (The) Ialorixá,[24] a (the) babalorixá[25] doing "black magic"? What's that? Why sell the rich heritage of our sacred spiritual heritage, at the very low price of necessity? Titles on the one hand and on the other, it doesn't matter if you dirty the name of a religion, besides playing with people's weaknesses? Then we don't want to be discriminated against, while we ourselves take care of denigrating and distorting the foundations, along with the sublime ritual essence.[26]

Andrade tries to establish a dichotomy between a group represented as "the others" and a group represented as "us." Using the dichotomous logic of Teun Van Dijk (1998), based on emphasizing that "the others" violate norms and values that are precious to us, is a way to make a distinction between groups. According to this, it id needed to assign positive terms to the group that includes the author of the speech and assign negative terms to the group that does not integrate the Umbandist community. At the same time, respecting and/or obeying certain religious practices that are accepted by leaders and community members allows one to belong to it. Disobeying rules that are unwritten but known by the practitioners implies to be rejected and deligitimized by the leaders.

Armando Ayala and Sausana Andrade have then been religious leaders who have struggled, trying to avoid the association of Afro-Brazilian religious with ethically reprehensible practices and even with rituals that aim to harm other people physically or spiritually. For this reason, Andrade tries to show that Pai Donatto and his practices are unrelated to the Umbandist community or to what is "authentically" religious. However, the very characteristics of this religious phenomenon make it extremely difficult for those who identify themselves as *pais* or *mães* to be forced to follow preestablished canons because there is no central and unified hierarchy that encompasses the Umbandist temples (Giobellina and González 1984, 2000).

Pai Donatto and his vision of the Umbanda community

Pai Donatto, according to his own statements, does not have a good relationship with the rest of the local Umbandist community and has a critical position toward it. Regarding the religious community, he considers that they "are managed as sects."[27] Donatto de Oxúm's words reveal that he is not accepted by most of his peers, because his public speech [what he says] and his practices [what he does] are not well received by the community leaders. Although he allows the media to present him as a *pae umbandista*, Donatto also expresses himself in third person when referring to other umbandists.[28] According to him, concerning his own life, he lived part of his life in Argentina, starting in the type of religious practices that he carries out during his stay in that country. He also makes it clear that religion, in his opinion, is a way to earn money and that his religious practices intend to cause harm to others.

In spite of his speech, there seems to be some interest in following the guidelines he proposes, since he claims to have sons of religion.[29] In any case, although this could be confirmed, it contradicts the logic with which he intends to link up with those who attend his temple. He does not intended to build a religious community once the relationship with those who use his religious services is a provider–customer type.

The trajectory of Pai Donatto, with high public exposure in the last decade defining itself as "mediatic,"[30] shows a new way of public speech by people who identify themselves with Afro-Brazilian religions in Uruguay. Donatto's case shows some particular characteristics such as the open challenge to the existing leaderships, the rejection of the traditional legitimacy guidelines, and the resistance to the integration of the organized community of Umbanda. In addition, the fact that disputes regarding Donatto's figure have a place in the media and, above all, that the religious practices of Pai Donatto have been accused to be criminal could indicate an incipient process of linking the "Black Magic" to criminal acts – similar issues happened in Argentina and Brazil in recent decades – to solve religious conflicts.

Conclusions

According to the current state of knowledge on the transnationalization of Umbanda to Uruguay, I consider that it constitutes a specific variation of the phenomenon of religious transnationalization due to the cultural characteristics of the border region between Uruguay and Brazil. This can be observed especially in those urban centers, close to both sides of the border and even more in areas of binational conurbation such as Santana do Livramento and Rivera. The border between Uruguay and Brazil has characteristics that make it dynamic and in movement, a zone in which cultural expressions are in constant contact and merging, and from which a cultural conjunction originated that is heir to both Uruguayan and Brazilian culture, but at the same time, it constitutes a different cultural space: the border culture.

The border area between the two countries has a high degree of cultural hybridization with its own dialects, common cultural expressions, and an indistinct movement of goods, ideas, and people to either side of the border, which distinguishes this area of Uruguayan territory from the rest of the country. Therefore, the Umbanda religion remained almost exclusively located in the border area of Uruguay during its first two decades of settlement in the country, before expanding to other regions of the country as explained above.

The characteristics of this region allowed a "transnationalization from below" of the religious phenomenon, in the border area from which both Brazilian and Uruguayan border dwellers expanded their worship to other parts of the country. It is also a case of transnationalization that took place without a diaspora, nor the establishment foreigners to promote this process. The border region was the center of Umbanda diffusion toward the rest of the country, so there was a regional transference from the border area between Uruguay and Brazil to the rest of Uruguay.

With regard to the African matrix of these religions, previous studies have shown that the Afro-Uruguayan population did not preserve the religious practices of their African ancestors. Rather, it retained other cultural patterns without religious content. Therefore, the discourse of identification with Umbanda and the claim that this religion is as a form of cultural resistance on the part of Afro-descendants, promoted by some community leaders, reproduces or emulates discourses of Afro groups in Brazil, for the collective interests and claims of these groups today.

In regard to the legitimacy of the ritual initiation in Brazil conferred to the practitioners of religion, although this continues to be important, it has gradually lost relevance, giving way to new leaderships that give little relevance or ignore this reference of prestige. The initiation by other Uruguayans is now prestigious enough, as long as the individuals can afford it.

At the same time, the case of Pai Donatto demonstrates how new forms of transnational Umbanda—including religious competition, mediatization, and commercialization—have traveled throughout the continent, especially between Brazil, Argentina, and Uruguay, showing competing "frontiers in movement" and shaping discussions about Umbanda's origins and authenticity. Pai Donatto calls himself an Umbandist leader, fostering religious competition and even confrontation with community leaders at a level of public exposure that is unprecedented in Uruguay.

From a historical perspective, the case of Uruguay exposes the connections, continuities, and ruptures in the circulation of Umbanda in Latin America, and how, through media and travels, Umbandist leaders move frontiers and adopt alternative spiritualities from Argentina and Brazil. This specific history of circulation between particular borders represents how the movement of people, things, and ideas is not only about hybridity, but also accounts for the obstacles and boundaries that emerge with regard to authority and origins; what does it make something or someone religious or spiritual in specific transnational circuits? In particular, religious mediating practices invoke discussions about how a relationship with spiritual powers is shaped through the investment of authority and meaning in certain words, actions, and transnational linkages.[31] For the time being, the discussions and contestations around Umbanda in Uruguay uncover how different transnational connections and histories can strengthen religious and cultural conflicts.

Sources

El Observador TV (2015), Montevideo

FM Del Sol (2006), Montevideo.

La República (2005–15), Montevideo.

Mil Voces (2015), Salto.

Montevideo Portal (2014), Montevideo.

Océano FM (2012), Montevideo.

Atabaque (2005–6), Montevideo.

Nuestra Umbanda (1994–2002), Montevideo.

The Constitution of a Transnational Sphere of Transcendence

The Relationship between the Irmãos Guerreiros Capoeira Angola Group and Ilê Obá Silekê in Europe

Celso de Brito

Introduction

Both Candomblé and Capoeira are cultural manifestations that are practiced in Brazil. Originating from different regions of Africa, they are the result of the transatlantic movement promoted by the Portuguese slave trade. In addition to both practices having a similar genealogy, they share some "fundamentals" such as the value of their ancestry, the circular formation of their rituals, as well as singing and dancing. From a sociopolitical point of view, both were criminalized in the Brazil and severely policed until the 1930s. Using historical documents, Soares (1994) analyzes the strategic union between practitioners of Capoeira and Candomblé during the nineteenth century and is able to perceive the strategic aim of this union, of them joining forces against a common enemy, being the elite whites who saw the practices of the black population as a threat (Azevedo 1987).

However, during much of the twentieth century (from 1930 to 1980), this practice underwent transformations that distanced it from a supposed Afro-religious organicity. During this period, Capoeira became nationalized according to a process of social and geographical expansion, to correspond with the values of the Brazilian white middle class (Frigerio 1989). It was reclassified as "national gymnastics" (Marinho 1982), much to the detriment of the complexity of Afro-Brazilian cultural practices, which could hardly be reduced to a sport/gymnastic. Thus, the Afro-religious aspects of Capoeira became folklore fables and Capoeira became immersed in a process of transformation" from a black art to a white sport" (Frigerio 1989).

The hegemonic model of Capoeira that emerged became one of the Brazilian symbols of national identity, marked by mixed races. However, in the end of 1980s, beginning of 1990s, when the practice of Capoeira expanded to the USA, it was transformed into a pan-African ethnic symbol, just as *feijoada*[1] would become "soul food" as Peter Fry's (1982) insightful description has shown.

The pan-Africanization of Capoeira (more specifically Capoeira Angola)[2] was a consequence of the alliances of the African–American intellectuals, who traveled to Bahia/Brazil in search of African practices in Brazil, and the Brazilian Black Movement that in turn built militant strategies with cultural groups (see Agier 1992).[3] These African–American intellectuals took some Capoeira *Mestres*[4] to workshops at African–American culture congresses in the United States and inserted them into an incipient transnational Capoeira market (Granada 2004, 2015). During this ethnicization and transnationalization of Capoeira Angola, there was an embrace of "mystery" and "sacredness," associating a kind of "traditional power" as "*Mandinga*" to Capoeira. Afro-Brazilian religiosity has become a source of diacritical signs of this "sacredness" in order to build an ethnic purity which meant a politicization of the ethnic identity of Capoeira Angola (Vassalo 2009).

Since then, the contemporary form of this practice is marked both by a transnational and transcendental configuration. The confluence between these two configurations (transnational and transcendental) needs to be better understood and this is what is proposed in this chapter, through the idea called the "transnational sphere of transcendence." The inspiration for this description lies in Peter Sloterdijk's notion of "spheres" (2016) and Thomas Csordas's idea of "transnational transcendence" (2009).

Using the image of the bubble, Sloterdijk presents spheres as shared spaces of experience that provide possibilities for self-realization and immunizations that are both recognizable as "religions" and as other "things" such as sports or artistic practices. What matters to us here is that the constitution of spheres such as Capoeira relies on performative practices with which practitioners create and experience the life-worlds in which they dwell. In line with Csordas (2009), these performative practices are constituted by an embodied phenomenology that takes otherness as a characteristic immanent to human existence. The same logic of otherness that constitutes subjectivity also constitutes collective subjectivities through elaborations of differences. In a transnational context, in which the breaching of the frontiers of collective (local/national) subjectivities is prevailing in the search for a certain universality, there seems to be, at the same time, the constitution of other frontiers in the field of transcendence. Csordas expands the possibilities of the establishment of otherness in transcendence beyond the field of classical religions, demonstrating the possibility, for example, of the capitalist economy itself and science to generate modes of transcendence. Therefore, for both Csordas and Sloterdijk, the transcendental experience and the construction of self-immunizing spheres can be achieved by practices recognized as nonreligious, such as dancing and music in the case of Capoeira, which then can become new resources that enable the reformation of religiocultural forms in Europe.

In this chapter, I will focus on the practices of the Irmãos Guerreiros Capoeira Angola Group[5] as a sphere, orbited by the Babalorixá[6] Muralemsibe, located in the surrounding areas of Kreuzberg in Berlin. I will argue that in this transnational Capoeira Angola Group, Afro-Brazilian religiosity is strategically institutionalized as a producer of particular transcendental experiences which in turn helps to expand the group to other European countries, creating a larger sphere of interrelated Capoeira bubbles.

Transnational configuration: The installation of an "exotic" religious culture in Germany

This research is based on a multisituated ethnography (Marcus 1995) done in different European capitals (Berlin, Lisbon, Warsaw, Vienna, and Paris) during the years of 2013 and 2014.[7] At the time I was researching the different ways in which Capoeira Angola expanded in Europe and the relationships that local groups established between themselves and the Brazilian *mestres* or masters (Brito 2017).

In trying to understand the transcendental strategies and senses produced by the members of the Grupo Irmãos Guerreiros group (based in Bremen, Germany) that have been able to install themselves in and expand to other European countries, the main focus of the analysis will be the strategic union of two people: Master Perna (Márcio Araújo), responsible for the Grupo Irmãos Guerreiros Group in Europe and Babalorixá Muralemsibe (Murah Soares), who was responsible for creating the first temple in Berlin (Ilê Obá Silekê, which means House of King Xangô Aganju), in 2003 and for founding the Forum Brazil *Interkulturelle Zentrum* (Forum Brazil Intercultural Center)[8] in 2005. In what follows, I will present, first, a brief analysis of the context in which both, Mestre

Perna and Babalorixá Muralemnsibe, came to Europe and, second, a synthesis of the strategy used by Babalorixá Murelemsibe to install *Candomblé* in Berlin and the overlapping of its trajectory with that of Mestre Perna.

Still in the 1990s, Babalorixá Muralemsibe worked with Mestre Rosalvo at the Jangada Academy[9] and both of them left Brazil motivated by the condition in which the country was. The national market for popular artists was not very promising, due mainly to the government's lack of support for popular ethnic culture, which leads us to the unfavorable political environment. Brazil had just come out of a dictatorship, which curtailed all social movements, including the Black Movement. During the 1980s, a change in the country's cultural policies began, but it only came to be consolidated after 2003 with the rise of the government of the President Luis Inácio Lula da Silva. Thus, between 1970 and the mid-2000s, many European countries presented better economic and political conditions for Brazilian Afro-descendent artists.

As Fernandes (2014) shows, Germany, especially Berlin, represented a welcoming ethnic market for Afro-Brazilian groups since the late 1960s, when Miécio Ascanasy inaugurated his show with the Brasiliana Group at the *Frederichstadt-Palast* theater, followed by Emilia Biancardi and her Parafolclórico Group, both made up of Brazilian capoeiristas and candomblecistas. In ethnic political terms, Germany was concerned with reversing the stigma attached to social nationalism, which made the country a safe and welcoming place for Afro-Brazilian artists (Fernandes 2014).

Both Mestre Rosalvo and Bablorixá Muralemsibe have performed ethnic performances for years in Germany, the first maintaining his academy with diverse ethnic activities that range from samba, hip-hop, and Capoeira, to Zumba, and salsa. Babalorixá Muralemsibe, in turn, established himself as the priest of Candomblé in Berlin thanks to his mastery as choreographer and dancer and to the market being favorable to its spatiality: Afro-Brazilian culture.

To articulate these two activities, Babalorixá Muralemsibe commonly separates his work in Europe into two dimensions: the cultural and the religious. To promote his work in Germany, Babalorixá Muralemsibe took a cultural management course, in which he learned to represent the cultural aspects of Brazil and to transform these into products for his ethnic dance company. At Forum Brazil, he presents workshops called *A força dos Orixás*[10] (the power of the Orixás—the African gods), for example. In addition to the characteristic dance steps of the Orixás, he teaches the meanings of the movements, the myths of the sacred pantheon, and the ways of *Candomblé*. About his work, Babalorixá Muralemsibe says:

I separate religion from culture in order to teach the Germans to feel what we, *Candomblé* Brazilians feel. They are very rational, you know? They need information before they can feel, and I realized that dance performances and workshops help to make them understand the Ilê religious festivals. They come here to watch, and only after that some become very slowly interested in the religion ... that is how I attract my *filhos de santo* [sons of the saint or Candomblé followers] here.

If we follow the division established by Babalorixá Muralemsibe, we see that there was in fact a double entry of Candomblé into Germany, which we can extend to other Afro-Brazilian cultural elements such as Capoeira. On the one hand, there was the formation of an ethnic market, where "the exotic" remains latent and helps disseminate the cultural element throughout Germany; on the other hand, a change took place where the element ceased to be perceived as exotic and began to take on meaning for the participants, as a familiar religious sense.

A similar analogy of this double insertion was described by Domínguez and Frigerio (2002) while studying the insertion of Capoeira in Argentina. The authors defined two categories of analysis: "exotic culture vendors" and "cultural workers." The first category refers to Brazilian immigrants, who make use of culture without worrying it might annul their exoticism, selling "exotic culture" as a more marketable product. The second category refers to Brazilian immigrants who build links between the society of origin and local participants, producing transnational identity connections that necessarily break with exoticization, creating a kind of "ethnopolitical" identity.

The significant difference between Buenos Aires and Berlin is that in Berlin, Babalorixá Muralemsibe represents both "exotic culture vendors" and "cultural workers." His performances can be understood as a *continuum* between Dominguez and Frigerio's (2002) two analytical categories. Orixá dance workshops appeal to the experience created by the exotic performances, in order to specifically seduce their participants and make them understand and feel Afro-Brazilian religiosity, thus breaking exoticization and establishing links with the Ilê Obá Silekê.

As mentioned previously, Babalorixá Muralemsibe worked with Master Rosalvo at Academia Jangada in the 1980s, the first Capoeira Angola academy in Europe, based in Berlin. Since then, he has maintained many connections with different groups and he is often invited to present workshops at Capoeira events.[11] The relationship between Master Perna from Irmãos Guerreiros Group and Babalorixá Muralemsibe was different. It began in 2006, when Master Perna participated in the Berlin Culture Carnival, where Babalorixá Muralemsibe held his annual presentation of *Afoxé Loni*.[12] The Irmãos Guerreiros Group in Europe was three years old at the time and only had one center, in Bremen.[13]

Master Perna and Babalorixá Muralemsibe quickly became friends. In the years that followed, Master Perna become an *Ogã*[14] through a process called *Suspensão de Ogã*,[15] and then given the task of playing the *atabaque*[16] in rituals at Ilê Obá Silekê. While Master Perna carried out his responsibilities as Ogã in Ilê Obá Silekê, Babalorixá Muralemsibe became to be considered as one of the Masters of the Irmãos Guerreiros Group, even though he does not practice Capoeira Angola. He is present at all the events organized by the Group in the different countries where their centers are located.[17] According to Master Perna, his role is to explain Afro-Brazilian religiosity to European *capoeiristas* (Capoeira practitioners), but more than that, to making them aware of the spiritual dimensions of Capoeira Angola. Babalorixá Muralemsibe teaches more about the movements, the myths, and the function of Candomblé, gradually introducing the European *capoeiristas* into the world of Afro-Brazilian religion.

The Mandinga in the transnational events of Capoeira Angola: The preparation of the European bodies for transcendental experiences

The aim of this section is to suggest, through the ethnographic description of an event of Capoeira Angola, that the Mandinga, a particular "magic" or seductive power (see further below), is an element strategically mobilized by Master Perna and Babalorixá Muralemsibe "to loosen up the bodies" of the Europeans and to add an Afro-religious sense to the practice of Capoeira Angola in Europe. As we shall see, I think that the notion of Mandinga assumes a central position in the discourse of both Masters during the Capoeira events in Europe, contributing to a phenomenological opening for re-elaborations between "sensations" (body) and "meanings" (spirit), sensitizing Europeans to transcendental experiences coming from the Afro-Brazilian tradition, thus consolidating what I call the "transnational sphere of transcendence."

The events of the Irmãos Guerreiros Group follow the same general format wherever they take place. Orixá dance lessons take place in the morning; in the afternoon, there is training in Capoeira Angola. At night, there is the ritual of the *Roda*[18] de Capoeira Angola. The annual calendar of the Irmãos Guerreiros Group includes at least seven events, one for each country in which the group has centers. Once a year, each center organizes an event that will host the Masters, including Babalorixá Muralemsibe, and *capoeiristas* from other centers. The Masters are thus moving around the transnational Capoeira circuit all year round.

The registration fee for the events is around 50 Euros per day, with most events occurring over weekends. A collection is taken to pay for the air fares, for the cultural work of the workshop speakers, their meals, and occasionally for the rental of the venue. If the amount collected is greater than the amount spent, it is saved in a fund to be spent on future events.

On these occasions, between 50 and 60 participants (on average) gather out of the 200 *capoeiristas* affiliated with the Group throughout Europe. The members of the Group are young men and women (mostly between twenty and thirty-five years of age), university students, artists, and independent professionals from different Europeans countries.[19] Most of them see Capoeira as a political position that is contrary to the "Occidental life-world," "Eurocentrism," and "Colonization"—it means the institutions and ideas connected with colonization in politics, economics, and religious terms. One of the main criticisms of the European *capoeiristas* on the Western way of life is the excessive individualism and suffering that it causes, which is healed by the social life of the Capoeira groups that, more than festivals, provide them with "religious experiences" within a religious picture that is far from that which exists in Europe. In the case of young German *capoeiristas*, this criticism is directed to the followers of social nationalism, above all the previous generations linked to social nationalism and Christianity.[20]

At least one of these events occurs at Ilê Obá Silekê in Berlin during a religious festival, generally on December 4th, during the feast of *Iansã*.[21] As stated above, the events have a preestablished schedule: Orixá Dance Workshops, Capoeira Angola Workshops, and the Roda de Capoeira Angola ritual.

Workshops are not split into separate theoretical and practical events. Babalorixá Muralemsibe concentrates on body movements and pauses when he believes an explanation is needed for what is being taught. Gradually, he explains the *modus operandi* of *Candomblé*, emphatically establishing the relationship between the filhos de santo and the musical instruments, the *atabaques*, in the religious ritual, and its structural parallels with the relationship between *capoeiristas* and the musical bow *berimbau*.[22]

Babalorixá Muralemsibe places the Masters/Ogãs next to the *atabaque*. He then teaches the first dance step and everyone repeats it, and then teaches the second step and students repeat it, he then moves on to the third step. Finally, he does all three steps in sequence, making sure that everyone has memorized them. He then says:

> Now you shall dance, but you have to listen to the *atabaque*. Even if you cannot perform the movements perfectly, obey the rhythm of the *atabaque*! The instrument is what directs the dance of the Orixás just as the *berimbau* directs the *capoeirista*'s moves. The *atabaque* and the *berimbau* are sacred instruments in Afro-Brazilian culture because they are what connect us to our ancestors. Do not ignore them!

The Masters/Ogãs begin to play the *atabaques* and everyone tries to repeat the entire choreographic sequence, following the movements of Babalorixá Muralemsibe. Gradually, the steps increase until the sequence for that class forms a complete choreography. This is then repeated for a few more hours, to the constant sound of instruments being played and songs being sung.

Babalorixá Muralemsibe's workshops aim at developing Mandinga in the European *capoeiristas*, both physically and spiritually. To "loosen up the body" is the first task for them. As Babalorixá Muralemsibe explains: "European bodies are usually stiff. They do not have the Mandinga that Brazilians learn as children and it is necessary for both Capoeira and Candomblé."

The movements taught by Babalorixá Muralemsibe are extremely articulated, based on spins and swings of the shoulders and hips, which European *capoeiristas* find difficult to learn. Therefore, Babalorixá Muralemsibe, ever since he started to participate in the Group in 2006, works with only one choreography at all of the events, based on the movements of certain Orixás (*Ogum e Oxum*).[23] These movements are repeated for about four hours. The workshop takes place at Ilê Obá Silekê hall, which is filled with African masks, pictures of Orixás, plants, straw, plates of food, candles, and certain characteristic elements of Candomblé—all serving as visual sensory stimuli that make up the Afro-religious atmosphere for the *capoeiristas*. In addition to the pictures of Orixás on the walls, the Ilê Obá Silekê provides other sensory stimuli, next to the hall where the workshop takes place, there is a large kitchen from where the aroma of the food being prepared for the Orixás wafts through the rooms, this mixed with the smoke from herbs in the burners contributes to the formation of an Afro-religious "multisensory image" (Csordas 2008).

In the workshop, Babalorixá Muralemsibe demonstrates some of Ogun's movements, paying particular attention to the force of the blows of his sword, represented by arm movements. He then demonstrates an Oxum movement emphasizing the seduction of a target moving in a mirror, building a bridge between the dance of the Orixás and the movements of Capoeira:

Capoeiristas should be like this, *mandingueiros* [holder/possessor of the Mandinga] [...] they should learn from the Orixás how to move, dancing beautifully and at the same time showing one's power. A *mandingueiro* is like that, isn't it? Power and seduction, Ogun and Oxum.

In Capoeira, *power* and *seduction* are the most common definitions of that which is called Mandinga. The term "Mandinga" is used in Afro-Brazilian religions as a synonym for spiritual work; however, it has a double meaning for *capoeiristas*. First, it is body movements according to a specific aesthetic standard which relates to the aesthetics of the dances of the Orixás. It is a standard of effectiveness in Capoeira; that which makes agile *capoeiristas* able to defend themselves and attack with great precision. Second, it is a spiritual force that protects *capoeiristas* from bad luck and the enchantments from other *capoeiristas*. As we have seen, Babalorixá Muralemsibe adapts this double meaning in his workshops, establishing a direct relationship between the dance movements and the divine characteristics of the Orixás: connecting, on the one hand, the "body" with the "spirit" and, on the other, Candomblé with Capoeira.

The workshop ends and the *capoeiristas* have an hour to eat a light lunch before they return to the Capoeira workshop taught by Master Perna. The *atabaques* are replaced by *berimbaus* and the workshop starts with some Orixá dance steps to warm up the *capoeiristas*. Gradually, everyone begins the *ginga* (the characteristic back and forth movement of Capoeira). Rotation and inversion movements are added and *capoeiristas* turn their bodies by flexing their joints, switching the support of their bodies from their hands to their legs and back again. While the *capoeiristas* spin and whirl, Master Perna continues to connect Capoeira to Candomblé, like Babalorixá Muralemsibe, through the idea of "loosening up one's body" and the notion of Mandinga: "Our goal is to be a *mandingueiro*, loosen your body as if we were in Brazil, in, under the sunshine. Tune into the sound of the *berimbau* and let it take you away, *ginga!*"

Ginga is a constant flow and the movements are taught sequentially, one at a time, moving from and returning to *ginga*. An attack and a defense, *ginga*, an attack, *ginga*, a defense ... Gradually, the attacks and defenses become a sequence of movements that are repeated many times, always interspersed by *ginga*. After this stage, another sequence forming process starts.

The movements are repeated to exhaustion, eventually causing a feeling of dizziness or a loss of sense of space and time for beginners (those who are in the workshops along with the more experienced *capoeiristas*). For the more experienced, it causes a sensation described by one of the students of the Irmãos

Guerreiros Group in Vienna as a "[...] dynamic meditation [...] a time to forget everything out there and have the body act on its own."

After a lot of repetition of the basic sequences, some alternative moves are demonstrated. Other moves are explored by the more experienced students in order to introduce improvization into the exercise without, however, deviating from the pace imposed by the *berimbau*. The uncertainty and insecurity of improvised movements cause some concern that the attacks might actually hit their target. If this occurs, it will break the Capoeira movements' harmony with the rhythm imposed by the *berimbau*.This should not happen, Master Perna warns: "[...] the rhythm must flow. Leave the body loose; let it obey the rhythm of the berimbau. Do not think about the movement that your partner will make, nor of the movement that you will make [...] Or rather [...] don't think, just feel!"

This teaching method suggests a deconstruction and reconstruction of corporeality through memorization, exhaustive repetition, and the subsequent spontaneous performing of movements. The spontaneous performance of the sequence is necessary so that the harmony with the rhythm of the *berimbau* will not be broken. To obtain this spontaneity, however, one must deal with doubts and fears without expressing physical or mental strain. The body must act on its own, and the attacks and defenses must be conducted through an unconscious logic. Here, Master Perna draws attention to the role of the *berimbau*:

> This is Mandinga. *Capoeiristas* cannot be tense, or else they cannot hear what the *berimbau* is saying and that is when they get out of rhythm and the other guy gets them. Trust the training, trust your Orixá, the ancestors of Capoeira Angola, trust Mandinga. Let your body go really loose!

The sensation (body) must be prioritized to the detriment of thought (reason). "Reason" must be abandoned so that Mandinga is embodied, so much so that it allows European *capoeiristas* to overcome rationality and to hear what the *berimbau* is saying. Thus, the embodiment of the Mandinga (loosening up of the body) appears as a transposition of the limits of perception imposed by an education based on rationality, making a re-elaboration of the perception relative to some physical sensations originating from the practice of Capoeira Angola possible.

To conclude this section of ethnographic description of a Capoeira Angola event, it is important to emphasize that Mandinga has proven to be a key factor in making Europeans able to perceive transnational Capoeira Angola as being a transcendental experience.

The transcendental configuration: The fusion of *Candomblé* and Capoeira Angola as a sphere of Afro-Brazilian religious experiences

After European *capoeiristas* undergo exhaustive and repetitive training that is capable of "loosening up the body" for new elaborations of their perceptions, a ritual begins to conclude the fusion between Capoeira Angola and Candomblé for the *capoeiristas* of the European Irmãos Guerreiros Group, the realization of a Roda de Capoeira Angola during a true Candomblé ritual.

The Candomblé ritual becomes a representation of a *Roda de Capoeira*—or vice versa. The responsive structure of the songs, the three *atabaques* (*rum, rumpi,* and *lê*), similar to the three *berimbaus* (*gunga, médio,* and *viola*), the harmony with which the Orixás moves when hearing the *atabaques,* and especially the shared leadership of Master Perna playing one of the *atabaques* and Babalorixá Muralemsibe beside him singing the *pontos* (invocation prayers) to the Orixás; all of this evokes the same aesthetics and ethics of the afternoon classes.

The worshippers occupy the center of the hall, some in a circle in the center, and others dancing while incorporating Orixás. The changing expressions of the *capoeiristas* who enjoy the ritual with seriousness and respect represent the changes in the expressions of the worshippers when they incorporate their Orixás. These changes denote that the participants in the ritual are experiencing the presence of spiritual entities in the hall.

After Babalorixá Muralemsibe's worshippers incorporate their Orixás and dance, the ritual changes and the *capoeiristas* enter the scene. Following the workshop format, the *atabaques* are removed and the *berimbaus* take their place. The *berimbau* players are exactly the same people as those who played the *atabaques*. Babalorixá Muralemsibe also remains in the same position he occupied during the dance of the Orixás: next to the instruments and singing. The worshippers become spectators and the *capoeiristas* take their place, both delimiting the sacred space and to perform in the center circle, just as the worshippers had done in the previous stage of the ritual. During the Roda de Capoeira, the *capoeiristas* express the same seriousness with which they previously observed the Orixás.

During the performance, one sees the movements that were taught during the workshops. The similarity between the salutation movements that greet the *atabaque* players and the movements used for greeting the *berimbau* players can also clearly be seen. In the beginners' movements, the recently learned sequences are easily visible due to their mechanical reproduction. In the movements of the more experienced students, however, one sees a more complex series of movements and the use of varied and improvised combinations, which change according to the situation. Some of the movements are completely innovative. When these movements occur, the Masters playing the *berimbaus* and the *capoeiristas* watching the game repeatedly scream out in collective ecstasy.

At such times, if the *capoeirista*'s Orixá is known by the Masters, he sings songs of that specific Orixá as a way to stimulate the *capoeirista*'s performance. This, in turn, addresses the *berimbau* and greets it with touches to the ground. Songs like *mandingueiro, mandingueiro, where is the mandingueiro?* It serves to recognize and legitimize the Mandinga of the *capoeirista* who has performed an innovative and improvised movement, causing collective ecstasy.

The songs are also for times when the game has no Mandinga. In such cases, songs like "let loose the Mandinga aê, let loose the Mandinga!" It serves to alert the *capoeirista* that their body is stiff/stuck, and they have to loosen up, to connect to the sound of the *berimbau*, and let the Mandinga emerge.

After the ritual, which ends at almost midnight, most *capoeiristas* go to one of the nearest bars (Kapadokia)[24] to drink and talk about the Capoeira games that had taken place. The comments turn to the moments of apparent danger that existed in the games, caused or prevented by improvised and innovative actions (precisely those moments which evoked collective emotion): efficient attacks and defenses through spinning, twirling, and twisting movements, especially when these keep in harmony with the rhythm of the *berimbaus*. Such actions are felt and recognized (subjectively and collectively) as manifestations of Mandinga.

It is possible to analyze the results of the experience accumulated in this type of ritual and manifestation of Mandinga by focusing on the answers of those who had the most appreciated performances and were acclaimed as *mandingueiros*. On the one hand, there are the less experienced *mandingueiros* who say things like, "at that moment I felt something that I cannot explain ... I simply did not think about anything or I have no idea how I did it," and on the other, the more experienced players attribute a more mystical meaning to their feelings, saying: "The energy in the roda was very strong ... I felt the ancestors there with me" or "I was not alone at that moment."

During these conversations, I asked the more experienced players if this was the first time that they had felt this transcendental force and they answered "no." But some of them agreed that in the Roda de Capoeira they always feel something. They were not sure what it was until they began to participate in the rituals with Master Perna and Babalorixá Muralemsibe together.

If we consider the process as a whole, we see that it is a deconstruction of a horizontal and static corporeality. Through this, new possibilities of bodily organization are then established, adopting other visual and sensory references. With a new bodily organization that is perceived as a space/time disorientation, something like a codirection is rebuilt between the "self" (conscious movements) and the "being outside the self" (unconscious movements), being understood as the presence of a transcendental force and legitimized by religious authorities.

One may understand the overlapping of these two rituals as a way of transposing Afro-Brazilian religious cosmology on the ritual of Capoeira Angola which, in turn, gradually establishes an Afro-Brazilian religious sense in the perceptions of the European *capoeiristas* during practice. A sense that is always present in the practice of the European *capoeiristas* thus gains a transcendental significance. In other words, everything leads us to think that this repetitive training process complemented by the transmission of connected meanings forges a sense of transcendence shared by the (intersubjective) group about an individual (subjective) physical sensation. With this, the already initiated process of re-elaboration perception (described in the second section of this chapter) adds to the transcendental experience of the Brazilian Afro-religion. One might even say that it is the accommodation or familiarization of a mode of exotic transcendence in European lands, from which it becomes possible more than just getting to know, but to feel the presence of Afro-Brazilian transcendental forces.

Conclusion

The workshops given at the Irmãos Guerreiros Group events seem to allow for a phenomenological opening for re-elaborations of the relationship between "sensation" (body) and "meaning" (spirit) through the special treatment attributed to the notion of Mandinga, which enables Europeans to have transcendental experiences originating from African–Brazilian traditions, thus consolidating the establishment of a significant cultural communication bridge that uses the body as the main way of transposing two frontiers: one between cultures, establishing a transnational connection and another between corporal and spiritual dimensions, establishing a transcendental connection.

This I call the "transnational sphere of transcendence," insofar as it is the condensation of two complementary configurations that are essential for the understanding of the phenomenon of religious globalization: (1) "Transnational configuration" formed by the relations between culture, politics, and economy of the country of origin and the country of destination and (2) "Transcendental configuration" formed by the strategies of transmission of religious meanings and their experiences/performances.

When Capoeira and Candomblé were brought to Europe at the end of the twentieth century, Germany presented itself as an interesting market niche to the "sellers of ethnic culture" such as Miécio Ascanasy and the 1960s Brasiliana Group, which allowed for the implementation of Afro-Brazilian culture in this country as an exotic culture. From a political standpoint, Brazil was still breaking free from a totalitarian nationalist regime, and the alternative movements were still incipient; in Germany, a critique of the social nationalism by the new generations was consolidated. This scenario facilitated the establishment of Afro-Brazilian culture in Germany. We can say that this transnational phenomenon, as a breaker of frontiers (or overcoming of a national "sphere") has led to the elaboration of a transcendental phenomenon, as the elaboration of a new frontier (or the constitution of a religious "sphere"), in turn also transposable.

The phenomenon analyzed herein allows us to understand that young German (and European) *capoeiristas* seek religious experiences characterized by a symbolic (more geographical) distance from religious experiences that are familiar to them, a desire that is only possible based on a given transnational configuration.

To conclude, the study carried out herein leads us to think that the comprehensiveness of this transnational sphere of transcendence that circumscribes the union between Capoeira Angola and Candomblé in Europe represents a new form of religiosity that corresponds to the lifestyles of the new generations of this continent: a religious experience guided by bodily sensations and activities that provides a certain degree of self-immunity in the face of existential and social crises, while at the same time circumventing the conservatism associated with traditional religions.

Notes

Chapter 1

1   *The Economist*, "So Near and Yet So Far, Special Report on Latin America," September 9, 2010.
2   *The Economist*, "Brazil's Classrooms Become a Battleground in a Culture War: Jair Bolsonaro and His Allies Crusade against Left-Leaning Teachers," November 29, 2018.
3   "United Nations World Economic and Social Survey," (2004: 36), available online: http://www.un.org/esa/analysis/wess/, accessed August 10, 2007. "The World Migration Report" (2018: 76) of the International Organization for Migration recognizes the large number of Brazilian migrants living in the United States and the high emigration rate more generally, despite the number of returning migrants—the second highest emigration country of Latin America countries after Colombia (ibid.: 81); the report is available online: https://publications.iom.int/system/files/ pdf/wmr_2018_en.pdf, accessed December 21, 2018. See also Ministério das Relações Exteriores (2015), Brasileiros no Mundo: Estimativas 2015, available online: http://www.brasileirosnomundo.itamaraty.gov.br/a-comunidade/estimativas-populacionais-das-comunidades/Estimativas%20RCN%202015%20-%20Atualizado. pdf, accessed December 13, 2018.
4   Anthropophagy can be described best as the cannibalistic appropriation of cultural forms (see Islam 2011).
5   The former Portuguese empire included among others the Portuguese-speaking countries Portugal, Brazil, Angola, Mozambique, Guinee-Bissau, Cape Verde, São Tomé e Principe and East Timor.
6   The term *butinage* differs from *bricolage* (Levi-Strauss 1989) as it does not necessarily mean that actors mix religious traditions but rather move dynamically between them (see also Premawardhana 2018).

Chapter 2

1   For more on how these religious artifacts are understood and used in diverse ways in different networks in the West, see Rocha 2017a passim. In particular, chapter 7 shows how white Australians and New Zealanders use these artifacts and concepts

derived from Spiritism to address their history of European colonization and consequent Indigenous peoples' exploitation, death, and dispossession of land and culture which continue to this day.

2   The Australian megachurch Hillsong has become a global phenomenon by blurring the boundaries between the religious and secular worlds, and making religion fun, fashionable, and trendy (Connell 2005; Goh 2008; Klaver 2015; Riches and Wagner 2017; Rocha 2017b). Hillsong has a global network of leaders and an assembly of over 100,000 adherents on five continents. Its worship band has multiple bestselling albums and its music is now sung weekly by an estimated 50 million people in sixty languages. Its band leaders have been featured in the secular media from the *New York Times* to *Harpers' Bazaar* and *GQ* magazines, and followers include Justin Bieber, Kendall Jenner, and others in the American music, fashion, and sports worlds. In 2016 the Hollywood film "Let Hope Rise" featured its worship band.

3   Since the publication "Lost Horizon" by British author James Hilton in 1933, in which he depicted the fictional Shangri-La located in the Himalayans as an earthly utopia, the term has become synonymous with any place constructed as perfect, where people live in harmony and eternal happiness.

4   However, as I show in my book (2017a), Western spiritual tourists' presence in John of God's healing center and in the town of Abadiânia is not without conflict. Locals contest foreigners' intrinsic power by asserting their own power—they may set strict rules for foreigners, raise prices, or mock them for their lack of understanding of spiritual matters.

5   There are also instances in which cultural translation does not work, particularly in the spread of this spiritual movement in the West, where John of God's wealth, his radical healing methods, and patriarchal stance are sources of friction.

6   For Bourdieu (1984: 135–37), "reconversion of capital" refers to those strategies employed by any sector of society to maintain or improve their class position. Typically, economic capital is converted into social and cultural capital, but the opposite is also true. For instance, I have shown elsewhere (Rocha 2006a) the ways in which Brazilian intellectuals convert cultural capital associated with knowledge of Buddhism into symbolic capital to gain prestige and recognition and to secure their dominant position within Brazilian society. At the same time such knowledge also guarantees their parity with their peers overseas, giving them a sense of multiple, transnational belonging.

7   Middle-class Brazilians do not leave home until they find professional jobs after finishing university. This is due to the country's enormous social inequality which, among other consequences, produces a rigid system of class distinction in which middle-class members will not take up unskilled jobs, and cannot live independently and maintain middle-class status without a full-time professional job.

Chapter 3

1   The name of the church in English is "The Universal Church of the Kingdom of God."

2   The research for this project (2015–17) was enabled by a postdoctoral fellowship financed by the Kreitman School for Advanced Studies at Ben Gurion University, Israel; as well as a grant from the Israel Science Foundation project titled "Guide my Sheep: Catholic Guides of Holy Land Pilgrims—Historical and Ethnographic Aspects" (Grant 291/13 awarded to Prof. Yvonne Friedman and Prof. Jackie Feldman). I thank Prof. Jackie Feldman for his unconditional support and excellent advice. I am grateful to Kurt Kaufman and Nelson Rozenbaum from Genesis Tours for their generosity and assistance. I accompanied about twenty organized tours and interviewed dozens of tour guides, travelers, and pastors. In 2016 I spent three months in the Brazilian state of Maranhão (where I worked previously on other issues) for a focused field research.

3   In the statistical data I obtained, Israeli authorities have not distinguished between Protestants and evangelicals. I therefore assume here that those who claimed they were "Protestant" are more likely to belong to neo-Pentecostal or Historical-Evangelical congregations.

4   *Fogueira Santa* involves the burning of requests to God sent from all around Brazil and brought to Israel. See further information below.

5   Some American neo-Pentecostal groups do purchase Jewish symbols, however (cf. Feldman 2014).

6   Israeli law obliges professional guides to complete a twenty-four-month training course. They are additionally required to master the languages of the main national groups they guide. While some guides are Arab–Palestinian, majority are Jewish Israelis, often with an immigration background. See Feldman (2007).

7   Since the political aspect of the journey is usually marginal—if it exists at all—I will not elaborate this point further. For more information on the Israeli–Palestinian conflict in Holy Land trips, see Feldman (2011 and 2016).

8   Jewish holidays are marked on a lunar calendar, which thus differ annually in relation to the Gregorian calendar.

9   Zechariah 14 (16): "Then the survivors from all the nations that have attacked Jerusalem will go up year after year to worship the King, the Lord Almighty, and to celebrate the Festival of Tabernacles."

10 Herod's palace dates back to the first century BCE. The Qumran Caves complex is believed to have been the main habitat of the first century Essenes Sect. It is where the oldest known copy of the Old Testament has been discovered in the 1950s.

11 According to Roman Catholic and Orthodox Christianity, the fourth-century Holy Sepulchre Cathedral is built on top of the hill where Jesus was crucified. Protestant

pilgrims, widely defined, nonetheless follow a nineteenth-century tradition that locates this event elsewhere, some kilometers to the east. The site in this place is kept by the Anglican Church and is known as the Garden Tomb.

12 This event took place during Rene Terranova's Holy Land *caravana* of the Sukkot Holiday in 2016, which included about 500 pilgrims.

13 *Oração* is best described as a direct approach to God commonly enacted among Brazilian evangelicals on multiple occasions. It is a mundane ritual that expresses both the vertical exteriorization of faith and the horizontal dispersion of a sense of togetherness that unites the group of listeners as an intimate community of equals (Sarró and Mafra 2009; Shapiro 2015).

14 "Pisando na Terra dos Milagres: A Caravana do Sobrenatural." See https://www. youtube.com/watch?v=Ygp002RHCuE

15 Elijah first orders the Baal Prophets to pray and ask Baal to light up the wood on the altar. When they fail, Elijah builds his own altar to the Lord (YHWA, in Hebrew) and orders the people of Israel to pour water on it. He then prays to God, who sends His fire to burn the wet wood, thus consuming the sacrificial meat. Elijah then captures the Baal Prophets and kills them. Following this incident, a heavy rain falls. Bispo Rodovalho does not read directly from the Bible in this case but refers to the verses metaphorically.

16 This is inaccurate. Rain falls regularly on Mount Carmel every year between September and April.

17 At times, this acquired almost comic dimensions. For example, in one of the *caravanas* I witnessed a pastor who kept repeating the term "kanta-le'hai," which, according to him, is the Hebrew term for "salvation." To the best of my knowledge this is not a Hebrew word although it is reminiscent of the Hebrew term for *resurrection*, which is "Tehiya." When such terms are being used confidently and with an air of authority, they are persuasive regardless of whether they are real words, or not.

18 See https://www.youtube.com/watch?v=p0rMYp1mCwA. Although Pastor Alvarenga connects the site to the biblical figure of King David, the structure of which the tower makes part—as well as the entire walls surrounding the Old City— have in fact been built by the Othman in the sixteenth and seventeenth centuries AD. While Pastor Alvarenga addresses this clip for his congregation in Portugal, for every other aspect it is representative of the IURD's consecration and transfer techniques as well as the Brazilian neo-Pentecostal Judaization trend at large. See Mariz (2009); Rodrigues (2014); Swatowiski (2010).

19 Anallisa Butticci (2016: 8–10) identifies a sacramental similarity between Roman Catholicism and neo-Pentecostalism in and around the "perceived real presences of divine and supernatural powers pulsating in the material world" (p. 8). Butticci argues that this generates a shared "aesthetic of presence," which she calls "Catholicity."

20 This makes part of a larger phenomenon taking place in recent years across the Iberian Peninsula and Latin America, wherein persons revert "back" to Judaism due to personal convictions they may be descendants of Jews forcefully converted into Christianity during the Spanish and Portuguese Inquisitions. For a recent analysis of this phenomenon see Leite (2017).

21 The term "religious southernization" describes the reverse of traditional missionary trajectories through a rigorous transnationalization of theological frameworks, which now move from the Global South into northern social milieus.

22 On Messianic Judaism as a mode of "authentic" or "original" Christianity, see Topel (2011) and Dulin (2013).

Chapter 4

1 According to the official site of the Universal Church in Brazil (www. igrejauniversal.org.br, accessed December 15, 2009), the international expansion of the denomination began in New York in 1980. However, according to the website of the Church in Portugal, the Universal Church was founded in the United States in 1986. Freston (2001) indicates that the denomination in fact began to establish official temples outside of Brazil in 1985, when it opened a church in Paraguay. He also states that in 1989, in addition to arriving in Portugal, the Universal Church established itself in Argentina and Uruguay. This expansion became more intense in the 1990s. It is estimated that there were 225 temples abroad in 1995; in 1998 there were 500; and by 2001, 1,000. According to the Universal Church's website, in 2015, the denomination had almost 8,000 temples in 105 countries (Oro and Tadvald 2015). South Africa and Angola are among the countries in which the Universal Church has significant scope, in addition to Argentina, Venezuela, Mozambique, Portugal, Great Britain, Ivory Coast and the United States (Oro et al. 2003; Oro and Tadvald 2015; van de Kamp 2016; van Wyk 2014).

2 From 2011 to 2013, I participated as a research collaborator in the international cooperation project "The Universal Church of the Kingdom of God, the theology of prosperity and human rights in Angola." The project included researchers from Brazil, Portugal, and Angola, under the coordination of Professor Clara Mafra of the State University of Rio de Janeiro, and had financing from the Brazilian funding agency CNPq. During the project, we conducted field excursions and international workshops in order to understand the dynamics of Angola's religious life, and specifically the introduction and operation of the Universal Church in the Angolan capital. I also have been doing research about the Universal Church in Brazil (since 2002) and Portugal (2007–2008).

3 Angola is a country with a long history of war. From 1961 to 1974, the Angolan people fought for independence from Portugal, which, under the Estado Novo

regime, maintained the African colonies of Angola, Mozambique, Guinea-Bissau, and Cape Verde. This period was marked by the rise of a variety of organized and militarized political fronts. In 1975, the Popular Movement for the Liberation of Angola (MPLA) achieved independence and established a Marxist–Leninist inspired regime. But the victory of the MPLA did not produce political consensus and triggered a long period of wars between 1975 and 1991. Civil war flared again from 1992–1994 and 1998–2002 in splits caused by political and economic disputes.

4   12.3 percent of the population declared themselves without religion. 0.6 percent animist, 0.4 percent Islamic, 0.2 percent Jewish and 7.4 percent belonging to other religions.

5   Regardless of their location in the network, Universal Church temples offer virtually the same religious services, that is, spiritual experiences connected to common human privations (Campos 1997; Freston 2001; Mafra 2002; Oro et al. 2003). On Monday, there is a meeting dealing with prosperity and financial matters; on Tuesday, a session of spiritual cleansing dealing with health problems; on Wednesday, a meeting of the "children of God" and the spiritual growth group; on Thursday, an event called "love therapy" which focuses on the family; on Friday a session on liberation (exorcism); on Saturday, activities around impossible causes and (again) love matters; and on Sunday, an encounter with God, as well as family encounters.

6   See Almeida (2000).

7   Initially, the Universal Church invested in the purchase of large old movie theaters for their meetings in Brazil and abroad. Because of this practice, the church was accused of implementing an active policy of destroying collective memory (Gomes 2011). In some cases, as in Portugal, the purchase of spaces originally intended for cultural activities was much criticized and the Universal Church faced strong resistance. From 1995 onwards, the church changed its strategy and began to buy large lots and build mega-cathedrals in strategic points of big cities (Almeida 2009; Gomes 2011; Mafra and Swatowiski 2008).

8   Available at https://sites.universal.org/templodesalomao/a-inspiracao/, accessed November 16, 2017.

9   Halbwachs (1971) affirmed that the concept of the Holy Land is the result of an imaginative projection of the Christian faithful on a certain place that is considered sacred and central to the construction of Christian collective memory. Objects, monuments, and elements of the landscape fix Christian memory in a material reality.

10 According to historical records, the temple erected by Solomon was destroyed by the Babylonians in 586 BCE. After seventy years, Israelites rebuilt the temple and, years later, it was destroyed again, this time by Romans.

Chapter 5

1   The former president of the United States Barack Obama, accompanied by Michelle Obama and the couple's two daughters, conducted a historic official visit to Havana while in office, from March 20–22, 2016.

2   On the opening page of its website, the institution presents itself as follows: "MCC is a global denomination that is a welcoming place for all of God's people. Founded in 1968, MCC has been at the vanguard of civil and human rights movements by addressing issues of race, gender, sexual orientation, economics, climate change, aging and global human rights." Text available at http://mcchurch.org/, accessed March 3, 2017.

3   The Martin Luther King Memorial Centre is an ecumenical entity founded by the pastors of the Ebenezer Baptist Church, Raúl Suarez and Clara Rodés, on April 25, 1997, in Marianao, a municipality linked to the Province of the City of Havana. Its history reaches back to the pacification process between the Cuban State and a group of national evangelical churches that sat at the negotiation table for the purpose of setting the conditions and terms for religious freedom on the island.

4   Apart from the Unites States and Canada, MCC has associate churches in 38 countries, according to the 2012 document available on the website: http://mcchurch.org/files/2009/08/MCC-GLOBAL-PRESENCE-as-of-June-23-2012.pdf. It is important to consider, however, that the 2012 list does not reflect the current distribution of communities. For example, MCC Uganda, founded in May 2016, does not appear on the list. For information on that specific national church, see Silva (2017). Cuba is on the list, though that initial experience of nucleation has not continued.

5   In Brazil and abroad, reports from people about how they had their first contact with MCC through the Internet are common. One of the means of access is the institution's homepage available at http://mcchurch.org/. Multiple testimonies tell stories of quests on web search engines that direct to the church's homepage or related websites by the combination of keywords such as "gay," "church," and "Christian."

6   Troy Perry, a Baptist pastor expelled from his community for coming out as homosexual, has been directly engaged in the struggle for civil rights in the United States by merging political and religious activism. He worked in the Human Rights Commission of Los Angeles, and his activism has yielded him various official distinctions, such as an invitation by then-president Jimmy Carter to discuss LGBT rights in the White House in 1977, and by President Bill Clinton, who hosted him in the White House during the Conference on Hate Crimes held there in 1997. Further information on his ideas and personal journey can be found in his two books: *The Lord Is My Shepherd and Knows I'm Gay* and *Don't Be Afraid Anymore*.

7   Troy Perry returned to Cuba in May 2017, when he received an award from the National Centre for Sexual Education (Cenesex) for his activism against homophobia.

8   During fieldwork, we learned of two other Cuban groups that were in contact with MCC. One of them had even received a visit from bishop Hector Gutierrez, but such contact had not yielded results.

9   On the dynamics of the Cuban post-revolutionary religious environment and the active participation of evangelical churches in the construction of the Cuban secularism, see Alonso (1997), Calzadilla (2000, 2004), and Massón (2006).

10 Available at https://www.apnews.com/682b93e8ebee417ca030245b861b9a7a, accessed May, 2018.

11 See, for example, the article published in Granma in September 2016, available at http://pt.granma.cu/cuba/2016-09-01/comunicado-do-conselho-de-igrejas-de-cuba, accessed May, 2018.

12 The text "Religious Activism Blesses a Cuba without Homophobia," by Ivet Gonzáles, is available on the website http://envolverde.cartacapital.com.br/ativismo-religioso-abencoa-uma-cuba-sem-homofobia/, accessed October 10, 2017.

13 During our visit to Matanzas, I followed the MCC leaders' visit to the organization.

14 The term refers to the political opposition stance of a minority that claimed autonomy for the then Free Associated State of Puerto Rico in relation to the United States.

15 Excerpt from the sermon recorded on the night of May 15, 2016 in Matanzas, Cuba.

16 Excerpt extracted from the introduction of the members of the theologist's group. Available at http://mccchurch.org/ministries/mcc-theologies-team/our-team/, accessed March 1, 2017. I have not had access to the dossier yet. The information was reported during an interview given by Margarita on May 16, 2017.

17 The text by La Fountain-Stokes (1999: 93) informs us that according to such law: "Every person that keeps sexual relationship with another person from the same sex or commits a crime against the nature with a human being shall be punished with imprisonment for a fixed period of ten (10) years."

18 A Hebraic term referring to wind or breath used in reference to the Holy Ghost. Ruah, a feminine word, allows for rendering the third person of the Trinity feminine.

19 Excerpt from the sermon recorded on the night of May 15, 2016 in Matanzas, Cuba.

20 A group of the Brazilian Social Democracy Party (PSDB) linked to the inclusive agenda of the so-called LGBTI population (Lesbians, Gays, Bisexuals, Trans, and Intersex).

21 He continuous his answer as follows: "Therefore, we have to make a stand on defence of the LGBT community rights, not just in the LGBT movement, but also in the black and feminist movements. So, when requested, or not (laughter), we find a way of showing up and positioning ourselves, of telling we are there making a stand. ICM is very militant. One difficulty sometimes people have approaching ICM is that there is no way of getting involved with the church's activities remaining inside the closet. Because we face up the challenges all the time, we participate all the time." Excerpt extracted from an interview published on *Mix Brasil*. The document is available on the website http://www.diversidadetucana.com.br/2011/08/entrevista-do-reverendo-cristiano.html, accessed February 3, 2017.

22 Excerpt extracted from the interview published on MixBrasil. The document is available on the website http://www.diversidadetucana.com.br/2011/08/entrevista-do-reverendo-cristiano.html, accessed February 3, 2017.

23 The MCC's participation in this parade and its strategy for increasing visibility for the "queer evangelism" platform was addressed in a previous text (Silva 2016).

24 It is important to note that Margarita and Cristiano do not represent the MCC project in its entirety. Drawing from their alliances and practices, they mobilize a competitive vision of church among others. After the fieldwork in Cuba we had the opportunity to participate in the MCC World Conference, held in Canada in July. Here we observed that different churches had different definitions of "radical inclusion" and ideas about homosexuality, transsexuality, religion, politics, etc.

Chapter 6

1 The IPDA was the research topic for my doctoral dissertation between 2006 and 2011. There are very few studies about this church as it is very difficult to gain access.

2 *Travesti* is the name commonly used in Brazil for people born male, who identify as women and who may perform bodily modifications on themselves, but who do not generally want to undergo genital reconstruction surgery. *Mãe* or *Pai de Santo* is a hierarchical position in Afro-Brazilian religions that is roughly comparable to a priest.

3 African–Brazilian spirits associated with nightlife and prostitution.

4 In my doctoral dissertation (Téchio 2011), I analyze religious performances as spectacles and look at the forms of narratives used by the pastors according to the audience and especially with regards to the presence of women who are not part of the church. Narrative resources include the citation of the main entities and *orixás* (African Gods) of the Afro-Brazilian religions.

5   To understand the concept of *pombagira*, see Bahia this same volume.

6   In the IPDA, there is no acceptable definition of spirits or entities: all are seen as the personification of evil by the pastors, so all are treated as demons. I think one can say that the existence and growth of the IPDA is mainly due to the existence of such Afro-Brazilian religions as Candomblé and Umbanda (see also Chesnut 1997: 45). If there were no *pombagira* so active, strong and present, threatening the purity of women and men, then preaching would basically be discouraging. Without a "mortal enemy," there would be no passion in speech. The fearsome *pombagira* is thus directly a sponsor or godmother of the enthusiasm we see in preaching and the faith workers are the frontline of combat against her. They must thus be completely sanctified through the punishment of their bodies in order to be able to expel *pombagira* and other spirits and *orixás* from the bodies of the faithful who are victimized by these entities.

7   Jerusalem is understood by Pentecostals to be the most sacred place in the world. Members dream about visiting the city and getting to know it. Some churches organize excursions to Israel as a way to reward dedicated pastors (see also Shapiro, this volume).

8   In an increasingly competitive religious market, Brazilian religious groups who aspire to establishing a presence in Europe (especially Portugal, given the lack of a language barrier), choose some kind of symbol that differentiates them from other groups. For example, the Christian Congregation Church of Brazil changed its name in its newly built temples in Portugal. Its women wear a full embroidered veil that becomes an object of ostentation, either due to the size of the embroidery in comparison with simpler veils, or due to its white color in comparison with veils yellowed by time. Both things are indicators of economic power. In the Christian Congregation, women display their economic and social status through the type of veil, bags, watches, shoes, and accessories they can use. The Universal church, which changed its name to Spiritual Help Center is the most creative and diversified of Brazilian religions in terms of making of sacred objects and rituals such as "ark-shaped key chains, bottles of water from the Jordan River, holy bonfires, walking on rock salt trails, love flowers, divine credit cards," etc.

9   Leach (1990) proposes that the heart of public symbolic behavior is that it is a means of communication. Given this, all women who follow the religious rules of the IPDA share in the meaning of the element of the "untouchable hair." In this case, inside the church, they wear their hair loose and long, reaching almost to their feet. This integrates these women and reinforces their networks of power and sociability. Outside the church, they wear their hair in a bun that serves to publicly communicate their adherence to the IPDA.

10 The case was reported by newspapers around the world using sensationalistic headlines: "Bragança mothers accuse Brazilians of causing 'a wave of madness' in

the city" by Helena Fidalgo (LUSA), May 1, 2003. The story was also on the cover of *Time* Magazine's European weekly edition in November 2003 titled "The New European Prostitution Quarter" by Amanda Ripley and Martha de La Cal. It had eight pages of text entitled "When the girls came to town." Read more in: http://www.cmjornal.pt/tv-media/detalhe/prostituicao-em-braganca-na-time, accessed December 10, 2018. The situation was also reported by Pais (2010, 2016).

11 See Sabaot Church, "Uma igreja pentecostal brasileira fundada em Milão, em 1994," by Brazilian pastor Roselen Boerner Faccio (http://www.sabaothchurch.com, accessed December 10, 2018).

Chapter 7

1   *Pombagira* represents a spirit of a woman who once worked in prostitution. She deals with cases of love, protects the women who seek her out, and is able to create any kind of love or sexual union. *Exús* and *pombagiras* are the owners of crossroads and the streets, being entities that are very close to humans because they have more attachment to material reality. They are considered less enlightened and less further along the path of spiritual evolution, but are extremely dangerous and powerful. *Pombagira* is a female spirit who symbolizes the dangers that female sexuality poses to a social order in which positions of formal power are occupied almost entirely by men. See Contins (1983) and Meyer (1993).

2   Candomblé is a religion that was constituted in the nineteenth century in the Brazilian state of Bahia, drawing upon the Yoruba tradition. Although many Candomblé *terreiros* only deal with the religion of the *orixás* (African gods), others engage with *Umbanda* spirits according to the needs of their *filhos de santo* (children of the saint) and organize sessions with *pombagiras* and *exús*, spirits that are held in a certain prestige by both Brazilians and Portuguese. *Umbanda* is a Brazilian religion based upon the notion of possession by spirits. Created in the beginning of the twentieth century in Rio de Janeiro, it blends African religions with Catholicism, Spiritism (the version created by Allan Kardec), and considerable indigenous lore. In Umbanda, one worships and incorporates spirits (not African gods as in Candomblé). The religious temples I study practice both Candomblé and Umbanda, and this sort of dual practice is one of the reasons why Umbanda is very well accepted in Portugal.

3   During my fieldwork realized in Brazil and Portugal, I observed that sex professionals and their clients interact with these spirits, often giving them offerings in their temples. These spirits are important to sex workers because *pombagira* attract men, *exus* attract money, and both "open the ways" and are important to maintaining profits in houses of prostitution.

4   "Hypersexual, happy con artist" is the general stereotypical portrayal of Brazilians by the Portuguese. These essentialist stereotypes have been around since colonial times, reproducing a portrayal of the two nations as not peers (being center and periphery). The Brazilian cultural tendency toward ambiguity and toward creating different rules of behavior in different social environments is often understood by Europeans to be permissive or dishonest. These stereotypes affect Brazilian women and transsexuals more than they do men (Machado 2009; Ribeiro 2010).

5   See endnote 2.

6   These are the spirits of the old native Brazilians who were chosen by Bantu slaves as the real "owners of the land." In this sense, then, when Indians take over the bodies of the Portuguese, possession rewrites history and transforms the Portuguese, in a certain sense, into Indians.

7   The *terreiro* head's direct assistant.

8   The head of the hierarchy in the family of the saints. It signifies religious kinship within the cult group.

9   Also called *jogo de búzios* or Dilogun, it is a divination method played by the father or mother-of-saint though which Exu (*orixá*) speaks directly to a person via the way the cowrie shells fall down.

10   Part of the prostitution circuit in which she worked has now become part of a brothel circuit where she attends to spiritual clientele.

Chapter 8

1   http://statline.cbs.nl/Startweb/lin, accessed December 19, 2014.

2   In this case, the data corresponds to the year 2012.

3   The names used in the text are fictitious to ensure the anonymity of respondents.

4   The Portuguese-speaking Catholic Church in The Hague is formed by members who come from the following lusophone countries: Angola, Brazil, Guinea-Bissau and Portugal. They use Portuguese as the official and common language.

5   See also https://www.ed.nl/overig/mannen-met-een-missie-in-handel~a2a34d22/, accessed November 29, 2018.

6   Activities of the prayer group are regularly announced on www. brasileirosnaholanda.com/novo/index.php, a site with diverse advertisements from the Brazilian Community in the Netherlands.

7   The concept of "reverse mission" has been used freely to summarize modalities of this phenomenon. For further understanding of the term and in what context it exists, look at: Freston (2010) and Koning (2011).

8   According to Godoy (2017: 54), the image of Our Lady of Aparecida was crowned in 1904 by Pope Pius X as "the Queen of Brazil." From that moment on, the saint has become more known and appreciated by Brazilians all over the country.

9 The mission of the Brazilian Carmelite Friars is also an example of "reverse mission" (Freston 2010).

10 To which they organized access by employing the hypermodern technology of transnational internet connectivity resulting in a radical transformation of their personal life projects.

Chapter 9

1 *Ayahuasca* is a tea of *Banisteriopsis caapi* brewed with *Psychotria viridis*.

2 According to the president of the Spanish Federation of Daime churches, "Spain reached the inquisitorial process to pursue our sacrament throughout Europe" (personal communication). "No more civil wars (we, in Spain, know a lot about this), no more inner fighting, no more endogamous movements, no more quarrels—please! Every people that uses plants of power is in the same boat, for better or for worse. In this beginning of a new millennium, there is no other way out than uniting ourselves and our beliefs, to fight together for true spiritual union" (http://www.santodaime.org/site-antigo/fardados_i/spain2.htm, accessed October 6, 2018). I also heard from many *ayahuasca* users about the feeling of living without religious freedom and persecution.

3 When SD church was formed in Spain its statute expressed as primary goal: the reconciliation of the Christian experiences, beliefs, and doctrines with those of the Indian cultures of Amazon (Pavillard 2008).

4 New Age refers to the spiritual beliefs and practices developed in the West from the 1970s.

5 Community of the SD church.

6 Currently responsible for the SD church San Juan de Madrid and president of the Spanish Federation of Daimist churches.

7 "The Enneagram emanates from traditions of great antiquity and offers an astonishingly precise map of personal development processes" (http://www.naranjo-sat.com/?pg=satprogr_e, accessed October 28, 2018).

8 Prenucleus are developing centers of worship that lack some physical infrastructure and usually have fewer members (Labate, Meyer and Anderson 2009).

9 Authorized distribution of Vegetal refers to a developing center of worship that has not yet reached the status of prenúcleo or núcleo (Labate, Meyer and Anderson 2009).

10 Juramidam Empire refers to a mythical affiliation: the mother is the Queen of the Forest (Our Lady of Conception) and the father is the Juramidam king (Jesus Christ).

11 This idea was shared in a personal communication with a Spanish UDV master in 2009.

12 Curiosity is false knowledge, speculation, superficiality (Labate, Meyer, and Anderson 2009).

13 Science refers to the body of UDV spiritual and material knowledge, the "true knowledge" (Labate, Meyer, and Anderson 2009).

Chapter 10

1   Umbanda (in Spanish "La Umbanda" or also simply "Umbanda") is a cult in which invocations are made through dances and chants intoned in Portuguese. Its original doctrinal system was based on spiritism, fundamentally on the postulates of Allan Kardec, later incorporating elements of Catholicism, African cults, and elements of indigenous origin. The first form of worship, called Umbanda Blanca (White), eliminated animal sacrifices, the use of drums and nonwhite clothing. Later, followers of the cult integrated those elements that were considered typical of African cults and the Umbanda Cruzada (Crossed) emerged, which is the predominant form in Uruguay.

2   Unless expressly stated otherwise, all translations of the original quotations in Spanish or Portuguese are mine.

3   Renzo Pi Hugarte preferred the term "possession cults" to refer to Afro-Brazilian religions, as he understood that the practice of "possession," that is, the bodily incorporation of spirits and entities, was the most characteristic aspect of these religious phenomena.

4   A transnational space has been defined as "configurations of social practices, artifacts and symbol systems that span different geographic spaces in at least two nation-states without constituting a new 'deterritorialized' nation-state" (Pries 2001: 18).

5   Cultural hybridization is defined as "sociocultural processes in which discrete structures or practices, which existed separately, combine to generate new structures, objects and practices" (García 2001: 14).

6   Examples of such cities are as follows: Bella Unión—Barra do Quaraí, connected by the Bella Unión—Barra do Quaraí International Bridge (road and rail). Artigas—Quaraí, united by the International Bridge of Concordia. Rivera—Santana do Livramento, joined by Av. 33 Orientales, on the Uruguayan side, and Av. João Pessoa, on the Brazilian side, and also by Av. Paul Harris, which has this name on both sides, in the one known as Frontera de la Paz.

7   Conurbation is that form of spatial growth of a city that forms a vastly built extension, in which the physical continuity is a fundamental aspect, which, nevertheless, does not prevent the differentiation of cities that form part of the conglomerate (Pujadas and Font 1998: 328).

8   Portuñol or Portunhol is an interlanguage spoken in several border regions between countries where Spanish and Portuguese are spoken. For more information on the use of the Portuguese language see Gutierrez Bottaro (2002).

9   For a glossary of adaptations of the original religious terms from Brazilian Portuguese to Spanish spoken in Uruguay see Pi Hugarte (1998).

10 The Charrúas were an Amerindian people, which based on testimonies of European explorers, we know that in the sixteenth century lived in the territory currently occupied by Uruguay. In the following centuries they also came to occupy part of the Province of Entre Ríos (Argentina) and the State of Rio Grande do Sul (Brazil). During the 1830s, the last inhabitants of this ethnic group to conserve their traditional way of life and culture were exterminated or integrated into other groups of Western culture in a voluntary or forced way. Currently, there are no Charrúa communities living according to their original culture and tradition. For more information see Bracco (2013) and Vidart (2012).

11 The *Banda Oriental* (the Eastern Bank) is the name given to the current territory of the Republic of Uruguay and part of the current State of Rio Grande do Sul in Brazil. It received its name from its location east of the Uruguay river.

12 Some aspects of Afro culture have survived in Uruguay, including some that originally had a mystical or transcendental meaning, but are now devoid of any religious connotation, as is the case of Candomble. These cultural phenomena have a strong identity component and are claimed as part of their legacy to Uruguayan culture by the Afro population of the country. The song and dance associated with Candomble has been transmitted generationally, as George Reid Andrews (2010) demonstrated.

13 Pi Hugarte (2003: 104) defines *charruísmo* as an ideological position characterized by the uncritical exaltation of what is related to *charrúas*, the rejection of objective knowledge and its substitution by irrational statements.

14 "Internal transfer", in this sense, means that the religion did not come from other countries or other regions of Uruguay; instead, Umbanda was mostly spread from the north to the rest of the country.

15 Segato (1996) places the introduction of Umbanda in Argentina in the 1950s, attributing a prominent role in this to some people who frequented the cities of Rivera and Livramento, which were linked to the sex trade.

16 A transnationalization without migration, in this case, means that there was not a massive Brazilian or Argentine migration that brought the religion. Umbanda was brought to Uruguay by sporadic visitors, traveling people, and individuals who lived in the border. Oro (2013) maintains that this happened with both Umbanda and Batuque, also in Argentina. I believe that the important role played by Uruguayans living in Argentina in bringing and strengthening this religion in Argentina, as described by Frigerio (2013) and other authors, leads me to conclude that the weight of migration was even less in Uruguay than in Argentina.

17 It means that Bolivians go to Brazil to practice Umbanda as if they were clients that use a (religious) service, instead of being part of a faithful community.

18 The term "Quimbanda" can be used to refer to a ritual variant of Umbanda as a synonym for Linha Cruzada, to refer to the ritual variant Linha de Exú, or to an autonomous religious system in which both exu and *pombagira* play a central

role (Leistner 2014). In the sense used by the expression, PI Hugarte refers fundamentally to those temples that practice crossed Umbanda.

19 The term "Batuque" refers generically to rhythms produced on percussion during cults whose mythological, axiological, linguistic and ritual elements are of African origin. The word "Batuque" can also allude to a religion of Afro-Brazilian origin, that worships twelve orixás and is divided into "sides" or "nations" (Oro 2002). The presence of this religion in Uruguay, with its first stable temples, can be dated to the 1950s.

20 The Argentine example analyzed by Alejandro Frigerio (1998) shows that, in that country, two different schools of Umbandist tradition are sources of legitimacy and prestige: the Uruguayan school and the Brazilian school.

21 Interview with Mai Susana Andrade by Andres Serralta Massonnier, March 9, 2017, Montevideo, Uruguay.

22 Radio Océano FM, September 12, 2012, Pae umbandista, cuenta su increíble historia de vida. Available online: https://oceano.uy/abrepalabra/lengua-larga/87-pae-donato-de-oxum_Gustavo Rey

23 Andrade, S. (2006), "Puntualizaciones sobre la magia negra", *La República*, December 4. Available online: http://www.lr21.com.uy/editorial/232068-puntualizaciones-sobre-la-magia-

24 *Ialorixá* is the woman who exercises the headship of the temple, to whom powers of medium are attributed and who is usually a "Mãe-de-santo" of middle age or even older; a High Priestess (Pinto 1971).

25 *Babaloxirá* is the man to whom powers of medium are attributed, who in addition is "Pai-de-Santo," who exercises as Head of at least one temple of Umbanda; a High Priest (Pinto 1971). Whoever is called *Babaloxirá*—or its feminine equivalent *Ialorixá*—is usually a person who enjoys a certain prestige and reputation within the religious community.

26 Andrade, S. (December 4, 2006), "Puntualizaciones sobre la magia negra", *La República*, available online: http://www.lr21.com.uy/editorial/232068-puntualizaciones-sobre-la-magia-negra

27 Radio Océano FM (September 12, 2012) *"Pae umbandista, cuenta su increíble historia de vida",* available online: https://oceano.uy/abrepalabra/lengua-larga/87-pae-donato-de-oxum_Gustavo Rey

28 Radio Océano FM (September 12, 2012) *"Pae umbandista, cuenta su increíble historia de vida",* available online: https://oceano.uy/abrepalabra/lengua-larga/87-pae-donato-de-oxum_Gustavo Rey

29 "Magia Negra (Parte 2)", by Mil Voces, Salto, https://www.youtube.com/watch?v=g4a72BLJtaE

30 Mediatic is a slang word used to refer to characters who achieve some degree of popularity in the mass media.

31 See also Espirito Santo and Tassi (2013).

Chapter 11

1   *Feijoada* is a traditional bean and meat stew that is widely popular in Brazil. The dish gets its name from *feijão*, the Portuguese word for beans. *Feijoada* is made with either beef or pork, which may be fresh or salt-cured.

2   Usually, two different forms of Capoeira are being distinguished: Capoeira Angola and Capoeira Regional. "The first [...] has to do with a distinctive conception of power [here this power is called "Mandinga"] held by practitioners of Capoeira Angola, and with the style's difference in the way it treats the body and magic. The second main difference is that Angola and Regional stand in an asymmetrical relation concerning their mutual influences in society. Regional outnumbers Angola in the number of practitioners and academies [...], as well as in visibility in the media and mass culture. The Angola style, which is situated in a relatively marginal position compared to Regional groups, has used this disadvantage to claim a closer involvement with African traditions, thereby perpetuating the idea that the style maintains a purer connection with its origins that has not yet been contaminated by the external influences of mainstream sports or other martial arts" (Varela 2017: 46–47).

3   In the 1980s and 1990s, social movements (such as the Feminist Movement, Black Movement, Indigenous Movement) gained greater visibility and mobilization strength due to the end of the dictatorial regime and the establishment of a constitution focused on the civil rights of minorities.

4   *Mestre* (master), the highest authority in a Capoeira group.

5   The Irmãos Guerreiros Group has three centers in Germany, two in Poland, one in France, one in Norway, one in Slovakia, two in Portugal and one in Austria.

6   Term of origin Yorubá *babalóòrisà* (father of the *orixás*) used to refer to the priest in Candomblé.

7   This research was funded by the Brazilian funding agency for scientific research CAPES.

8   The Forum has been studied by Bahia (2014) and Graeff (2013).

9   Mestre Rosalvo runs the Jangada Academy together with his German wife, and Contramestra Suzy. *Jangada* means rustic boat. For more information on the arrival of Capoeira Angola in Berlin, see Brito (2015).

10 Divinities of Candomblé.

11 These participations maintained a purely folkloric character: a dance class.

12 "[...] Afoxé, also popularly called *Candomblé de Rua* (Street Candomblé), is a cultural manifestation based on the African doctrines of the Orixás Cult, which in the diaspora for Brazil was called Candomblé. Therefore, each group adopts an Orixá as a guide and is guarded by religious leadership. It is this person who guides the group in all aspects, and its participants, even if not believers of Candomblé, must respect the hierarchy, the religious foundations and must have discipline, obeying the criteria of operation of the Terreiro [Temple] to which the group belongs" (Souza 2008: 1).

13 Arrival of Master Perna in Germany.

14 Ogã is a function/position in Candomblé "[...] exercised only by men who are
    not incorporated by Orixás (trances) in order to always be aware and attentive
    to the progress of the rituals. The different functions/positions of *ogans* include:
    ogan'illu (responsible for playing the atabaques), *axogã* (responsible for the sacrifice
    of animals) and *Ogã Cipá* (Responsible for the care of sacred things, order and
    maintenance of the sanctuary). We understand then that cutting, caring and
    playing are specific 'gifts' attributed to particular men. These 'gifts' are provided by
    the gods, who also require a differentiated position in the inner fabric of religion.
    This position is that of *Ogã*" (Germano 2017: 127).

15 The "Suspensão de Ogã" ("elevation" of Ogã) is a part of the Candomblé ritual in
    which an "incorporated" Orixá chooses a man present at the ritual and invites him
    to walk by his side. He is then taken to a chair and is sat down beside the Ogãs
    that have already been *confirmado* (confirmed), to be *suspendido* (elevated) both
    physically (two Ogãs lift up the chair and the man) and symbolically (from then on,
    he is considered to hold the title of Ogã in the temple).

16 The atabaque is a single-head membranophone, a musical instrument from
    northeastern Brazil where it is associated with a number of Afro-Brazilian sacred
    and secular traditions (example: Candomblé, Capoeira, and samba).

17 The Irmãos Guerreiros Group has three centers in Germany, two in Poland, one in
    France, one in Norway, one in Slovakia, two in Portugal and one in Austria.

18 A space circumscribed by people and used to define the ritual performance area,
    characteristic of both the Capoeira ritual and the Candomblé ritual. The "Roda de
    Capoeira" was registered as an Intangible Cultural Heritage of Brazil in 2008, and as
    a Humanity Cultural Heritage in 2014 (Brazil 2014).

19 See note 5.

20 See Brito (2012, 2015, 2017). Some of the French *capoeiristas* position themselves
    as follows: "Capoeira provides the possibility of redeeming the Europeans from the
    guilt that derives from having been involved in colonization, the slave trade and
    other forms of exploitation" (Brito 2012: 117–18).

21 Iansã is the deity of the winds, hurricanes, and storms; she is connected to the river
    Niger. Iansã has a strong temper and gets angry very easily. She was married to
    Ogum, but left him to become Xangô's first wife.

22 Musical bows, a musical instrument of African origin, which has become
    Capoeira's greatest symbol.

23 Both Orixás correspond to stereotyped movements of men and women: Oxum
    as graceful and seductive movements of a fertility queen, Ogum with strong and
    aggressive movements of a great warrior.

24 I thank Nina Graeff for reminding me of the name of the bar.

References

Chapter 1

Abreu, M. J. A. de (2005), "Breathing into the Heart of the Matter: Why Padre Marcelo Needs No Wings," *Postscripts*, 1 (2/3): 325–49.

Almeida, R. de and C. Gutierrez (2015), "Universal Church in France: Demonization, Prosperity and Globalization," Paper presented at the Conference of the International Society for the Sociology of Religion, Louvain-la-Neuve, July 2–5, 2015.

Andrade, O. de (1990), *A Utopia Antropofágica: Obras Completas de Oswald de Andrade*, Globo: São Paulo.

Appadurai, A. (1996), *Modernity at Large: Cultural Dimensions of Globalization*, Minneapolis and London: Minnesota Press.

Badone, E. and S. R. Roseman (2004), "Approaches to the Anthropology of Pilgrimage and Tourism," in E. Badone and S. R. Roseman (eds), *Intersecting Journeys: The Anthropology of Pilgrimage and Tourism*, 1–23, Urbana: University of Illinois Press.

Bahia, J. (2014), "Under the Berlin Sky. Candomblé on German Shores," *Vibrant*, 11 (1): 326–69.

Bahia, J. (2016), "Dancing with the Orixás: Music, Body and the Circulation of African Candomblé Symbols in Germany," *African Diaspora*, 9 (1–2): 15–38.

Bastide, R. (1978), *The African Religions in Brazil: Toward a Sociology of the Interpenetration of Civilizations*, Baltimore: Johns Hopkins University Press.

Becci, I. M. Burchardt and J. Casanova, eds (2013), *Topographies of Faith: Religion in Urban Spaces*, Leiden: Brill.

Bendix, R. (2009) "Heritage between Economy and Politics: An Assessment from the Perspective of Cultural Anthropology," in N. Akagawa and L. Smith (eds), *Intangible Heritage*, 253–69, London: Routledge.

Beserra, B. (2003), *Brazilian Immigrants in the United States: Cultural Imperialism and Social Class*, El Paso: LFB Scholarly Publishing LACK.

Beserra, B. (2006), "Entre as demandas de Deus e as da sobrevivência. Os brasileiros adventistas de Chino," *Revista Travessia*, XIX (55): 17–22.

Beyer, P. (2006), *Religions in Global Society*, London: Routledge.

Birman, P. and D. Lehmann (1999), "Religion and the Media in a Battle for Ideological Hegemony: The Universal Church of the Kingdom of God and TV Globo in Brazil," *Bulletin of Latin American Research*, 18 (2): 145–64.

Cahen, M. (2013), "Is 'Portuguese-speaking' Africa Comparable to 'Latin' America? Voyaging in the Midst of Colonialities of Power," *History in Africa*, 40 (1): 5–44.

Campos, L. S. (1997), *Teatro, Templo e Mercado: Organização e Marketing de um Empreendimento Neopentecostal*, Rio de Janeiro: Vozes.

Casanova, J. (2001), "Religion, the New Millennium, and Globalization," *Sociology of Religion*, 62 (4): 415–41.

Cohen, R. (2008), *Global Diasporas: An Introduction*, London: Routledge.

Coleman, S. and J. Eade, eds (2004), *Reframing Pilgrimage: Cultures in Motion*, London: Routledge.

Coleman, S. and K. Maier (2013), "Redeeming the City: Creating and Traversing 'London-Lagos'," *Religion*, 43 (3): 353–64.

Comaroff, J. and J. L. Comaroff (1991), *Of Revelation and Revolution, Volume I, Christianity, Colonialism, and Consciousness in South Africa*, Chicago: University of Chicago Press.

Couldry, N. (2003), *Media Rituals: A Critical Approach*, London: Routledge.

Csordas, T. J. (2009), "Introduction: Modalities of Transnational Transcendence," in T. J. Csordas (ed.), *Transnational Transcendence: Essays on Religion and Globalization*, 1–29, Berkeley: University of California Press.

Da Matta, R. (1991), *Carnivals, Rogues, and Heroes: An Interpretation of the Brazilian Dilemma*, Notre Dame: University of Notre Dame Press.

Davie, G. (2013), "Belief and Unbelief: Two Sides of a Coin," *Ecclesiastical Law Journal*, 15: 259–66.

DeLanda, M. (2016), *Assemblage Theory*, Edinburgh: Edinburgh University Press.

Deleuze, G. and F. Guattari (1987), *A Thousand Plateaus: Capitalism and Schizophrenia*, trans. B. Massumi, Continuum: London.

Dias, G. (2006), "Expansão e choque: a IURD em Portugal," in I. Machado (ed.), *Um mar de identidades. A imigração brasileira em Portugal*, 299–312, São Paulo: Edufscar.

Eade, J. and M. J. Sallnow (1991), *Contesting the Sacred. The Anthropology of Christian Pilgrimage*, Urbana: University of Illinois Press.

Freston, P. (2010), "Reverse Mission: A Discourse in Search of Reality?," *Pentecostudies*, 9 (2): 153–74.

Garbin, D. and A. Strhan, eds (2017), *Religion and the Global City*, London: Bloomsbury.

Geschiere, P. and B. Meyer (1998), "Globalization and Identity: Dialectics of Flow and Closure: Introduction," *Development and Change*, 29 (4): 601–15.

Gez, Y. N., Y. Droz, E. Soares and J. Rey (2017), "From Converts to Itinerants: Religious Butinage as Dynamic Identity," *Current Anthropology*, 58 (2): 141–50.

Glick Schiller, N. and N. B. Salazar (2013), "Regimes of Mobility across the Globe," *Journal of Ethnic and Migration Studies*, 39 (2): 183–200.

Greenfield, S. M. and A. Droogers (2003), "Syncretic Processes and the Definition of New Religions," *Journal of Contemporary Religion*, 18 (1): 25–36.

Groisman, A. (2009), "Trajectories, Frontiers, and Reparations in the Expansion of Santo Daime to Europe," in T. Csordas (ed.), *Transnational Transcendence: Essays on Religion and Globalization*, 185–204, Berkeley: University of California Press.

Heck, G. (2013), "Worshipping at the Golden Age Hotel: Transnational Networks, Economy, Religion, and Migration of the Congolese in Istanbul," in J. Becker, K. Klingan, S. Lanz and K. Wildner (eds), *Global Prayers: Contemporary Manifestations of the Religious in the City*, 275–89, Zurich: Lars Müller Publishers.

Hess, D. (1991), *Spirits and Scientists: Ideology, Spiritism, and Brazilian Culture*, University Park: Penn State University Press.

Hüwelmeier, G. and K. Krause, eds (2009), *Traveling Spirits: Migrants, Markets and Mobilities*, London: Routledge.

Islam, G. (2011), "Can the Subaltern Eat? Anthropophagic Culture as a Brazilian Lens on Post-Colonial Theory," *Organization*, 19 (2): 159–80.

Jenkins, P. (2011), *The Next Christendom: The Coming of Global Christianity*, Oxford: Oxford University Press.

Keim W., Ç. Ercüment, C. Ersche and V. Wöhre (2014), *Global Knowledge Production in the Social Science: Made in Circulation*, Aldershot [etc.]: Ashgate.

Kong, L. (2005), "Religious Processions: Urban Politics and Poetics," *Temenos*, 41 (2): 225–49.

Kramer, E. (2005). "Spectacle and the Staging of Power in Brazilian Neo-Pentecostalism," *Latin American Perspectives*, 32 (1): 95–120.

Krause, K. and R. van Dijk (2016), "Hodological Care among Ghanaian Pentecostals: De-Diasporization and Belonging in Transnational Religious Networks," *Diaspora*, 19 (1): 97–115.

Lambek, M. (2014), "Afterworld: Recognizing and Misrecognizing Spirit Possession," in P. Johnson (ed.), *Spirited Things: The Work of Possession in Afro Atlantic Religions*, London: University of Chicago Press.

Lanz, S. and M. Oosterbaan (2016), "Entrepreneurial Religion in the Age of Neoliberal Urbanism," *International Journal of Urban and Regional Research*, 40 (3): 1–21.

Latour, B. (2005), *Reassembling the Social: An Introduction to Actor-Network Theory*, Oxford: Oxford University Press.

Lee, L. (2015), *Recognizing the Non-Religious: Reimagining the Secular*, Oxford: Oxford University Press.

Lee L. (2017), "New and Alternative Careers in *Butinage*: A Comment on Gez et al.," *Current Anthropology*, 58 (2): 152–53.

Levi-Strauss, C. (1989), *Des Symboles et leurs Doubles*, Paris: Plo.

Levitt, P. (2007), *God Needs No Passport. Immigrants and the Changing American Religious Landscape*, New York and London: New Press.

Levitt, P. and Glick Schiller, N. (2004), "Conceptualizing Simultaneity: A Transnational Social Field Perspective on Society," *International Migration Review*, 38 (3): 1002–39.

Mafra, C. (2001), *Os Evangélicos*, Rio de Janeiro: Jorge Zahar Editor.

Mareels, E. (2016), "Migration et Pentecôtisme Brésiliens entre le Brésil et la Belgique: une Analyse à Partir des Enjeux du 'Relationnement'," Ph.D. diss., Laap/Université Catholique de Louvain, Louvain-Neuve.

Martes, A. (1999), "Os imigrantes brasileiros e as igrejas em Massachusetts," in T. Sales and R. Reis (eds), *Cenas do Brasil Migrante*, 87–122, São Paulo: Boitempo.

Massey, D. (1993), "Power-Geometry and a Progressive Sense of Place," in J. Bird, B. Curtis, T. Putnam, G. Robertson and L. Tickner (eds), *Mapping the Futures: Local Cultures, Global Change*, 59–69, London: Routledge.

Mazzarella, W. (2004), "Culture, Globalization, Mediation," *Annual Review of Anthropology*, 33: 345–67.

Meyer, B. (2004), "Christianity in Africa: From African Independent to Pentecostal-Charismatic Churches," *Annual Review of Anthropology*, 33: 447–74.

Meyer, B. (2009), "Introduction: From Imagined Communities to Aesthetic Formations: Religious Mediations, Sensational Forms, and Styles of Binding," in B. Meyer (ed.), *Aesthetic Formations: Media, Religion, and the Senses*, 1–28, New York: Pallgrave.

Meyer, B. (2014), "Lessons from 'Global Prayers': How Religion Takes Place in the City," in J. Becker, K. Klingan, S. Lanz and K. Wildner (eds), *Global Prayers: Contemporary Manifestations of the Religious in the City*, 590–99, Zürich: Lars Müller Publishers.

Meyer, B. and D. Houtman (2012), "Introduction: Material Religion—How Things Matter," in B. Meyer and D. Houtman (eds), *Things: Religion and the Question of Materiality: Religion and the Question of Materiality*, 1–23, New York: Fordham University Press.

Meyer B. and M. van de Port (2018), *Sense and Essence: Heritage and the Cultural Production of the Real*, Oxford: Berghahn Books.

Meyer, B. and M. de Witte (2013), "Heritage and the Sacred: Introduction," *Material Religion*, 9 (3): 274–80.

Miller, R. and A. Anderson (2003), "Britain," in A. Corten, J. P. Dozon and A. P. Oro (eds), *Les nouveaux conquérants de la foi. L'Eglise universelle du royaume de Dieu*, 151–57, Paris: Karthala.

Miller, D. E. and T. Yamamori, eds (2007), *Global Pentecostalism: The New Face of Christian Social Engagement*, Berkeley: University of California Press.

Moreira, L. V. de C. (forthcoming), "The Secularisation of Demons—Exorcisms by the Universal Church of the Kingdom of God in Madrid," *Journal of Contemporary Religion*, forthcoming in 2019.

Naro, N. P., R. Sansi-Roca and D. H. Treece (2007), *Cultures of the Lusophone Black Atlantic*, Basingstoke and New York: Palgrave Macmillan.

Oliveira Assis, Gláucia and T. Martins (2010a), "As representações sobre os novos imigrantes brasileiros rumo à Europa: gênero, etnicidade e preconceito," Trabalho apresentado na Abant. Porto Seguro. Mimeo.

Oliveira Assis, Gláucia and T. Martins (2010b), "Criminalização das migrações contemporâneas: as brasileiras na mídia europeia no período entre 2003 e 2009," Work presented at the Fazendo Gênero 9, University of Santa Catarina. Mimeo.

Oliveira Assis, G. (2013), "Os Pequenos Pontos de Partida: As Mobilidades Contemporâneas Rumo à Europa nesse Início de Séc. XXI," Paper presented at Anpuh, Universidade do Rio Grande do Norte.

Oosterbaan, M. (2011), "Virtually Global: Online Evangelical Cartography," *Social Anthropology*, 19 (1): 56–73.

Oosterbaan, M.. (2014), "Religious Experiences of Stasis and Mobility in Contemporary Europe: Undocumented Pentecostal Brazilians in Amsterdam and Barcelona," *Social and Cultural Geography* 15 (6): 664–82.

Oosterbaan, M. (2017), *Transmitting the Spirit: Religious Conversion, Media and Urban Violence in Brazil*, University Park: Penn State University Press.

Openshaw, K. (2018), "I am Universal: Transnational Material Networks of Spiritual Capital in the Australian Universal Church of the Kingdom of God," Ph.D. diss., Western Sydney University, Sydney.

Oro, A. P. and D. Rodrigues, eds (2015), *Transnacionalização Religiosa: Religiões em Movimento*, 265–89, Porto Alegre: CirKula.

Padilla, B. (2006), *Brazilian Migration to Portugal: Social Networks and Ethnic Solidarity*, Lisbon: CIES-ISCTE.

Patarra, N. L. (2005), "Migrações internacionais de e para o Brasil contemporâneo: Volumes, fluxos, significados e políticas," *São Paulo em Perspectiva*, 19 (3): 23–33.

Pinxten, R. and L. Dikomitis, eds (2009), *When God Comes to Town: Religious Traditions in Urban Contexts*, Oxford: Berghahn Books.

Pontes, Luciana. (2004), "Mulheres Brasileiras na Mídia Portuguesa," *Cadernos Pagu*, 23 (23): 229–56.

Povoa Neto, Helion. (2007), "Migração na Europa: desafios na Itália e nos países da área Mediterrânea," in O. Da Cruz Paiva (ed.), *Migrações internacionais: desafios para o século XXI*, 51–63, São Paulo: Memorial do Imigrante (Série Reflexões, v. 1).

Premawardhana, D. (2017), "Comments on: From Converts to Itinerants: Religious Butinage as Dynamic Identity," *Current Anthropology*, 58 (2): 153–54.

Premawardhana, D. (2018), "Spirit(s) in Motion: Pentecostalism, Pluralism, and Everyday Life," *PentecoStudies*, 17 (1): 37–53.

Reis Santos, L. (2018), "Ser Universal: crentes engajados e práticas cotidianas na cidade de Maputo," Ph.D. diss., State University of Rio de Janeiro, Rio de Janeiro.

Rial, C. (2012), "The 'Devil's Egg': Football Players as New Missionaries of the Diaspora of Brazilian Religions," in C. Rocha and M. A. Vásquez (eds), *The Diaspora of Brazilian Religions*, 91–115, Leiden: Brill.

Rickli, J. (2016), "Narratives, Movements, Objects," in M. Svasek and B. Meyer (ed.), *Creativity in Transition: Politics and Aesthetics of Cultural Production across the Globe*, 267–89, New York: Berghahn Books.

Robertson, R. (2012), "Globalisation or Glocalisation?," *Journal of International Communication*, 18 (2): 191–20.

Robbins, J. (2004), "The Globalization of Pentecostal and Charismatic Christianity," *Annual Review of Anthropology*, 33: 117–43.

Rocha, C. (2005), *Zen in Brazil: The Quest for Cosmopolitan Modernity*, Honolulu: University of Hawaii Press.

Rocha, C. and M. A. Vásquez, eds (2013), *The Diaspora of Brazilian Religions*, Leiden: Brill.

Roett, R. (2010), *The New Brazil*, Washington: Brookings Institution Press.

Roy, A. and A. Ong, eds (2011), *Worlding Cities: Asian Experiments and the Art of Being Global*, Malden, MA, and Oxford: Wiley-Blackwell.

Sales, T. (1999), *Brasileiros longe de casa*, São Paulo: Cortez Editora.

Sarró, R. and R. Blanes (2009), "Prophetic Diasporas: Moving Religion across the Lusophone Atlantic," *African Diaspora: A Journal of Transnational Africa in a Global World*, 2 (1): 52–72.

Schinkel, W. and L. Noordegraaf-Eelens (2011), "Peter Sloterdijk's Spherological Acrobatics: An Exercise in Introduction," in W. Schinkel and L. Noordegraaf-Eelens (eds), *In Medias Res: Peter Sloterdijk's Spherological Poetics of Being*, 7–28, Amsterdam: Amsterdam University Press.

Sherringham, O. (2013), *Transnational Religious Spaces: Faith and the Brazilian Migration Experience*, Basingstoke: Palgrave Macmillan.

Siqueira, D. (2002), "Novas Religiosidades na Capital do Brasil," *Tempo Social*, 14 (1): 177–97.

Siqueira, D. (2003), "Novas Religiosidades, Estilo de Vida e Sincretismo Brasileiro," in D. Sequeira and R. Barbosa Lima (eds), *Sociologia das Adesões: Novas Religiosidades e a Busca Místico-Esotérica na Capital do Brasil*, 107–69, Goiânia: Editora Vieira.

Siqueira, S. (2014), "Brasileiros em Portugal e a percepção das diferenças culturais e preconceito," Paper presented at the Conference of Portuguese Sociology, University of Évora, April 14.

Sloterdijk, P. (2003), *Sferen*, trans. Hans Driessen, Amsterdam: Boom.

Sloterdijk, P. (2009), *Sferen: Schuim*, trans. Hans Driessen, Amsterdam: Boom.

Smith, M. P. (2005), "Transnational Urbanism Revisited," *Journal of Ethnic and Migration Studies*, 31 (2): 235–44.

Soares, E. (2009), *Le Butinage Religieux: Pratiques et Pratiquants au Brésil*, Paris: Karthala.

Stephens, N. and S. Delamont (2013), "Mora Yemanjá? Axé in Diasporic Capoeira Regional," in C. Rocha and M. Vásquez (eds), *The Diaspora of Brazilian Religions*, 271–88, Leiden: Brill.

Tsing, A. (2000), "The Global Situation," *Cultural Anthropology*, 15 (3): 327–60.

Tweed, T. A. (2006), *Crossing and Dwelling: A Theory of Religion*, Cambridge, MA: Harvard University Press.

Van de Kamp, L. (2016a), *Violent Conversion: Brazilian Pentecostalism and Urban Women in Mozambique*, Woodbridge, UK: James Currey, Religion in Transforming Africa Series.

Van de Kamp, L. (2016b), "Introduction: Religious Circulation in Transatlantic Africa," *African Diaspora*, 9 (1/2): 1–13.

Van de Kamp, L. (2017), "The Transnational Infrastructures of Luso-Pentecostal Mega-Cities," *New Diversities*, 19 (1): 1–17.

Velho, O. (2009) "Missionization in the Postcolonial World: A View from Brazil and Elsewhere," in T. J. Csordas (ed.), *Transnational Transcendence: Essays on Religion and Globalization*, 31–54, Berkeley: University of California Press.

Vries, H. de (2008), "Introduction: Why Still 'Religion'?," in H. de Vries (ed.), *Religion: Beyond a Concept*, 1–99, New York: Fordham University Press.

Wambacq, J. and S. van Tuinen (2017), "Interiority in Sloterdijk and Deleuze," *Palgrave Communications*, 3 (17072): 1–7.

Wimmer, A. and Glick Schiller, N. (2003), "Methodological Nationalism, the Social Sciences, and the Study of Migration: An Essay in Historical Epistemology," *The International Migration Review*, 37 (3): 576–610.

Witte, M. de (2009), "Modes of Binding, Moments of Bonding. Mediating Divine Touch in Ghanaian Pentecostalism and Traditionalism," in B. Meyer (ed.), *Aesthetic Formations: Media, Religion, and the Senses*, 183–205, New York: Pallgrave.

Chapter 2

Ang, I. and J. Stratton (1996), "Asianising Australia: Notes towards a Critical Transnationalism in Cultural Studies," *Cultural Studies Journal*, 10 (1): 16–36.

Antunes, A. (2013), "The Richest Pastors in Brazil," *Forbes*, January 17. Available online: https://www.forbes.com/sites/andersonantunes/2013/01/17/the-richest-pastors-in-brazil/#7b4d762e5b1e (accessed August 15, 2014).

Aparicio, F. and S. Chávez-Silverman (1997), *Tropicalizations Transcultural Representations of Latinidad*, London: University Press of New England.

Appadurai, A. (1996), *Modernity at Large: Cultural Dimensions of Globalization*, Minneapolis: University of Minnesota Press.

Barros, G. (2002), "Tudo funciona em Sydney, até o trânsito," *Folha de São Paulo*, April 1. Available online: http://www1.folha.uol.com.br/fsp/turismo/fx0104200206.htm. (accessed May 1, 2002).

Bourdieu, P. (1984), *Distinction: A Social Critique of the Judgement of Taste*, trans. R. Nice, Cambridge, MA: Harvard University Press.

Bourdieu, P. (1986), "The Forms of Capital," in J. Richards (ed.), *Handbook of Theory and Research in the Sociology of Education*, 241–58, Westport, CT: Greenwood Press.

Boym, S. (2007), "Nostalgia and Its Discontents," *The Hedgehog Review*, 9 (2): 7–18.

Bruner, E. (1989), "Of Cannibals, Tourists, and Ethnographers," *Cultural Anthropology*, 4 (4): 438–45.

Bruner, E. (2005), *Culture on Tour: Ethnographies of Travel*, Chicago: University of Chicago Press.

Chakrabarty, D. (2000), *Provincializing Europe: Postcolonial Thought and Historical Difference*, Princeton, NJ: Princeton University Press.

Connell, J. (2005), "Hillsong: A Megachurch in the Sydney Suburbs," *Australian Geographer*, 36 (3): 315–32.

Conrad, J. (1995 [1899]), *Heart of Darkness*, Ware, UK: Wordsworth Classics.

Cunningham, H. (2004), "Nations Rebound?: Crossing Borders in a Gated Globe," *Identities: Global Studies in Culture and Power*, 11 (3): 329–50.

Freston, P. (2010), "Reverse Mission: A Discourse in Search of Reality?," *PentecoStudies*, 9 (2): 153–74.

García Canclini, N. (1995), *Hybrid Cultures: Strategies for Entering and Leaving Modernity*, trans. C. Chiappari and S. López, Minneapolis: University of Minnesota Press.

Goh, R. (2008), "Hillsong and 'Megachurch' Practice: Semiotics, Spatial Logic and the Embodiment of Contemporary Evangelical Protestantism," *Material Religion*, 4 (3): 284–304.

Hall, S. (1992), "The West and the Rest: Discourse and Power," in S. Hall and B. Gieben (eds), *Formations of Modernity*, Cambridge: Polity Press.

Hearn, A. (2016), *Diaspora and Trust: Cuba, Mexico, and the Rise of China*, Durham, NC: Duke University Press.

Hess, D. and R. DaMatta (1995), *The Brazilian Puzzle: Culture on the Borderlands of the Western World*, New York: Columbia University Press.

Klaver, M. (2015), "Media Technology Creating 'Sermonic Events.' The Hillsong Megachurch Network," *CrossCurrents*, 65 (4): 422–33.

Levitt, P. (2007), *God Needs No Passport*, Boston, MA: The New Press.

Loes, J. and R. Cardoso (2016), "O Declínio da Igreja da Bispa Sônia," *Isto É*, January 21. Available online: https://istoe.com.br/158676_O+DECLINIO+DA+IGREJA+DA+BI SPA+SONIA/ (accessed March 30, 2016).

Massey, D. (1993), "Power-Geometry and a Progressive Sense of Place," in J. Bird et al. (eds), *Mapping the Futures: Local Cultures, Global Change*, 59–69, London and New York: Routledge.

Mosquera, G. (2003), "Alien Own/Own Alien: Notes on Globalization and Cultural Difference," in N. Papastergiadis (ed.), *Complex Entanglements: Art, Globalization and Cultural Difference*, 18–30, London: Rivers Oram.

O'Dougherty, M. (2002), *Consumption Intensified: The Politics of Middle-Class Daily Life in Brazil*, Durham, NC: Duke University Press.

Oliven, R. (2000), "Brazil: The Modern in the Tropics," in V. Schelling (ed.), *Through the Kaleidoscope: The Experience of Modernity in Latin America*, 53–72, London and New York: Verso.

Oro, A. (2014), "South American Evangelicals' Re-Conquest of Europe," *Journal of Contemporary Religion*, 29 (2): 219–32.

Ortiz, Renato (2000), "Popular Culture, Modernity and Nation," in V. Schelling (ed.), *Through the Kaleidoscope: The Experience of Modernity in Latin America*, London and New York: Verso.

Pellegrino-Estrich, R. (2001 [1997]), *The Miracle Man: The Life Story of João de Deus*, Goiânia: Terra.

Prado, L. (2017), "Australia," *Folha Online*, October 31. Available online: http://www1.folha.uol.com.br/folha/turismo/oceania/australia.shtml (accessed October 31, 2017).

Riches, T. and T. Wagner (2017), *The Hillsong Movement Examined: You Call Me Out upon the Waters*, NY: Palgrave Macmillan.

Ricke, A. (2018), "Producing the Middle Class: Domestic Tourism, Ethnic Roots, and Class Routes in Brazil," *The Journal of Latin American and Caribbean Anthropology*, 23 (2): 281–300.

Rocha, C. (2006a), *Zen in Brazil: The Quest for Cosmopolitan Modernity*, Honolulu: Hawaii University Press.

Rocha, C. (2006b), "Two faces of God: Religion and Social Class in the Brazilian Diaspora in Sydney," in P. Patrap Kumar (ed.), *Religious Pluralism in the Diaspora*, 147–60, Leiden: Brill.

Rocha, C. (2009), "Conexiones Sur-Sur: Vivir entre Australia y Brasil," in C. Solé et al. (eds), *Nuevos Retos del Transnacionalismo en el Estudio de las Migraciones*, 113–27, Barcelona: Ministerio de Trabajo e Imigración.

Rocha, C. (2013), "Transnational Pentecostal Connections: An Australian Megachurch and a Brazilian Church in Australia," *Pentecostudies*, 12 (1): 62–82.

Rocha, C. (2014), "Triangular Circulation: Japanese Brazilians on the Move between Japan, Australia and Brazil," *Journal of Intercultural Studies*, 35 (5): 493–512.

Rocha, C. (2017a), *John of God: The Globalization of Brazilian Faith Healing*, New York: Oxford University Press.

Rocha, C. (2017b), "The Come to Brazil Effect: Young Brazilians' Fascination with Hillsong," in T. Riches and T. Wagner (eds), *The Hillsong Movement Examined: You Call Me Out upon the Waters*, 125–41, New York: Palgrave Macmillan.

Rocha, C. (2019), "'God Is in Control': Middle-Class Pentecostalism and International Student Migration," *Journal of Contemporary Religion*, 34 (1): 21–37.

Rocha, C. and M. Vásquez, eds (2013), *The Diaspora of Brazilian Religions*, Leiden: Brill.

Schelling, V. (2000), "Introduction: Reflections on the Experience of Modernity in Latin America," in V. Schelling (ed.), *Through the Kaleidoscope: The Experience of Modernity in Latin America*, 1–33, London and New York: Verso.

Seyferth, G. (1990), *Imigração e Cultura no Brasil*, Brasília: UnB.

Souza Martins, J. (2000), "The Hesitations of the Modern and the Contradictions of Modernity in Brazil," in V. Schelling (ed.), *Through the Kaleidoscope: The Experience of Modernity in Latin America*, 248–73, London and New York: Verso.

Torresan, A. (2012), "A Middle Class Besieged: Brazilians' Motives to Migrate," *The Journal of Latin American and Caribbean Anthropology*, 17 (1): 110–30.

Tsing, A. (2005), *Friction: An Ethnography of Global Connection*, Princeton, NJ: Princeton University Press.

Turner, B. (2007), "The Enclave Society: Towards a Sociology of Immobility," *European Journal of Social Theory*, 10 (2): 287–303.

Tweed, T. (1997), *Our Lady of the Exile: Diasporic Religion at a Cuban Catholic Shrine in Miami*, Oxford: Oxford University Press.

van de Kamp, L. (2016), *Violent Conversion: Brazilian Pentecostalism and Urban Women in Mozambique*, Suffolk, UK: James Currey.

Vásquez, M. and M. F. Marquardt. (2003), *Globalizing the Sacred: Religion across the Americas*, New Brunswick, NJ and London: Rutgers University Press.

Wulfhorst, C. (2011), "Intimate Multiculturalism: Blurring the Boundaries between Brazilians and Australians in Sydney," Ph.D. diss., University of Western Sydney.

Young, R. (1995), *Colonial Desire: Hybridity in Theory, Culture and Race*, London: Routledge.

Zaluar, A. (2014), "Etos Guerreiro e Criminalidade Violenta," in R. Lima et al. (eds), *Crime, Polícia e Justiça no Brasil*, 35–50, São Paulo: Contexto.

Chapter 3

Almeida, R. (2004), "Religião na Metrópole Paulista," *Revista Brasileira de Ciências Sociais*, 19 (56): 15–27.

Bajc, V. (2006), "'Christian Pilgrimage Groups in Jerusalem: Framing the Experiences through Linear Meta-narrative," *Journeys*, 7 (1): 101–28.

Bajc, V. (2007), "Creating Ritual through Narrative, Place, and Performance in Evangelical Protestant Pilgrimage in the Holy Land," *Mobilities*, 2 (3): 395–412.

Birman, P. (2009), "Feitiçarias, Territórios e Resistências Marginais," *Mana*, 15 (2): 321–483.

Birman, P. (2012), "O Poder da Fé, o Milagre do Poder: Mediadores Evangélicos e Deslocamento de Fronteiras Sociais," *Horizontes Antropológicos*, 18 (37): 133–53.

Bowman, G. (1991), "Christian Ideology and the Image of a Holy Land: The Place of Jerusalem Pilgrimage in the Various Christianities," in J. Eade and M. J. Sallnow (eds), *Contesting the Sacred: The Anthropology of the Christian Pilgrimage*, 98–121, Urbana: University of Illinois Press.

Butticci, A. (2016), *African Pentecostals in Catholic Europe: The Politics of Presence in the Twenty-First Century*, Cambridge, MA: Harvard University Press.

Casanova, J. (2013), "Religious Associations, Religious Innovations and Denominational Identities in Contemporary Global Cities," in I. Becci Irene, M. Burchardt and J. Casanova (eds), *Topographies of Faith: Religion in Urban Spaces*, 112–27, New York. Brill.

Chesnut, A. (2007), *Competitive Spirits: Latin America's New Religious Economy*, New York: Oxford University Press.

Coleman, S. (2004), "The Charismatic Gift," *Journal of the Royal Anthropological Institute*, 10 (2): 421–42.

Coleman, S. and J. Eade (2004), "Introduction: Reframing Pilgrimage," in S. Coleman and J. Eade (eds), *Reframing Pilgrimage: Culture in Motion*, 1–25, London and New York: Routledge.

de Abreu, Maria José A. (2015), "Worldings: The Aesthetics of Authority among Catholic Charismatics in Brazil," *Culture and Religion*, Online First. http://dx.doi.org/10.1080/14755610.2015.1058529.

Dulin, J. (2013), "Messianic Judaism as a Mode of Christian Authenticity. Exploring the Grammar of Authenticity through Ethnography of a Contested Identity," *Anthropos*, 108: 35–51.

Dulin, J. (2015), "Reversing Rupture: Evangelical's Practice of Jewish Rituals and Processes of Protestant Inclusion," *Anthropological Quarterly*, 88 (3): 601–346.

Durkheim, É. (2001), *The Elementary Forms of Religious Life*, Oxford and New York: Oxford University Press.

Feldman, J. (2007), "Constructing a Shared Bible Land: Jewish Israeli Guiding Performances for Protestant Pilgrims," *American Ethnologist*, 34 (2): 351–74.

Feldman, J. (2011), "Abraham the Settler, Jesus the Refugee: Contemporary Conflict and Christianity on the Road to Bethlehem," *History and Memory*, 23 (1): 62–95.

Feldman, J. (2014), "Changing Colors of Money: Tips, Commissions and Ritual in Christian Pilgrimage to the Holy Land," *Religion and Society*, 14 (5): 143–56.

Feldman, J. (2016), *A Jewish Guide in the Holy Land: How Christian Pilgrims Made Me Israeli*, Bloomington: University of Indiana Press.

Freston, Paul. (1999). "Neo-Pentecostalism" in Brazil: Problems of Definition and the Struggle for Hegemony. *Archives de sciences sociales des religions*, 44 (105): 145–162

Fry, P. and N. Howe (1975), "Duas respostas à aflição: umbanda e pentecostalismo," *Debate e Crítica*, 6: 75–94.

Giumbelli, E. (2013), "Cultura pública: evangélicos y su presencia en la sociedad brasileña," *Sociedad y Religión*, XXIII (40): 13–43.

Gonçalvez, V. (2007), "Neopentecostalismo e Religiões Afro-Brasileiras: Significados do Ataque aos Símbolos da Herança Religiosa Africana no Brasil Contemporâneo," *Mana*, 13 (1): 207–36.

IMTSS (2013), *Israeli Ministry of Tourism 2013 Statistical Survey* (IMTSS): 1–38.

Instituto Brasileiro de Geografía e Estatistica (IBGE). https://www.ibge.gov.br/. Accessed in 2017.

Jenkins. (2002), *The Next Christendom: The Coming of Global Christianity*, Oxford: Oxford University Press.

Kaell. H. (2014), *Walking Where Jesus Walked: American Christians and Holy Land Pilgrimage*, London and New York: NYU Press.

Kaell, H. (2016), "Can Pilgrimage Fail? Intent, Efficacy, and Evangelical Trips to the Holy Land," *Journal of Contemporary Religion*, 31 (3): 393–408.

Kramer, E. (2002), "Making Global Faith Universal: Media and a Brazilian Prosperity Movement," *Culture and Religion*, 3 (1): 21–47.

Kramer, E. (2005), "Spectacle and the Staging of Power in Brazilian Neo-Pentecostalism," *Latin American Perspectives*, 32 (1): 95–120.

Leite, N. (2017), *Unorthodox Kin: Portuguese Marranos and the Global Search for Belonging*, Berkeley: University of California Press.

Mafra, C. (2001), *Os Evangélicos*, Rio de Janeiro: Jorge Zahar.

Mariano, R. (2004), "Expansão Pentecostal no Brasil: O caso da Igreja Universal," *Estudos Avançados*, 18 (52): 121–38.

Mariz, C. L. (2009), "Missão religiosa e migração: "novas comunidades" e igrejas pentecostais brasileiras no exterior," *Análise Social*, 44 (190): 161–87.

Mapril, J. and R. Blanes (2013), "Introduction," in J. Mapril and R. L. Blanes (eds), *Sites and Politics of Religious Diversity in Southern Europe: The Best of All Gods*, 1–15, Leiden: Brill.

Maués, R. H. (2013), "A Mãe e o Filho Como Peregrinos: Dois Modelos de Peregrinação Católica no Brasil," *Religião e Sociedade*, 33 (2): 121–40.

Meyer, Birgit. (2015), "How to Capture the 'Wow': R.R. Marett's Notion of Awe and the Study of Religion," *Journal of the Royal Anthropological Institute* (N.S.) (22): 7–26.

Oosterbaan, M. (2011), "Virtually Global: Online Evangelical Cartography," *Social Anthropology/Anthropologie Sociale*, 19 (1): 56–73.

Oro, A. P. (2005), "O 'Pentecostelismo Macumbeiro," *Revista USP*, 68: 319–32.

Pype, K., S. van Wolputte and A. Mélice (2012), "The Interdependence of Mobility and Faith: An Introduction," *Canadian Journal of African Studies/La Revue canadienne des études africaines*, 46 (3): 355–65.

Reinhardt, B. (2007), *Espelho ante Espelho: A troca e a Guerra entre o Neopentecostalismo e os Cultos Afro-Brasileiros em Salvador*, São Paulo: Attar.

Robbins, J. (2004), "The Globalization of Pentecostal and Charismatic Christianity," *Annual Review of Anthropology*, 33 (1): 117–43.

Rocha, C. and M. Vásquez (2014), "O Brasil na Nova Cartografia Global da Religião," *Religião e Sociedade*, 34 (1): 13–37.

Rodrigues, D. (2014), "Ethnic and Religious Diversities in Portugal: The Case of Brazilian Evangelical Immigrants," in H. Vilaça, E. Pace, I. Furseth and P. Pettersson (eds), *The Changing Soul of Europe: Religions and Migrations in Northern and Southern Europe*, 133–47, London and New York: Routledge.

Ron, A. (2009), "Towards a Typological Model of Contemporary Christian Travel," *Journal of Heritage Tourism*, 4 (4): 287–97.

Sansi-Roca, R. (2007), "The Fetish in the Lusophone Atlantic," in R. Sansi-Roca, N. Priscilla-Haro and D. Treece (eds), *Cultures of the Lusophone Black Atlantic*, 19–40, London: Palgrave Macmillan.

Sarró, Ramon and Ruy Blanes. (2009), "Prophetic Diasporas: Moving Religion Across the Lusophone Atlantic," *African Diaspora* 2: 52–72.

Selka, S. (2010), "Morality in the Religious Marketplace: Evangelical Christianity, Candomblé, and the Struggle for Moral Distinction in Brazil," *American Ethnologist*, 37 (2): 291–307.

Shapiro, F. (2011), "The Messiah and Rabbi Jesus: Policing the Jewish–Christian border in Christian Zionism," *Culture and Religion*, 12 (4): 463–77.

Shapiro, M. (2015), "Curving the Social, or, Why Antagonistic Rituals in Brazil Are Variations on a Theme," *Journal of Royal Anthropological Institute*, 22 (1): 47–66.

Shapiro, M. (forthcoming), "Brajisalem: Biblical Cosmology, Power Dynamics and the Brazilian Political Imagination," *Ethnos*, forthcoming in 2019.

Swatowiski, C. (2010). "Igreja Universal em Portugal: tentativas de superação de um estigma," *Intratextos*, 1: 169–92.

Topel, M. (2011), "A Inusitada Incorporação do Judaísmo em Vertentes Cristãs Brasileiras: Algumas Reflexões," *Revista Brasileira de História das Religiões*, IV (10): 35–50.

Turner, V. and E. Turner (1978), *Image and Pilgrimage in Christian Culture*, New York: Columbia University Press.

Vásquez, M. (2011), *More than Belief: A Materialist Theory of Religion*, Oxford: University Press.

von Sinner, Rudolf. (2012), "Pentecostalism and Citizenship in Brazil: Between Escapism and Dominance," *International Journal of Public Theology*, 6 (2012): 99–117.

Chapter 4

Africa Progress Panel (2013), *Africa Progress Report 2013*, Geneva: Africa Progress Panel. Available online: https://www.letemps.ch/sites/default/files/media/2013/05/16/2.1.1323106478.pdf (accessed December 14, 2018).

Almeida, R. (2000), "Religião na metrópole paulista," *Revista Brasileira de Ciências Sociais*, 19 (56): 15–27.

Almeida, R. (2009), *A Igreja Universal e seus demônios: um estudo etnográfico*, São Paulo: Terceiro Nome.

Anderson, B. (1983), *Imagined Communities: Reflections on the Origin and Spread of Nationalism*, London: Verso.

Barbosa, C. A. (2017), "Jerusalém é aqui! Espaços de disputa e jogo de poder: O Templo de Salomão da IURD," Ph.D. diss., Pontifícia Universidade Católica de São Paulo, São Paulo.

Birman, P. (2003), "Imagens religiosas e projetos para o futuro," in P. Birman (ed.), *Religião e Espaço Público*, São Paulo: Attar.

Birman, P. (2006), "Future in the Mirror: Media, Evangelicals, and Politics in Rio de Janeiro," in B. Meyer and A. Moors (eds), *Religion, Media and Public Sphere*, 52–72, Indianapolis: Indiana University Press.

Blanes, R. L. (2014), *A Prophetic Trajectory: Ideologies of Place, Time and Belonging in an Angolan Religious Movement*, New York: Berghahn Books.

Campos, L. (1997), *Teatro, templo e mercado*, Petrópolis: Vozes.

Comaroff, J. and J. Comaroff (2001), "Millennial Capitalism: First Thoughts on a Second Coming," in J. Comaroff and J. Comaroff (eds), *Millenial Capitalism and the Culture of Neoliberalism*, 1–56, Durham, NC: Duke University Press.

Contins, M. and E. C. Gomes (2007), "Os percursos da fé: uma análise comparativa sobre as apropriações religiosas do espaço urbano entre carismáticos e neopentecostais," *Ponto Urbe: Revista do núcleo de antropologia urbana da USP*, 1: 1–17.

Contins, M. and E. C. Gomes (2008), "Edificações religiosas e autenticidade: Comparando a IURD e os carismáticos católicos," *Revista Anthropológicas*, 19 (1): 169–99.

Fonseca, A. (2003), "Fé na tela: características e ênfases de duas estratégias evangélicas na televisão," *Religião & Sociedade*, 23 (2): 33–52.

Freston, P. (2001), "The Transnationalisation of Brazilian Pentecostalism. The Universal Church of the Kingdom of God," in A. Corten and R. Marshall-Fratani (eds), *Betweeen Babel and Pentecostalism. Transnational Pentecostalism in Africa and Latin America*, 196–215, London: Hurst & Company.

Freston, P. (2005), "The Universal Church of the Kingdom of God: A Brazilian Church Finds Success in Southern Africa," *Journal of Religion in Africa*, 35 (1): 33–65.

Gomes, E. (2011), *A era das catedrais: a autenticidade em exibição*, Rio de Janeiro: Garamond.

Gonçalves, J. R. (1988), "Autenticidade, memória e ideologias nacionais: o problema dos patrimônios culturais," *Revista Estudos Históricos*, 1 (2): 264–75.

Halbwachs, M. (1971), "La topographie légendaire des évangiles en terre sainte," in *The conclusion to La topographie is translated in On Collective Memory*, Paris: Presses Universitaires de France.

INE (2016), *Resultados definitivos. Recenseamento geral da população e habitação 2014*, Luanda: Instituto Nacional de Estatística de Angola.

Kramer, E. (2001), "Possessing Faith. Commodification, Religious Subjectivity, and Collectivity in a Brazilian Neo-Pentecostal Church," Ph.D. diss., University of Chicago, Chicago.

Levi-Strauss, C. (1963), "The Effectiveness of Symbols," in *Structural Anthropology*, New York: Basic Books.

Macedo, E. (2014), *Nada a perder*, Livro 1, São Paulo: Plana.

Mafra, C. (2002), *Na posse da palavra. Religião, conversão e liberdade pessoal em dois contextos nacionais*, Lisboa: Imprensa de Ciências Sociais.

Mafra, C. (2011), "A 'arma da cultura' e os 'universalismos parciais'," *Mana*, 17 (3): 607–24.

Mafra, C. and C. Swatowiski (2008), "O balão e a catedral: trabalho, lazer e religião na paisagem carioca," *Antropológicas*, 19 (1): 141–67.

Mafra, C., C. Swatowiski and C. Sampaio (2013), "Edir Macedo's Pastoral Project: A Globally Integrated Pentecostal Network," in C. Rocha and M. Vasquez (eds), *The Diaspora of Brazilian Religions*, 45–68, Leiden and Boston: Brill.

Messiant, C. (2008), *L'Angola postcolonial: Guerre et paix sans démocratisation*, vol. 1, Paris: Karthala.

Oosterbaan, M. (2011), "Virtually Global: Online Evangelical Cartography," *Social Anthropology*, 19 (1): 56–73.

Oro, A. P., A. Corten, J. Dozon, eds (2003), *A Igreja Universal do Reino de Deus: os novos conquistadores da fé*, São Paulo: Paulinas.

Oro, A. P. and M. T. Batista (2015), "A Igreja Universal do Reino de Deus e a reconfiguração do espaço público religioso brasileiro," *Ciencias Sociales y Religión*, 17 (23): 76–113.

Rickli, J. (2016), "Narratives, Movements, Objects," in M. Svasek and B. Meyer (eds), *Creativity in Transition: Politics and Aesthetics of Cultural Production across the Globe*, 267–89, New York: Berghahn Books.

Sarró, R. (2018), "Religious Pluralism and the Limits of Ecumenism in Mbanza Kongo, Angola," *Journal of Southern African Studies*, 44 (2): 239–51.

Schubert, B. (2000), *A Guerra e as Igrejas: Angola, 1961–1991*, Basel: Schlettwein Publishing.

Swatowiski, C. (2006), "Igreja Universal na 'Capital Nacional do Petróleo': considerações sobre as dinâmicas da comunicação de massa 'a serviço de Deus'," MA diss., Universidade do Estado do Rio de Janeiro, Rio de Janeiro.

Swatowiski, C. (2007), "Texto e contextos da fé: o discurso mediado de Edir Macedo," *Religião & Sociedade*, 27 (1): 114–31.

Swatowiski, C. (2013), *Novos cristãos em Lisboa: reconhecendo estigmas, negociando estereótipos*, Rio de Janeiro: Garamond.

Swatowiski, C. (2015), "Igreja Universal do Reino de Deus em Luanda," in I. C. Silva, S. Frangella, S. Aboim and S. Viegas (eds), *Ciências sociais cruzadas entre Portugal e o Brasil. Trajectos e investigações no ICS*, Lisboa: ICS. Imprensa de Ciências Sociais.

van de Kamp, L. (2016), *Violent Conversion: Brazilian Pentecostalism and Urban Women in Mozambique*, Woodbridge, UK: James Currey.

van Wyk, I. (2014), *The Universal Church of the Kingdom of God in South Africa: A Church of Strangers*, Cambridge, UK: Cambridge University Press.

Viegas, F. (1988), *Panorama Religioso em Angola: dados estatísticos (1987–1997)*, Luanda: Edição da autora.

Viegas, F., V. Bernardo and I. Marques (2008), *Panorâmica das religiões em Angola independente (1975–2008)*, Luanda: Instituto Nacional Para os Assuntos Religiosos.

Chapter 5

Alonso, A. (1997), *Iglesia e politica en Cuba revolucionaria*, La Havana: Editorial de Ciencias Sociales.

Arendt, H. (2010), *A condição humana*, Rio de Janeiro: Forense Universitária.

Butler, J. (2015), *Relatar a si mesmo*, São Paulo, etc.: Grupo Autêntica.

Butler, J. (2016), *Quadros de guerra: quando a vida é passível de luto?* Rio de Janeiro: Civilização Brasileira.

Calzadilla J. R. (2000), *Religión y relaciones sociales*, Havana: Editorial Academia.

Calzadilla J. R. (2004), "Laicismo y liberdad de religión em Cuba," *Primera Quincena*, 17, September.

Cefaï, D. (2002), "¿Qué es una arena pública? Algunas pautas para un acercamiento pragmático," in D. Cefaï and I. Joseph (eds), *La herencia del pragmatismo. Conflictos de urbanidad y pruebas de civismo*, La Tour d'Aigues: Editions de l'Aube.

Cefaï, D. (2009), "Como nos mobilizamos? A contribuição de uma abordagem pragmatista para a sociologia da ação coletiva," *Dilemas-Revista de Estudos de Conflito e Controle Social*, 2 (4): 11–48.

Cefaï, D. (2017), "Públicos, problemas públicos, arenas públicas … : O que nos ensina o pragmatismo (Parte 1)," *Novos Estudos*, 36 (1): 187–213.

Hymes, D. (1974), *Foundations in Sociolinguistics: An Ethnographic Approach*, New Jersey: University of Pennsylvania Press.

Kiesling, S. F. and C. B. Paulston, eds (2008), *Intercultural Discourse and Communication: The Essential Readings*, Malden etc.: Blackwell.

La Foutain-Stoke, L. (1999), "1898 and the History of a Queer Puerto Rican Century: Gay Lives, Island Debates, and Diasporic Experience," *Centro Journal*, 11 (1): 91–109.

Massón, C. (2006), *La revolución cubana en la vida de pastores y creyentes evangélicos*, La Habana: Ediciones La Memoria.

Montero, P. (2006), "Índios e missionários no Brasil: para uma teoria da mediação cultural," in P. Montero (ed.), *Deus na aldeia: missionários, índios e mediação cultural*, 31–66, São Paulo: Editora Globo.

Perez, L. F. (2012), "Acreditar em acreditar com Gianni Vattimo," *Numen. Revista de Estudos e Pesquisa da Religião*, Juiz de Fora, 15 (1), 187–215.

Searle, J. R. (1969), *Speech Acts: An Essay in the Philosophy of Language*, Cambridge: Cambridge University Press.

Silva, A. L. (2016), "Uma igreja em marcha. Relato etnográfico da participação da ICM na 20ª Parada do Orgulho LGBT de São Paulo," *Ponto Urbe—Revista do núcleo de antropologia urbana da USP*, 19, doi: 10.4000/pontourbe.3314.

Silva, A. L. (2017), "Ser ou não ser em nome de Deus—Notas sobre um missão LGBTI em Uganda," *Revista Geral do Arquivo do RJ* (12): 201–27. http://wpro.rio.rj.gov.br/revistaagcrj/wp-content/uploads/2017/08/12_Dossi%C3%AA-2_Artigo-4.pdf.

Silva, A. L., P. Montero and L. Sales (2018), "Fazer Religião em Público: encenações religiosas e influência pública," *Horizontes Antropológicos*, forthcoming in 2019.

Vattimo, G. and E. C. Neves (1998), *Acreditar em acreditar*, Lisbon: Relógio d'Água.

Chapter 6

Bahia, J. (2015a), "A descoberta de Putamagal pelo caboclo Pena Dourada," in A. P. Oro and D. Rodrigues (eds), *Transnacionalização Religiosa: religiões em movimento*, 265–89, Porto Alegre: CirKula.

Bahia, J. (2015b) "Exu na mouraria: a transnacionalização das religiões afro-brasileiras e suas adaptações, trocas e proximidades com o contexto português," *Revista Eletrônica Métis. História e Cultura.*UCS, 14 (28): 111–31.

Barth, F. (1976), *Los grupos étnicos e sus fronteras. La organización social e sus diferencias culturales*, México: Fondo de Cultura Económica.

Chesnut, A. (1997), *Born Again in Brazil: The Pentecostal Boom and the Pathogens of Poverty*, New Brunswick, NJ: Rutgers University Press.

Deleuze, G. and F. Guattari (2004), *A Thousand Plateaus*, trans. Brian Massumi, London: Continuum.

Freston, P. (1993), "Protestantes e política no Brasil: da Constituinte ao impeachment," Ph.D. diss., Universidade Estadual de Campinas, Instituto de Filosofia e Ciências Humanas, Campinas.

Galbraith, J. (1986), *Anatomia do poder*, trans. Hilário Torloni, São Paulo: Pioneira.

Geertz, C. (1978), *A interpretação das culturas*, Rio de Janeiro: Zahar Editora.

Gouveia, E. H. (1998), "Imagens femininas: a reengenharia do feminino pentecostal na televisão," Ph.D. diss., Programa de Pós Graduação em Ciências da Religião da Pontifícia Universidade Católica, São Paulo.

Halbwachs, M. (1990), *A memória coletiva*, São Paulo: Vértice.

Leach, E. R. (1990), *Cultura e comunicação*, Lisbon: Ed. 70.

Machado, I. (2006), "Estereótipos e encarceramento simbólico no cotidiano de imigrantes brasileiros no Porto," in I. J. R. Machado (ed.), *Um mar de identidades: a imigração brasileira em Portugal*, São Carlos: EduFSCar.

Machado, M. das D. C. (1996), *Os efeitos da adesão religiosa na esfera familiar*, São Paulo: ANPOCS.

Machado, M. das D. C. (2003), "Neopentecostalismo: continuidades e descontinuidades nas representações e relações de poder entre os gêneros," *Caminhos*, 1 (2): 67–82.

Machado, M. das D. C. and C. Mariz (1997), "Mulheres e prática religiosa nas classes populares: uma comparação entre as igrejas pentecostais, as Comunidades Eclesiais de Base e os grupos carismáticos," *Revista Brasileira de Ciências Sociais*, 12 (34): 71–87.

Mariz, C. (1996), "Libertação e ética: uma análise do discurso dos pentecostais que se recuperam do alcoolismo," in A. Antoniazzi, C. Mariz, I. Sarti, J. Bittencourt Filho, P. Sanchis, P. Freston, R. Valle, R. C. Fernandes and W. Gomes (eds), *Nem Anjos Nem Demônios: Interpretações Sociológicas do Pentecostalismo*, 204–24, Petrópolis, RJ: Vozes.

Pais, J. Machado (2010), "'Mães de Bragança' e feitiços: enredos luso-brasileiros em torno da sexualidade," *Revista de Ciências Sociais*, 41 (2): 9–23.

Pais, J. Machado (2016), *Enredos sexuais, tradição e mudança: as mães, os zecas e as sedutoras de além-mar*, Lisbon: Imprensa de Ciências Sociais (ICS).

Pontes, L. P. (2006), "Mulheres imigrantes brasileiras em Lisboa," in I. J. R. Machado (ed.), *Um mar de identidades: a imigração brasileira em Portugal*, São Carlos: EduFSCar.

SALEM, Tânia. (1981), "Mulheres faveladas: com a venda nos olhos," in B. Franchetto, M. L. V. C. Cavalcanti, M. L. Heilborn and T. Salem (eds), *Perspectivas Antropológicas da Mulher 1*, 49–99, Rio de Janeiro: Zahar. Perspectivas antropológicas da mulher, 1. Rio de janeiro, Zahar.

Sloterdijk, P. (2011), *Spheres I: Bubbles*, trans. Wieland Hoban, Los Angeles, CA: Semiotext(e).

Téchio, K. (2006), "Pizza sabor identidade: brasileiros evangélicos em um restaurante na Costa da Caparica," in I. J. R. Machado (ed.), *Um mar de identidades: a imigração brasileira em Portugal*, paginas, São Carlos: EduFSCar.

Téchio, K. (2011), "Transformando a água em sangue: uma análise sobre a exportação evangélica brasileira através das performances da IPDA," PhD diss., Universidade Nova de Lisboa, Lisbon. Available online: https://run.unl.pt/.

Chapter 7

Agustín, L. (2005), "La industria del sexo, los migrantes y la familia europea," *Cadernos Pagu*, 25: 7–128.

Augras, M. (2009), *Imaginário da Magia: magia do imaginário*, Petrópolis: Vozes.

Bahia, J. (2015), "A descoberta de Putamagal pelo caboclo Pena Dourada," in A. P. Oro and D. Rodrigues (eds), *Transnacionalização Religiosa: religiões em movimento*, 265–89, Porto Alegre: CirKula.

Benedetti, Marcos Renato. (2005), *Toda feita: o corpo e o gênero das travesties*. Rio de Janeiro: Garamond.

Bethencourt, F. (2004), *O Imaginário da Magia: feiticeiras, adivinhos e curandeiros em Portugal no século XVI*, São Paulo: Companhia das Letras.

Contins, M. (1983), "O Caso da pombagira: reflexões sobre crime, possessão e imagem feminina," MA diss., Federal University of Rio de Janeiro, Rio de Janeiro.

de Barros, M. L. (2013), "'Os deuses não ficarão escandalizados': ascendências e reminiscências de femininos subversivos no sagrado," *Estudos Feministas*, 21 (2): 509–34.

de Mello e Souza, Laura (1986), *O Diabo e a terra de Santa Cruz. Feitiçaria e religiosidade popular no Brasil colonial*, São Paulo: Companhia das Letras.

Espírito Santo, M. (1988), *Origens Orientais da Religião Popular Portuguesa*, Lisboa: Assírio e Alvim.

Espírito Santo, M. (1993), *Origens do Cristianismo Português: precedido de "A Deusa Síria, de Luciano de Samoçata"*, Lisbon: Universidade Nova de Lisboa.

Feldman-Bianco, B. (2010), "Brasileiros em Lisboa, portugueses em São Paulo. Construções do mesmo e do outro," in B. Feldman-Bianco (ed.), *Nações e Diásporas: estudos comparativos entre Brasil e Portugal*, 57–105, Campinas: Unicamp.

Hayes, K. (2011), *Feminity, Sexuality and Black Magic in Brazil*, Califórnia: University of California Press.

Kulick, D. (2008), *Travesti: prostituição, sexo, gênero e cultura no Brasil*, Rio de Janeiro: Fiocruz.

Lambek, M. (2014), "Afterworld: Recognizing and Misrecognizing Spirit Possession," in P. Johnson (ed.), *Spirited Things: The Work of Possession in Afro Atlantic Religions*, Londres: University of Chicago Press.

Latour, B. (2005) *Reassembling the Social: An Introduction to Actor-Network Theory*, Oxford: Oxford University Press.

Machado, I. J. (2009), *Cárcere Público: processo de exotização entre imigrantes brasileiros no Porto, Brasil*, Lisboa: Imprensa de Ciências Sociais.

Mafra, C. (2002), *Na Posse da Palavra*, Lisbon: Imprensa de Ciências Sociais.

Mcclintock, A. (1995), *Introduction in Imperial Leather: Race, Gender and Sexuality in the Colonial Context*, Londres: Routledge.

Mcclintock, A. (2003), "Couro imperial: raça, travestismo e o culto da domesticidade," *Cadernos Pagu*, 20: 7–85.

Meyer, M. (1993), *Maria Padilha e Toda a Sua Quadrilha: de amante de um rei de Castela a pomba-gira de umbanda*, São Paulo: Duas Cidades.

Pelúcio, L. (2009), *Abjeção e Desejo: uma etnografia travesti sobre o modelo preventivo de Aids*, São Paulo: Annablume/Fapesp.

Pelúcio, L. (2010), "Exótica, erótica e travesti: nacionalidade e corporalidade no jogo das identidades no mercado transnacional do sexo," in A. L. Castro (ed.), *Cultura Contemporânea, Identidades e Sociabilidades: olhares sobre corpo, mídia e tecnologia*, São Paulo: Cultura Acadêmica.

Perlongher, N. (2008), *O Negócio do Michê: prostituição viril em São Paulo*, São Paulo: Perseu Abramo.

Piscitelli, A. (2008), "Interseccionalidades, categorias de articulação e experiências de migrantes brasileiras," *Sociedade E Cultura*, 11 (2): 263–274.

Piscitelli, A., G. de O. Assis, J. M. N. Olivar (2011), "Introdução: transitando além de fronteiras," in A. Piscitelli, G. de O. Assis and J. M. N. Olivar (eds), *Gênero, Sexo, Afetos e Dinheiro: mobilidades transnacionais envolvendo o Brasil*, 5–30, Campinas: Unicamp/Pagu,Coleção Encontros.

Qualls-Corbett, N. (2005), *A Prostituta Sagrada: a face eterna do feminino*, trans. I. F. Leal Ferreira, São Paulo: Paulus.

Ribeiro, G. S. (2010), "Portugueses do Brasil e no Brasil: laços de irmandade e conflitos identitários em dois atos (1822 e 1890)," in B. Feldman- Bianco (ed.), *Nações e Diásporas: estudos comparativos entre Brasil e Portugal*, 27–55, Campinas: Unicamp.

Stoller, A. (2002), *Carnal Knowledge and Imperial Power: Race and the Intimate in Colonial Rule*. Berkeley and Los Angeles: University of California Press

Vartabedian, J. (2018), *Brazilian Travesti Migrations. Gender, Sexualities and Embodiment Experiences*, London: Palgrave Macmillan.

Chapter 8

Appadurai, A. (1996), *Modernity at Large: Cultural Dimensions of Globalization*, Minneapolis, London: Minnesota Press.

Brettel, C. (2003), *Anthropology and Migration: Essays on Transnationalism, Ethnicity and Identity*, US: Altamira Press.

Carranza, B. (2011), *Catolicismo Midiático*, Aparecida, São Paulo: Ed. Idéias e Letras.

Carranza, B. and C. Mariz (2013), "Catholicism for Export: The Case of Canção Nova," in C. Rocha and M. Vásquez (eds), The Diaspora of Brazilian Religions, 137–62, Leiden: Brill.

Centraal Bureau voor de Statistiek (2014), http://statline.cbs.nl/Startweb/publication. Accessed on December 19, 2014.

de Almeida, L. P. (2008), *Para além das nossas fronteiras: mulheres brasileiras imigrantes na Holanda*, São Paulo: Ed. Unesp.

de Hart, J. (2013), "Samenleven in meervoud: Nederlanders over een 'nieuw wij'," in M. Kalsky (ed.), *Alsof ik thuis ben – Samenleven in een land vol verschillen*, 33–49, Almere: Uitgeverij Parthenon.

de Theije, M. E. M. (2011), "Local Protest and Transnational Catholicism in Brazil," in T. Salman and M. E. M. de Theije, *The Globalization of Local Conflicts and the Localization of Global Interests: Local Battels, Global Stakes*, 61–78, Amsterdam: VU University Press.

Duyvendak, J. W. (2011), *The Politics of Home: Belonging and Nostalgia in Western Europe and the United States*, UK: Palgrave Macmillan.

Euser, H., K. Goosen, M. De Vries and S. Wartena (2006), *Migranten in Mokum: De betekenis van migrantenkerken voor de stad Amsterdam*, Amsterdam: Vrije Universiteit Drukkerij.

Freston, P. (2010), "Reverse Mission: A Discourse in Search of Reality?" *Pentecostudies*, 9 (2): 153–74.

Glick-Shiller, N. and G. E. Fouron (2001), *Georges Woke Up Laughing: Long-Distance Nationalism & the Search for Home*, Durham, London: Duke University Press.

Godoy, A. (2017), "O papa é o melhor prefeito que a cidade já teve: uma etnografia da paisagem urbana na capital da fé," *Religião e Sociedade*, 37 (2): 38–63.

Harvey, D. (1973), *Social Justice and the City*, Baltimore, Maryland: The Johns Hopkins University Press.

Kalsky, M ed. (2013), *Alsof if thuis ben – Samenleven in een land vol verschillen*, Almere: Uitgeverij Parthenon.

Koning, D. (2011), "Importing God: The Mission of the Ghanian Adventist Church and Other Immigrants Churches in the Netherlands," Amsterdam, Ph.D. diss., Vrije Universiteit Amsterdam.

Levitt, P. (2001), *The Transnational Villagers*, California: University of California Press.

Mareels, E. (2016), *Migration et pentecôtisme brésiliens entre le Brésil et la Belgique Une analyse à partir des enjeux du relationnement*. Doctoral Dissertation, Belgium: Louvain-Neuve University.

Margolis, M. L (1994), *Little Brazil: An Ethnography of Brazilian Immigrants in New York City*, Princeton, New Jersey: Princeton University Press.

Mariz, C. L. (2006), "Catolicismo contemporâneo no Brasil: reavivamentos e diversidade," in F. Teixeira and R. Menezes (eds), *As religiões no Brasil*, 53–68, Petrópolis, Rio de Janeiro: Ed. Vozes.

Martins, A. D. (2012), "Relocalização da religião em contexto transnacional: o caso da igreja católica de língua portuguesa em Haia, Holanda," in A. Oro and C. Steil and J. Rickli João (eds), *Transnationalização da religião: fluxos e redes*, 145–56, São Paulo: Ed. Terceiro Nome.

Miranda, M. E. (2009), "Brazilian Migrants in the Netherlands," MSc diss., International School for Humanities and Social Sciences, University of Amsterdam, Amsterdam.

Oosterbaan, M. (2010), "Virtual Re-Evangelization: Brazilian Churches, Media and the Post-Secular City," in A. L. Molendijk and J. Beaumont and J. Christoph (eds), Exploring the Postsecular: The Religious, The Political and the Urban, *International Studies in Religion and Society* (13): 281–310.

Piscitelli, A. (2007), "Sexo tropical em um país europeu: migração de brasileiras para a Itália no marco do 'turismo sexual' internacional," *Estudos Feministas*, 15 (3): 717–44.

Reesink, M. (2013), Minha Língua, Minha Igreja: comunidades católicas de língua portuguesa e imigrantes oriundos dos PALOP na Holanda, Recife: seminar paper.

Reis, R. and T. Sales, eds (1999), *Cenas do Brasil Migrante*, São Paulo: Boitempo Editorial.

Ribeiro, G. L. (1999), "O que faz o Brasil, Brazil: jogos identitários em São Francisco," in R. Reis and T. Sales (eds), *Cenas do Brasil Migrante*, 45–85, São Paulo: Boitempo Editorial.

Rosa, R. de M. (2000), "Vivendo um conto de fadas: o imaginário de gênero entre cariocas e estrangeiros," in M. Goldenberg (ed.), *Os novos desejos – seis visões sobre mudanças de comportamento de homens e mulheres na cultura brasileira contemporânea*, 147–83, São Paulo: Editora Record.

Salman, T. and M. E. M. de Theije (2011), "Introduction," in *The Globalization of Local Conflicts and the Localization of Global Interests: Local Battles, Global Stakes*, 7–17, Amsterdam: VU University Press.

Sheringham, O. (2010) "A Transnational Space? Transnational Practices, Place-Based Identity and the Making of 'Home' among Brazilians in Gort, Ireland," *Portuguese Studies*, 26 (1): 60–78.

Sheringham, O. (2013), *Transnational Religious Space: Faith and the Brazilian Migration Experience*, Oxford, UK: Palgrave Macmillan.

Theije, M. E. M. de (1999), *All That Is God's Is Good: An Anthropology of Liberationist Catholicism in Garanhuns, Brazil*, Maastricht: Shaker Publishing.

van de Kamp, L. (2016), *Violent Conversion: Brazilian Pentecostalism and Urban Women in Mozambique*, Woodbridge, UK: James Currey.

Vásquez, M. A and J. C. S. Alves (2013), "The Valley of Dawn in Atlanta, Georgia: Negotiating Incorporation and Gender Identity in the Diaspora," in C. Rocha and M. A. Vásquez, 313–73, *The Diaspora of Brazilian Religions*, Leiden-Boston: Brill.

Vásquez, M. A and M. F. Marquardt (2003), *Globalizing the Sacred: Religion across the Americas*, New Brunswick, New Jersey and London: Rutgers University Press.

Wetenschappelijke Raad voor het Regeringsbeleid (2007), *Identificatie met Nederland*, Amsterdam: Amsterdam University Press, WRR.

Chapter 9

D'Andrea, A. A. F. (1996), "O Self Perfeito e a Nova Era: Individualismo e Reflexividade em Religiosidades Pós-Tradicionais," MA diss., Instituto Universitário de Pesquisas do Rio de Janeiro, Rio de Janeiro.

Deleuze, G. and F. Guattari (1987), *A Thousand Plateaus: Capitalism and Schizophrenia*, Minneapolis: University of Minnesota Press.

Deleuze, G. (1997), *Essays Critical and Clinical*, Minneapolis: University of Minnesota Press.

Elias, N. (1994), *The Civilizing Process*, Oxford: Blackwell.

Elias, N. (2001), *A sociedade de corte: investigação sobre a sociologia da realeza e da aristocracia de corte*, Rio de Janeiro: Jorge Zahar.

Foucault, M. (1979), *Microfisica do poder*, Rio de Janeiro: Graal.

Greganich, J. (2010), "'Entre a Rosa e o Beija-Flor': Um estudo antropológico de trajetórias na União do Vegetal (UDV) e no Santo Daime," MA diss., Federal University of Rio Grande do Sul (UFRGS), Porto Alegre.

Groisman, A. (1999), *Eu venho da floresta: um estudo sobre o contexto simbólico do uso do Santo Daime*, Florianópolis, SC: Editora UFSC.

Groisman, A. (2013), "Transcultural Keys: Humor, Creativity, and Other Relational Artefacts in the Transposition of a Brazilian Ayahuasca Religion to the Netherlands," in C. Rocha and M. A. Vásquez (eds), *The Diaspora of Brazilian Religions*, 363–86, Leiden: Brill.

Hervieu-Leger, D. (1999), *Le pèlerin et le converti: la religion en movement*, Paris: Flammarion.

Kaufman, R. L. (2015), How might the ayahuasca experience be a potential antidote to Western hegemony: A mixed methods study. (Unpublished doctoral thesis). PhD thesis in Education. Fielding Graduate University. Santa Barbara, California. USA.

Labate, B. C. (2004), *A reinvenção do uso da ayahuasca nos centros urbanos*, Campinas: Mercado das Letras.

Labate, B. C., M. Meyer and B. Anderson (2009), Short Glossary of the Terms Used in the União do Vegetal, https://erowid.org/chemicals/ayahuasca/ayahuasca_info12.shtml, accessed July 30, 2009.

Labate, B. C. and K. Feeney (2012), "Ayahuasca and the Process of Regulation in Brazil and Internationally: Implications and Challenges," *International Journal of Drug Policy*, 23 (2): 154–61.

Léger, D. and B. Hervieu (1983), *Des communautés pour lês temps difficiles: neo-ruraux ou nouveaux moines*, Paris: Editions du Centurion.

Ortner, S. (2007), "Poder e Projeto: Reflexões sobre agência," in M. P. Grossi, M. Pillar, C. Eckert and P. Fry (eds), *Conferências e Diálogos: Saberes e Práticas Antropológicas*, 45–80, Blumenau: Nova Letra Gráfica e Editora.

Pavillard, S. L. (2008), "Recepción de la ayahuasca em España," MA diss., Universidad Computense de Madrid, Madrid.

Tonkonoff, S. (2017), *From Tarde to Deleuze and Foucault: The Infinitesimal Revolution*, London: Palgrave.

Chapter 10

Albuquerque, J. L. C. (2008), "Fronteiras e identidades em movimento: fluxos migratórios e disputa de poder na fronteira Paraguai-Brasil," *Cadernos Ceru*, 1: 49–63.

Andrade, S. (2006), "Puntualizaciones sobre la magia negra," *La República*, December 4. Available online: http://www.lr21.com.uy/editorial/232068-puntualizaciones-sobre-la-magia

Andrews, G. R. (2010), *Negros en la nación blanca: historia de los afro-uruguayos 1830–2010*, Montevideo: Linardi y Risso.

Arocena, F. and M. Gamboa (2011), "Estado de situación y perspectivas para la regionalización cultural," in F. Arocena (ed.) *Regionalización cultural del Uruguay*, 383–414, Montevideo: Udelar.

Bahia, J. (2015), "E o preto-velho fala alemão: espíritos transnacionais e o campo religioso na Alemanha," *Revista del Cesla*, 18: 181–212.

Bracco, D. (2013), Con las armas en la mano Charrúas, Guenoa-Minuanos y Guaraníes, Montevideo: Planeta.

Caetano, G. and R. Geymonat (1997), *La secularización uruguaya (1859-1919). Catolicismo y privatización de lo religioso*, Montevideo: Obsur—Taurus.

Clemente, I. (2010), "La región de frontera Uruguay-Brasil y la relación binacional: pasado y perspectivas," *Revista Uruguaya de Ciencia Política*, 19 (1): 165–84.

Copstein, G., J. M. S. Gonçalves and C. M. Jacobs (1989), "Aglomerações urbanas fronteiriças. Problemática urbana," *Anales Encuentro de Geógrafos de America Latina*, 2: 223–31.

Cristiano, J. (2011), "Identidades étnicas y regionalización cultural," in F. Arocena (ed.), *Regionalización cultural del Uruguay*, 263–90, Montevideo: Udelar.

Dantas, B. G. (1982), "Repensando a pureza nagô," *Religião e Sociedade* 8: 15–20.

Espirito Santo, D. and N. Tassi (eds) (2013), *Making Spirits: Materiality and Transcendence in Contemporary Religions*, London: I.B. Tauris.

Frigerio, A. (1998), "El rol de la 'escuela uruguaya' en la expansión de las religiones afrobrasileñas en Argentina," in R. Pi Hugarte (ed.), *Los cultos de posesión en Uruguay: Antropología e Historia*, 75–98, Montevideo: Ediciones de la Banda Oriental.

Frigerio, A. (2002), "La expansión de religiones afrobrasileñas en Argentina: representaciones conflictivas de cultura, raza y nación en un contexto de integración regional," *Archives de sciences sociales des religions* 117: 127–50.

Frigerio, A. (2007), "Exportando guerras religiosas: as respostas dos umbandistas à IURD na Argentina e no Uruguai," in Vagner Gonçalves Da Silva (eds), *Intolerância religiosa: Conflitos entre pentecostalismo e religiões afro-brasileiras*, 71–117, São Paulo: Universidade de São Paulo.

Ferreira, J. (2011), "Transnacionalización y (re)apropiación en las religiones afro-brasileñas: una reconstrucción de la historia de vida de un pai-de-santo," *Maguaré*, 25 (2), 41–63.

Frigerio, A. (2013), "A transnacionalização como fluxo religioso na fronteira e como campo social: Umbanda e Batuque na Argentina," *Debates do Ner*, 14 (23): 15–57.

García, N. (2001), *Culturas Hibridas. Estrategias para salir y entrar de la modernidad*, Buenos Aires: Paidós.

Giobellina, Fernando and Elda González. (1984), "Umbanda. Notas sobre un fenómeno religioso brasileño," *Revista española de antropología americana*, 14: 227–42.

Giobellina, Fernando and Elda González. (2000). *Umbanda, el poder del margen: Un estudio de religiosidad popular y experiencia social.* Cádiz: Servicio de Publicaciones de la Universidad de Cádiz.

Gutierrez Bottaro, S. (2002), "El fenómeno del bilingüismo en la comunidad fronteriza uruguayo-brasileña de Rivera," *Actas del Segundo Congreso Brasileño de Hispanistas*, San Pablo, São Paulo, São Paulo (SPSPSP, Brazil) [online], http://www.proceedings.scielo.br/scielo.php?script=sci_arttext&pid=MSC0000000012002000100053&lng=en&nrm=iso.

Hübel, A. (2011), "La región fronteriza uruguayo-brasileña y el portugués en la prosa contemporánea uruguaya," *Revista Eletrônica Celpcyro*, 2: 1–5.

Leistner, R. M. (2014), "Os outsiders do além: um estudo sobre a Quimbanda e outras 'feitiçarias' afro-gaúchas," Ph.D. diss., Universidade do Vale do Rio dos Sinos, São Leopoldo.

Locane, J. (2015), "Disquisiciones en torno al Portunhol selvagem. Del horror de los profesores a una 'lengua pura,'" *Perífrasis*, 6 (12): 36–48.

Oro, A. (2002), "Religiões Afro-Brasileiras do Rio Grande do Sul: Passado e Presente," *Estudos Afro- Asiáticos*, 24 (2): 345–843.

Oro, A. (2013), "Transnacionalização religiosa sem migração no Cone Sul," *Debates do NER*, Porto Alegre, ano 14 (23): 61–72, January/June 2013.

Pallavicino, M. (1988), *Umbanda. Investigación sobre religiosidad afro- brasileña en Montevideo*, Montevideo: Pettirossi Hnos.

Pereda Valdés, I. (1965), *El negro en el Uruguay. Pasado y Presente*, Montevideo: Instituto Histórico y Geográfico del Uruguay.

Persia, A. (2010), "Frontera como recurso, frontera como límite: una perspectiva antropológica," *Estudios Históricos*, 2 (4), http://www.estudioshistoricos.org/libros/adriana-persia.pdf.

Pi Hugarte, Renzo. (1992), "La Iglesia Pentecostal 'Dios es Amor' en el Uruguay," *Cadernos de Antropologia* (Porto Alegre), 9: 63–96.

Pi Hugarte, R. (1997), "Transnacionalização da religião no cone-sul: o caso do Uruguai," in A. Oro and C. Steil (eds), *Globalização e Religião*, 201–18, Petrópolis: Vozes.

Pi Hugarte, R. (1998), *Los cultos de posesión en Uruguay: Antropología e Historia*, Montevideo: Ediciones de la Banda Oriental.

Pi Hugarte, R. (2003), "Sobre el charruismo. La antropología en el sarao de las seudociencias," in *Anuario Antropología Social y Cultural en Uruguay (2002–2003)*, 103–21, Montevideo: Nordan Comunidad and UNESCO.

Pinto, A. (1971), *Dicionário da Umbanda: contendo o maior número de palavras, usadas na Umbanda no Candomblé e nos cultos afro-brasileiros*, Rio de Janeiro: Editorial Eco.

Pollak–Eltz, A. (1993), *Umbanda en Venezuela*, Caracas: Fondo Editorial Acta Científica Venezolana.

Pries, L. (ed.) (2001), *New Transnational Social Spaces. International Migration and Transnational Companies*, London: Routledge.

Pujadas, R. and J. Font (1998), *Ordenación y planificación territorial*, Madrid: Síntesis.

Segato, R. (1996) "Frontiers and Margins. The Untold Story of the Afro-Brazilian Religious Expansion to Argentina and Uruguay," *Critique of Anthropology*, 16 (4): 343–59.

Serralta Massonnier, A. (2015), "La Umbanda en un país laico. La pugna umbandista por el espacio público uruguayo," *Ciencias Sociales y Religión*, 17 (23): 34–50.

Silva, C. A. B. and M. d. P. Vasconcellos (2012), "Saravá, Opá: Bruxaria, Etiologias e um terreiro de Umbanda em Portugal," *Ponto Urbe*, 11: 1–19.

Solla, H. (1992), *Umbanda*, Montevideo: Eppal.

Van Dijk, Teun A. (1998), *Ideology a Multidisciplinary Approach*. London: Thousand Oaks-New Delhi: Sage Publications.

Vidart, D. (2012), *Uruguayos, quiénes somos, cómo somos, dónde estamos*, Montevideo: Ediciones B.

Viegas, A. C. M. M. and S. R. Oliveira (2015), "A Religiosidade Afro-Brasileira na Fronteira: os terreiros de Umbanda em Corumbá-MS," *Revista GeoPantanal*, 18: 205–17.

Chapter 11

Agier, M. (1992), "Ethnopolitique: Racisme, statuts et mouvement noir à Bahia," *Cahiers d"études africaines*, 125, XXXII–I: 53–81.

Bahia, J. (2014), "Under the Berlin Sky: Candomblé on German Shores," *Vibrant – Virtual Brazilian Anthropology*, 11 (2): 326–69.

Brazil. (2014), "Roda de Capoeira recebe título de Patrimônio da Humanidade," http://www.brasil.gov.br/editoria/cultura/2014/11/roda-de-capoeira-recebe-titulo-de-patrimonio-da-humanidade, accessed February 11, 2015.

Csordas, T. (2008), [2002], *Corpo/Significado/Cura*, Porto Alegre: Editora da UFRGS.

Csordas, T. (2009) *Transnational Transcendence: Essays on Religion and Globalization*, Berkeley: University of California Press.

de Azevedo, C. M. M. (1987), *Onda negra, medo branco – o negro no imaginário das elites do século XIX*, Rio de Janeiro, Paz e Terra.

de Brito, C. (2012), "*Berimbau*'S 'Use Value' and 'Exchange Value': Production and Consumption as Symbols of Freedom in Contemporary Global Capoeira Angola," *Vibrant – Virtual Brazilian Anthropology*, 9 (2): 104–27.

de Brito, C. (2015), "O processo de transnacionalização da Capoeira Angola: Uma etnografia sobre a geoeconomia política nativa," Ph.D. diss., Federal University of Rio Grande do Sul, Porto Alegre.

de Brito, C. (2017), *A roda do Mundo: a Capoeira Angola em tempos de globalização*, Curitiba: Editora Appris.

Domínguez, M. E. and A. Frigerio (2002), "Entre a brasilidade e a afro-brasilidade: Trabalhadores culturais em Buenos Aires," in A. Frigerio and G. L. Ribeiro, *Argentinos e brasileiros: encontros, imagens e estereótipos*, Petrópolis, RJ: Vozes.

Fernandez, F. A. (2014), *Capoeiragem in Between: um estudo etnográfico sobre a prática da Capoeira na Alemanha*, Florianópolis: Federal University of Santa Catarina

Frigerio, A. (1989), "Capoeira: De arte negra a esporte branco," *Revista Brasileira de Ciências Sociais*, 4 (10): 1–20.

Fry, P. (1982), "Feijoada e soul food: notas sobre a manipulação de símbolos étnicos e nacionais," in P. Fry (ed.) *Para inglês ver: Identidade e política na cultura brasileira*, Rio de Janeiro: Zahar.

Germano, P. (2017), "A constituição da pessoa Ogã no Xangô Renovado de Pernambuco (modelo Ilê Obá Aganjú Okoloyá)," *REIA- Revista de Estudos e Investigações Antropológicas*, 4 (2): 126–49.

Graeff, N. (2013), "Transmitiendo y preservando lo 'inmaterial' en una casa de Candomblé en Berlín," *Ensayos. Historia y teoría del arte. Bogotá*, XVII (25): 22–37.

Granada, D. F. da S. (2004), "Brasileiros nos Estados Unidos: Capoeira e identidades transnacionais: aspectos da interação social entre brasileiros e estadunidenses nos grupos da Fundação Internacional de Capoeira Angola," Ph.D. diss., Federal University of Rio de Janeiro, Rio de Janeiro.

Granada, D. F. da S. (2015), *Pratique de la capoeira en France et au Royaume-Uni*, Paris: L'Harmattan.

Marinho, I. P. (1982), *A ginástica brasileira*, Brasília: o Autor.

Sloterdijk, P. (2016), *Esferas I: bolhas*, São Paulo: Estação Liberdade.

Soares, C. E. L. (1994), *A negregada instituição: Os capoeiras no Rio de Janeiro (1850–1890)*, Rio de Janeiro: Secretaria Municipal de Cultura.

Souza, E. M. (2008), "Poder Feminino e Relações de Gênero no contexto dos Afoxés de Pernambuco," *Anais Fazendo Gênero*, Florianópolis: UFSC.

Varela S. G. (2017), *Power in Practice: The Pragmatic Anthropology of Afro-Brazilian Capoeira*, New York: Berghan Books.

Vassalo, S. P. (2009), "A 'ancestralidade africana' da Capoeira e do Candomblé: A contribuição da Capoeira ao imaginário da África no Brasil," paper presented at the 8th Meeting of the Anthropology of Mercosul, Buenos Aires, September 29– October 2, 2009.

Index

Abramovic, M. 28, 29
active faith 66
Afro-Brazilian religions. *See specific entries*
Afro-spiritualism 19
agency 16, 26, 66, 75, 115, 118, 119, 129,
    131, 132, 136, 137, 139, 142, 143–7,
    151
Alfredo, P. 140–1
Alvarenga, P. 46, 186 n.19
Andrade, S. 162, 163, 164–5
Andrews, G. R. 197 n.12
anointment rituals 46, 52, 54
antisyncretism 10
Aparicio, F. 28
Appadurai, A. 26, 118
Araújo, M. 171–2
Archangel Michael 18, 128, 129, 130
Ark of the Covenant 15, 37, 64–7
    replica of 64–7
Arocena, F. 156
artificial insemination 75–6
Ascanasy, M. 172, 182
assemblages 3, 7, 9, 10, 11, 12, 13, 102,
    135–51
    spheres and 11–12
Assemblies of God 14
Australia-Brazil transnational Pentecostal
    connections 23–36
    CJC, Brazilian diasporic church 31–5
    global power geometry, flows and
        patterns 25–8
    media and migration 26
    significant attractions for migration
        23–8, 31–2
authenticity 3, 13, 15, 18, 19, 24, 46, 49, 53,
    54, 61, 62, 63, 121, 126, 165, 167
authoritarianism 148
awe, power of 38, 50–3, 54, 55
axé 9
ayahuasca religions 8, 19, 28, 135, 138–43,
    145, 146, 147, 150, 151
Ayala, A. 162, 163, 165

Babalorixá 20, 164, 171–7, 179, 180
Babalorixá Murelemsibe 20, 164, 169,
    171–7, 179, 180
baptism 41, 98, 127
Baptists 75, 76, 80, 189 n.3, 189 n.6
Baroque 5
Bartolomeu, J. 66
belonging, sense of 7, 18, 29, 33, 63, 71, 76,
    117–32, 149, 157, 165, 184 n.6
Bethencourt, F. 114
Biancardi, E. 172
biblical symbolism 47, 50–3
biopower 136, 139, 143, 151
black magic 163, 164, 166
Black Movement 170, 172, 199 n.3
Boym, S. 29
Brasiliana Group 172, 182
Brazilian Catholic Charismatic Renewal
        Movement, Netherlands 117–32
    background of Brazilian migrant
        women 119–20
    and "Dutch identity" 121, 124
    "home": belonging and bonding 120–2
    mission expansion 126–7
    personal stories through interviews
        122–6
    Servants of Love prayer group 126–30
Brazilian migrant women
    Catholic charismatics 117–32
    Pentecostal identity 85–99
    sex workers 101–16
Brazilian religions, globalization of 1–20
    effects of emigration 1–2
    multipolar connections 4–8
    religious forms and traditions 3–4
BRICS countries 2
Bruner, E. 24, 35–6
Buddhism 4, 5, 144, 184 n.6
butinage 9–10, 19, 135–51

caboclos 104, 105
Candomblé 1, 5, 8, 9, 18, 20, 101, 102, 107,

109, 110, 111, 164, 169, 172–82, 192
  n.6, 193 n.2
Capoeira 1, 3, 4, 8, 9, 20, 88, 169–82, 199
  n.2, 200 n.16, 200 n.18, 200 n.20,
  200 n.22
caravanas (expeditions) 15, 40, 42, 44–5,
  50, 52, 55, 63, 186 n.13, 186 n.18
Carmelites 127, 129–30, 131, 195 n.9
carnival 8, 156, 174
Carranza, B. 127
Carter, J. 189 n.6
casting out devils. *See* exorcism
Castro, F. 74
Castro, R. 71, 74
catharsis 40
Catholicism 1, 5, 8, 15, 30, 40, 42, 46, 52,
  59, 62, 66, 67, 76, 77, 114, 137, 138,
  141, 150, 159, 185 n.11, 186 n.19,
  193 n.2, 194 n.4, 196 n.1
  Charismatic Catholics 24, 54, 117–32
CEFLURIS 138, 140, 142, 143
Céu das Estrelas Church 141
Céu do Mar Church 140
Charismatic Christianity. *See under*
  Catholicism
Charrúapeople 19, 158, 159, 197 n.10, 197
  n.13
Charruism 158, 197 n.13
Chávez-Silverman, S. 28
Chosen People 38, 45, 47–50, 53–4
Christian Congregation 93, 192 n.8
Christian values 13
Clinton, B. 189 n.6
Constitution, Spanish 138
Corrente, C. 141
corruption 2, 24
cosmology 28, 30, 35, 38, 39, 47, 51, 52,
  53, 54, 59, 78, 150, 181
cosmopolitanism 25, 27, 31, 32, 33, 35
Couldry, N. 14
Credere di credere 80, 81
Crivella, M. 61
Csordas, T. 170–1
Cuban Communist Party 74
Cuban Council of Churches (CIC) 75
Cuban Journey Against Homophobia and
  Transphobia 72, 75
Cuban National Centre for Sexual
  Education (Cenesex) 72, 74, 190 n.7

cultural capital 31, 34, 119, 184 n.6
cultural hybridization 8, 154, 155, 156,
  161, 166, 196 n.5
Cunningham, H. 25

Dantas, B. 159
da Silva, L. I. L. 2, 172
Delamont, S. 9
Delanda, M. 12
Deleuze, G. 3, 11, 19, 88, 135–7, 150
demonic manifestation 51
deterritorialization 19, 136–9, 143, 150–1,
  196 n.4
de Theije, Marjo 120
Deus é Amor Pentecostal church, Portugal
  (IPDA) 16
diaspora 4, 20, 24, 58, 102, 161, 167, 199
  n.12
Discalced Carmelites 127, 131
dispensationalism 38
Diversidade Tucana 80–1
divine essence 44, 55
divine intervention. *See* miracle
divorce 92, 149
DMT (dimethyltryptamine) 142
doctrines 5, 6, 39, 51, 52, 54, 86, 96, 135,
  138, 143–5, 148, 149–51, 195 n.3,
  199 n.12
Domínguez, M. E. 173
Donatto, P. 162–6, 167
drug trafficking 103, 138, 141, 142

eclecticism 61, 138, 143–4, 149–51
Ecletismo Evolutivo (Evolutionary
  Eclecticism) 143
Ecletismo Involutivo (Involutionary
  Eclecticism) 144
effervescence 51
egalitarian marriage 83
eguns (gods) 137
embeddedness 10, 16, 29, 42, 50, 52, 78,
  123
Enlightenment 27
entrepreneurialism 13
esoteric movements 8
Espín, M. C. 74–5
Espín, V. 74
Espírito Santo, M. 114
Essenes Sect 185 n.11

Eurocentrism 175
European Union 103
exorcism 13, 40, 51, 90, 91, 188 n.5
exoticism 8, 9, 25, 26, 28, 29, 30, 35, 106,
    171–4, 181, 182
exus 89, 102, 111, 113, 193 nn.1–3

Facebook 32, 33
faith 29, 42, 53, 61, 66, 75, 96, 98, 109, 127,
    128, 138, 186 n.14
faith healers 14, 23, 28, 35, 86, 127, 192 n.6
family 32, 48, 76, 83, 86, 87, 88, 92, 97, 99,
    110, 119, 126, 149, 188 n.5
Ferreira, J. 161
fetishization 54, 115
Fidalgo, H. 193 n.10
First Baptist Church, Matanzas 75
Fogueira Santa rituals 40, 49–50, 52, 185 n.5
Forum Brazil 171, 172
freedom, notion of 124, 125, 131, 149,
    150, 151
Freston, P. 24, 127
Frigerio, A. 153, 160–1
Fry, P. 170

Gabriel, M. 138, 143, 145, 149, 150
Galbraith, J. 95
Gamboa, M. 156
Garner, D. O. 74
Gay Pride parades 83
Gays, Lesbians, Bisexuals, Crossdressers,
    and Transsexuals (GLBT) National
    Conference 81
genetics 49
Geschiere, P. 10
Gestalt Therapy 140
Gez, Y. N. 9, 10, 11
Ghana 47, 54
globalization
    concept of 1, 10, 25
    and migration 119
    problems of 5–6
God is Love Pentecostal Church (IPDA)
    85–99
    feminine migration and religious
        attractions 92–3
    punishment 93
    reconstruction of Brazilian women's
        identity 93–9
    religious cultural continuity 85–6
    sacred-secular divide 94–5
    sacred symbols linking home 94
    status disputes 96
    structure, Internal Regulations, and
        identity 86–92
    women as pillars 85
Gonzáles, I. 75
Groisman, A. 135, 143, 150
guardian angels 137
Guatemala 54
Guattari, F. 11, 136
Gutierrez, H. 74, 190 n.8

Hail Mary (prayer) 30
headcaps 47
healing 4, 24–5, 28, 30, 40, 41, 43, 51, 90,
    127, 138, 184 nn.4–5
Hernandes, E. 41
heteronormativity 116
heuristics 40, 46, 53
Hillsong 14, 23, 33–4
hip-hop 172
Holocaust Memorial of Yad Vashem 42
Holy Fire Ceremony 40, 49–50
Holy Land 15
Holy Land/Holy land tours 15, 37–55,
    62–4, 68, 185 n.8, 186 n.13, 188 n.9
Holy See 8
Holy Spirit 54, 60, 66, 72, 78, 114
    gifts of 90, 127
home *vs.* house 11, 18, 117–32
homogenization 5, 18, 27, 120–1
homophobia 16, 74, 75, 83, 190 n.7
homosexuality 12, 16, 76, 82, 107, 111,
    149, 189 n.6, 191 n.24
hupa 48
hybridism 8, 116, 154, 155, 156, 161, 166,
    167, 196 n.5
hyperindividualization 150

Iansã 109, 116, 175, 200 n.21
idolatry 54
Igreja Universal do Reino de Deus. *See*
    Universal Church of the Kingdom
    of God/Universal Church
Ildefonso Pereda Valdés 158
Ilê Obá Silekê 171, 173, 174, 175, 176
imagination, concept of 118

imagined community 60
immanence 38, 51, 170
Imperial, J. 65
individualism 175
initiation 96, 110, 145, 162, 167
International Organization for Migration 2, 183 n.2
Irmãos Guerreiros Capoeira Angola Group, Germany 20, 169–82
  Babalorixá Murelemsibe/Master Perna/Master Rosalvo workshops 171–4
  Candomblé-Capoeira fusion 179–81
  transcendental experiences during exotic events 174–8
  transnational configuration 171–4
Islam 5, 121

Jackson, J. 75
Jerusalem Crosses 40
Jesus Christ 38, 44, 45, 46, 48, 53, 54, 55, 66, 72, 78, 80, 127, 146, 185 n.11
Jesus March 41
"Jewish" objects 37, 40, 52–3, 54–5
John of God 1, 23–5, 28–30, 35, 127, 129, 184 nn.4–5
Juan Carlos de la Cal 140, 141, 142, 147
Judaism 38, 48–9, 50, 54, 66, 187 n.21, 187 n.22
Judaization 38, 54, 186 n.19

Kardec, A. 8, 144, 196 n.1
kenosis 81
ketuba 48
Kronberg, J. 162, 164
Kulick, P. 102, 110

Labate, B.C. 138, 139
La Fountain-Stokes 80, 190 n.18
Levitt, P. 7
LGBT community 12, 13, 16, 71–84, 189 n.6, 190 n.20, 191 n.22
liberation 12, 53, 59, 81, 82, 83, 188 n.5
Liberation Theology 76–7
Llanos, C. 74
Lord, M. 83
Lord's Prayer 30. *See also* prayer
Luis, D. 33
lusosphere

biblical lusosphere 53–5, 67
concept of 3, 10–13, 14, 19
creation of 3–4, 25, 35, 73
expansion of, 28, 53–4, 103–7

Macedo, B. E. 37, 57, 60, 61, 64
Machado, I. 85, 86
mãe de santo (mother of saint) 17–18, 88, 89, 101–2, 107–15, 198 n.22
magic 52–4, 63, 66, 98, 105, 162, 174, 199 n.2
makeup 87, 89, 93, 94
malandragem 103, 106
mandinga (seductive spiritual power) 20, 170, 174–81, 199 n.2
Mareels, E. 125
Marett, R. R. 50, 51
Maria Joana (sorceress) 114
Maria Padilha 108–9, 112–16
Mariz, C. L. 86, 98, 127
marketing techniques 34
Marquardt, M. 131
Marquezine, B. 33
Mary 129
Mass (Eucharist celebration) 122, 128
Massey, D. 25
mass media 8, 9, 26, 83, 163
MCC Brazil 71, 81, 82
McClintock, A. 104, 105–6
media pilgrimages. *See* pilgrimages
medium-entity relationship 109–10
Mestre Perna 171–4, 177
mestres (capoeira teachers) 20, 171
Metropolitan Community Church (MCC) 12
  communities as social technology 82–4
  establishment of 71, 73
  "radical inclusion" of segregated groups (LGBT) 71, 73, 75–6
  transnational network/expansion 71–84
Metropolitan Community Church (MCC) Cuba 71–84
  arrival and transnational network 73–6
  communities of sense 80–2
  Cristiano's leadership 80–2, 83–4
  Elaine's role and activism 74–7
  ethnography 73–6

Pentecost service 72, 76–82
Sanchez's role and public campaigns 77–80
Mexico 54, 79
Meyer, B. 10, 18, 50–1, 53
michês 106, 108
migration, motivation for 31–2, 122–3
miracle 8, 39, 42–5, 48, 52–3, 80, 109
Miranda, M. E. 120
missionaries 2, 4, 8, 72, 127, 128, 129–30, 187 n.22
Mix Brasil 81, 191 n.22
modernity 25, 27, 32, 35, 57, 60
modernization 29
mulatinhas 106
mysticism 8

Naranjo, C. 140
National Coalition of Black Lesbians and Gays (NCBLG) 74
neoliberal ideology 13
neo-Pentecostalism. *See specific entries*
Neto, D. 83
New Age 30, 35, 140, 145, 149, 150, 151, 195 n.4
nondenominational churches 38
Noordegraaf-Eelens, L. 11, 12

Obama, B. 71, 189 n.1
Obama, M. 189 n.1
obreiras (Brazilian sisters assisting pastors) 86–97
Ogun 176–7
Old Testament 14–15, 37, 50, 185 n.11
Omolu 109
online dating 123
Opening Breaches of Colours 74
orixás (African Gods) 16, 102, 109, 172, 176–7, 179, 191 n.4, 192 n.6, 193 n.2, 198 n.20, 199 n.6, 199 n.12, 200 n.14, 200 n.23
Oro, A. 153, 158, 161
Our Lady of Aparecida 18, 128, 129, 194 n.8
Our Lady of Fatima 129
Oxum 163–5, 176–7, 200 n.23

Paco (Francisco de la Cal) 140
pais de santo 111, 113

Pallavicino, M. 153
Papal Authority 150
Pentecost 72, 78, 80
Pentecostalism. *See specific entries*
peregrination 78
Perez, L. F. 81
perfume 94
Perry, T. D., Jr. 74, 189 n.6, 190 n.7
Persia, A. 155
Peru 54
piety 49, 52, 62
Pi Hugarte, R. 153–4, 157–9, 162–3, 196 n.3, 197 n.13, 197 n.17
pilgrimage, notion of 13–14
Pollak-Eltz, E. 160
pombagira (sexual spirit) 17, 89, 91, 93, 101–16, 192 nn.5–6, 193 nn.1–3, 197 n.16
Pope Pius X 194 n.8
popular culture 8, 162
Portunhol dialect 19, 157, 196 n.8
power, redefined 95, 145
prayers 30, 37, 41, 44, 46, 50, 53, 65, 80, 85, 87, 90, 91, 95, 114, 119, 128, 179
prayer shawls, Jewish 37, 40, 45, 47, 48, 50
Premawardhana, D. 10
privatization 159
progress, idea of 27
prosperity gospel 13, 16, 38, 51
prostitution, Brazil-Portugal migratory flows and 88, 89, 96, 101–16
    colonial and economic impact 103–7
    and disease 109
    and femininity 116
    pombagiras and *mãe de santo* 107–14
    religious association/identity 106–7, 110
    Sandra/Maria Padilha case 108–12
Protestantism 8, 62
psychedelics 140, 142
psychoactive substances 19, 138, 150
purification 43, 89, 91, 95

Qumran Caves 41, 185 n.11

radio broadcasts 59, 90, 164
rebirth. *See* baptism
redemption 81
Rede Record television 59

reflexivity 78, 150
Reformation 27, 171
religion, definition of 10–11
religion in Brazil. *See also* Brazilian
    religions
    fusions of 8–9
    Protestantism and Pentecostalism 8–9
religious artefacts. *See* ritual objects
religious studies 10
repentance 81
Replacement Theology (Supercessionism)
    54
reterritorialization 19, 136, 138–40, 143, 151
reverse mission 6, 24, 127, 131, 194 n.7,
    195 n.9
Ribeiro, F. 141
ritual objects 2, 3, 12, 15, 18, 23, 28, 30,
    38, 39, 40, 44, 45, 46, 47, 50, 52–4,
    57–8, 66–8, 77, 94, 104–5, 128, 131,
    136, 140, 188, 192 n.8
    agency of 64–7
Roberto, P. 140
roda (circle) 20, 174
Rodés, C. 189 n.3
Rosa, R. 123
Rosalvo, M. 172, 173, 199 n.9
Rosemblat, O. 64–5
Rousseff, D. 61

sacrament 38, 53, 142, 186 n.19, 195 n.2
sacred music 6
sacred objects. *See* ritual objects
sacrifice/sacrificial offering 51–3
saints, agency and power of 8, 16, 18, 67,
    128, 137, 158
Salazar, N. 10
Salman, T. 120
salsa 172
salvation 38, 82, 87, 186 n.18
samba 172, 200 n.16
Sánchez de León, C. M. 77, 78–9, 80, 84
Santeríacults 76
Santo Daime (SD) 1, 4
    arrival and legalization in Spain 140–2
    expansion of 138
    founding of 138
    internal structure and power relations
        138–9
    membership and practices 147–50
    structure and agency in Brazil 144–7

Saralegui, E. 74–6
SAT (Seekers after Truth) 140
SAT Babia 140, 142–3
Schiller, N. G. 7, 10
Schinkel, W. 11
scientism 19
Sebastião, P. 138, 140, 146
Second Vatican Council 76
secularization 20, 29, 81
Segato, R. 153, 157
self-acceptance 82
self-account technologies 82–4
self-actualization 13
self-destructive behaviours 96
self-immunization 170, 171, 182
self-realization 170
self-spirituality 30, 35
sexualization, of Brazilian women 96–7
shamanism 137, 138, 139, 140
Shema Yisrael 48
Sheringham, O. 118, 131
Silva, C. 156
Sloterdijk, P. 11, 12, 170, 171
Soares, M. 171–2
social media 23, 24, 25, 26, 31, 32, 54,
    98–9, 123
social morphology 120, 125, 131
social nationalism 172, 175
Solla, H. 153
Souza, L. de Mello 114
sphere, notion of. *See* lusosphere
Spiritism 150, 184 n.1, 193 n.2, 196 n.1
spirits, agency and power of 16
spiritual presence 6
Stephen, N. 9
stereotypes 18, 87–8, 94, 103–4, 106, 107,
    194 n.4, 200 n.23
strategic antisyncretism 10
Suarez, R. 75, 189 n.3
subjectivation 63–4, 78
superstitions 105
syncretism 8, 10, 114, 137, 141

taboos 94
television broadcasts 59
Temer, M. 61
Temple of Solomon, São Paulo 15, 37,
    49–50, 57–8, 60–4
    architectural design and construction
        61–3

capacity 61
replica of Solomon's first temple 61
as site for religious experience 63
Ten Commandments 64
Terranova, R. 41, 42, 186 n.13
Time magazine 97, 193 n.10
tolerance 76, 107, 110, 142
tongues, gift of 90, 127
Topel, M. 38, 53
transcendence 3, 20, 28, 51, 81, 140, 170, 174–82
transformation 6, 10, 18, 38, 39, 59, 65, 80, 97, 108–10, 124, 125, 136, 138, 144, 146–8, 169–70, 195 n.10
transnationalism. *See under specific topics*
transnational transcendence 170–1
transphobia 16, 72, 74, 75, 83
travestis 16, 17, 88, 89, 101–16, 191 n.2
tropicalization 28, 104
tryptic discourse 79
Tsing, A. 6
Tweed, T. 10–11
2001 attacks 2

Umbanda in Uruguay 8, 19, 153–68
adaptation of 162–6
comparative perspective 160–1
cultural identity 155–9
PaiDonatto'scase 163–6
secular state 159–60
transnationalizationof 160–1
UN Commission on Narcotics 142
undocumented migrants 120
União do Vegetal (UDV) 8, 135–51
arrival and expansion in Spain 142–3
founding of 137–8
membership and practices 143, 147–50
structure and agency in Brazil 143–7
United Evangelical Church of Puerto Rico 77
United Nations 2
United States
Anglo culture in 28
attractions for migration to 31
Brazilian immigrants in 31
fashionable "biblical symbols" 47
Holy Land tours 40, 41
Universal Church in 187 n.1

Universal Church of the Kingdom of God (UCKG)/Universal Church 6, 7, 8, 37–55
and Catholicism 67
consecration of oil/religious articles 44, 46
Edir Macedo, founder 57, 60
Holy Land tours 38–47
intersections with/incorporation of Judaism 47–50
linkage with Israel and its ritual practices 37–8
rapid expansion 57
spiritual "awe" 38, 50–3
Universal Church, Angola 57–68
Alvaladechurch 60
caravanas (expeditions) 63
circulation of the Ark 64–8
establishment and expansion 59–60
global network 64
historical background of Angola 57–8
Marçal church 60, 63
media 59, 60
Ureta, H. 160
"us-them" dichotomy 121, 164–5

Valdés, P. 158
Valério, C. 77, 80–4
van de Port, M. 18
Van Dijk, T. 164–5
van Tuinen, S. 11
Vasconcellos, M. 156
Vasquez, M. A. 26, 131
Vattimo, G. 80, 81–2
Vidart, D. 158
Vienna Convention 142
vigils 85, 95
Vilvert, L. 65
visual cultures 6

Wambacq, J. 11
Weber, M. 95
Whatsapp 16, 44, 83
will 95–6
Wimmer, A. 7
Winfrey, O. 28
wiretapping 141
Word of God 38, 51
"work of the imagination" 26, 118, 119, 126, 130, 132

"worlding process" 7
World Trade Center 2
worldview 18, 26, 94, 97
worship practices 40, 47, 54

yarmulkes 37, 40, 48, 49
Yoga 20

Yom Kippur 41
Yoruba 5, 193 n.2, 199 n.6
YouTube 48

Zionism 38, 42, 54
Zumba 172